# AN INDIAN COMMENTARY

# AN INDIAN COMMENTARY

G. T. GARRATT

GYAN

*Published by*

GYAN

Gyan Publishing House
5, Ansari Road
Daryaganj, New Delhi-110002
Phone: 011-47034999, 9811692060
E-mail: books@gyanbooks.com

*Distribution Network*
gyanbooks.com
India, USA, Canada, UK, Australia



ISBN: 978-93-7014-108-7 (PB)

First Published, 1930

2nd Impression 2025

*Printed at:* Gyan Press, Delhi.



**AN INDIAN COMMENTARY**
Author: G. T. GARRATT

# AN INDIAN COMMENTARY

# AN INDIAN COMMENTARY

by

G. T GARRATT

JONATHAN CAPE
THIRTY BEDFORD SQUARE
LONDON

# CONTENTS

# CONTENTS

## PART IV

## THE FUTURE

# INTRODUCTION

A FAMOUS Indian legend describes how Gods and Demons churned the Ocean of Milk to obtain the nectar which alone could make them immortal. Their efforts were on the true epic scale. One demon, with tail neatly curled round a mountain, obligingly acted as the 'worker'. At length their task was done, but they found not only nectar but poison as well. To-day the vast silent ocean of Indian life is being slowly stirred into activity. The wisest have little idea of the end, some are certain about the nectar, others equally sure of the poison. Possibly the old legend gives the true analogy, good and evil results will follow in abundance. The process has, however, begun, and must be completed. The tragedy of modern India is that the two chief parties in this great work, the educated classes of England and India, remain hopelessly estranged.

Those who know both countries must have noticed how men of each nationality, whose training and outlook should have made them sufficiently akin to understand each other, almost invariably fail to find any common basis on which to discuss the future of India. The Indian thinks the Englishman's caution hypocritical. To the Englishman much of the Indian's nationalism seems perverse. There appears to be a need for restating the whole problem in a way which a layman can understand, for these troubles cannot be exorcised by a few politicians and specialists.

The object of this book is to describe and explain the problem rather than offer a solution. The first part will deal with the main classes into which the people of India are divided to-day, attempting to give some idea of their standard of living, their prospects, and their relative importance. The second part discusses the relations between the English and India, and the growth of the nationalist movement which has brought the whole question to a head. The third part will describe and attempt to place in their proper perspective the difficulties which are likely to arise if some form of autonomous government is constituted. The last part of the book will suggest the probable lines of political development, and deal with certain economic and social questions which are apt to be forgotten in the heat of political controversy.

A final chapter has been added to this edition in order to discuss the Simon Report, and the events leading up to the Round Table Conference.

As some controversy was aroused by views expressed in the second part of this book, the writer would like to take the opportunity to explain his position. It is impossible to understand the nationalist movement without discussing certain recent events which have deeply impressed the minds of all educated and many uneducated Indians. The Englishman's interest in his Empire is dissipated over a large field, and he is apt to forget certain unhappy incidents, the memory of which will linger for years in the countries where they occurred. The manner in which these old grievances survive was shown in America, where Mr. Gandhi's recent violation of the Salt Law immediately aroused memories of the Boston Tea Party. Any book which describes the relations between English and Indians must deal with occurrences which are almost forgotten in England, but are a very poignant memory in India. A writer immediately finds himself faced by the practical difficulties of justifying before an English law court statements made about events which occurred in India some years ago. Dr. Thompson in his recent work, *The Reconstruction of India*, discusses this difficulty.

'If we are to be fair in our judgment of the present situation, when the Indian National Movement seems so hysterical and childishly unreasonable, we must consider carefully the Punjab Tradition and the War. Unfortunately frank discussion must be left to a fairly distant posterity. It has been foreclosed by a famous trial, that of Sir Sankaran Nair for having libelled Sir Michael O'Dwyer, Lieutenant-Governor of the Punjab during the War. In that trial the Judge stated emphatically that the Hunter Commission had wrongly condemned General Dyer's action at Amritsar.'

The effect of this judgment has been to impose a censorship upon discussion which, though indirect, is quite as effective as any administrative order.

The course of events in the Punjab and elsewhere is discussed at some length in this book. The writer has no wish to raise any personal issue, and for this reason has expunged a personal reference to which objection was taken. He would like to apologise quite freely if the original insertion caused any pain. Two other disputed passages, on pages 118 and 152, have been left as they were. The writer believes them to be true. The reader must however realise that the overwhelming majority of the House of Lords took the opposite view, and Mr. Justice McCardie, summing up in the case mentioned by Dr. Thompson, stated that 'General Dyer, in the grave and exceptional circumstances, acted rightly, and, in my opinion, upon the evidence he was wrongly punished by the Secretary of State'. The reader who is interested in this question must find his way, without a guide, through the dusty files containing the evidence given before the Hunter Committee, which sat in India shortly after the occurrences upon which Mr. Justice McCardie pronounced judgment some years subsequently. The Committee contained three Indians and five Englishmen. The latter included a Major-General, a Judge, and a prominent member of the Civil Service. The Commission divided along racial lines. The Majority Report, which Mr. Justice McCardie rejected, was the work of the five Englishmen. It should be read through, but one quotation is given to justify the views expressed upon General Dyer's action.

'In continuing firing as long as he did, it is evident that General Dyer had in view not merely the dispersal of the crowd that had assembled contrary to orders, but the desire to produce a moral effect in the Punjab. . . . In our view this was unfortunately a mistaken conception of his duty. If necessary a crowd that has assembled contrary to a proclamation issued to prevent or terminate disorder may have to be fired upon; but continued firing upon that crowd cannot be justified because of the effect such firing may have upon people in other places.' [1]

As regards the administration of martial law, the reader must form his opinion from the evidence given before the Commission, evidence which has a certain historical value even if it has no legal validity in England.

[1] Report of Committee on Disturbances in the Punjab, 1920 Cmd. 681, p. 30.

# PART I

# MODERN INDIA

## CHAPTER I

# THE STRUCTURE OF SOCIETY

MANY Englishmen, sincerely anxious to learn something of the countries which they govern vicariously, find India incomprehensible. They are used to the small and comparatively homogenous nations of Western Europe, and to the free social life of the twentieth century. India conjures up a country without form or unity, of a vast population of diverse peoples living uneasily together. Her three hundred million inhabitants are of many races, all at different stages of civilisation, they adhere to several conflicting religions, and are remarkable for the variety of languages in which they express themselves. The population is divided into innumerable groups, the members of which do not intermarry, and have very little social intercourse with each other. In no area of the world can one find men so poor and so rich, so ignorant and so educated, so primitive and so civilised. To add to the confusion over a fifth of her people are still under the rule of princes who are more or less independent, and provinces so alien as Burma and Baluchistan have, for administrative purposes, to be considered as part of India.

It would be easy to enlarge upon the complexity of Indian life, but many features which seem peculiar to India can be found in any area inhabited by an illiterate and scattered agricultural population. Different English dialects have existed for centuries within a few miles distance, and we know that in Tudor times a man of Kent could hardly understand a Yorkshireman. Again, in many parts of Eastern Europe we find religious communities, like the Mohammadans in Russia or the Jews in

Poland, living amongst people of another religion, but keeping their separate identity, and not intermarrying with their neighbours. Southern Germany in the eighteenth century was ruled by irresponsible princelings in much the same archaic fashion as are parts of Central India and Kathiawar to-day. If we keep before us the history of Europe, especially of Eastern Europe, it is not difficult to visualise India 'marching in uneven stages through all the centuries from the fifth to the twentieth'.

The institution of caste, which lays down for every Hindu certain rules as to his marriage, food, and occupation, is another subject which must be kept in its proper perspective. The Englishman is inclined to think of it chiefly in connection with the bad treatment meted out to certain lowly castes, whereas it is a rigid social system which dates from the earliest Aryan invasions, and was primarily intended to prevent the invaders being absorbed by the hordes of aborigines who surrounded them. In India, as in most early civilisations, the family is the unit. Religion and public opinion combine to keep the system in force, and the son steps into his father's place, adopting his occupation, caste, and place in society. Such a society is obviously more stable than one founded upon individuals, and it is only recently that family and caste have lost much of their importance in Europe. Even in Victorian times England was divided into a number of classes between whom marriage was almost unthinkable. It was firmly believed by all classes that a man should 'keep his proper station', and that this system had some divine sanction. The earlier German, English, and French missionaries found little remarkable in the caste system, and the famous Abbé Dubois wrote, over a century ago, 'I believe caste division to be in many respects the *chef-d'œuvre*, the happiest effort, of Hindu legislation'. We no longer care to sing about 'the rich man in his castle, the poor man at his gate', or believe that the Almighty divided mankind into classes, and 'orders their estate', but the change is very recent. The Englishmen who went to India as administrators and soldiers during the nineteenth century, came from families which saw nothing incongruous in such a conception of the Deity, or unnatural in such a society. It is clear from the letters and diaries of men like Nicholson, Outram, and the Lawrences that they found many aspects of India much less strange and remote than would a modern educated Englishman brought suddenly into the society of the Talukdars of Oudh, or into the life of an Indian State. The War and the influence of America have hastened in England a mental process which began with our industrial development, so that we are apt to forget the important part played by caste in our own social life, especially in country villages.

Caste is, of course, a Hindu institution. Such a rigid system, imposing great restraints and hardships on millions, could hardly exist without religious support. *Tantum religio potuit suadere malorum.* But it does more than order the lives of the 220 millions who profess the Hindu religion. Hinduism is probably the most absorbent, it is certainly the most comprehensive system in the world. 'Agnostics, pantheists, devil-worshippers – all alike lay claim to a place within the fold, and their claim is undisputed.' [1] It enforces no dogma, and lays down no

[1] Macnicol, *The Making of Modern India*, p. 213.

rules of conduct. It only demands that men should take their assigned position in society, and accept their caste as an index of the stage they have reached in their spiritual progress. Placing before them the twofold doctrine of *karma* and transmigration, it leaves them to make their own way through the 'eighty-four lakhs of births and rebirths' which is their earthly pilgrimage. Hinduism defies summary treatment, and because it is the genuine philosophy of a primitive agricultural people it has a permanence which the European finds difficulty in understanding.

Not only has Hinduism absorbed Buddhism, but even those Indians whose religions draw strength and inspiration from outside are profoundly affected by it. We find Brahman Christians in Madras,[1] and the Moslems of the Deccan adopt innumerable Hindu conventions and ceremonies. It must be remembered that the Mohammadans of Bengal and Madras are almost entirely descendants of converts from Hinduism, and only about 15 per cent. of those in the Punjab are of foreign blood. Many of the former left their old faith unwillingly, and they and their descendants still retain something of the Hindu mentality. In most Provinces, except Bengal and the Punjab, they form a small backward minority with a disproportionate number living in the poorer parts of towns. Hinduism dominates the village life of India. It works through the slow dull minds of 'illiterate peasants, whose mental

[1] 'Striking as has been the success of Christian missions, it must be admitted that this great success has been nullified and vitiated to a great extent by the admission of caste into Christianity.' – Rev. J. A. Sharrock, *Hinduism Ancient and Modern*, p. 177.

outlook is coloured by the physical facts of India, the blazing sun, the enervating rains', the peasants whose 'placid pathetic contentment' was deplored by Mr. Montagu. It has covered India with a framework no less powerful because it is invisible.

In its earliest and simplest form the Indian village has three main features. The community of agricultural families with rights in the soil. The Headman, half elective and half hereditary. The lower castes, attached to the village, sometimes working on the land, but with no rights in the soil. Some rough organisation of this kind may have existed before the coming of the Aryans. The latter certainly developed it. The agricultural families would still be the bulk of the population, and in very early times the head of the family was husbandman, warrior, and priest for his household. Gradually these functions were separated. The man skilled in the composing of Vedic hymns gave up his husbandry, and his descendants became the priestly Brahmans. The keenest fighters developed into a special caste, the Kshattriyas. This was the beginning of the great Four Caste system – the agricultural families or Vaisyas, the warriors or Kshattriyas, the priests or Brahmans, and finally the lowly Sudras, the landless workers and servants. Of these four castes only the Kshattriyas have no real counterpart in modern India, for they have been absorbed into agriculture, while the priestly caste, distinguished by their ability to read and their sedentary habits, have of course been joined by others, for their special characteristics are a feature of all recent civilisation, and the goal of many men's ambition.

There remains, then, a threefold division of the population, which can be taken as a basis. The great bulk of Indians are villagers, and by grouping them according to the status which they would have in a village it is possible to get a truer picture, and one more in accordance with Indian ideas. Our analysis therefore will not deal primarily with religions, languages, or races. To use an economist's phrase, the division will be horizontal rather than vertical. The first group will be the 'cultivators', the descendants of the Vaisyas or agricultural families, men owning or renting land which they work themselves. In the next will be included every kind of landless manual worker, including that fairly large section of the population which has no means of support except casual labour and begging. The last group, which is numerically insignificant, but potentially of great importance, will contain all the clerical and professional classes, also those who live on rents and investments, and the business men who have risen above actual retailing.

To the European it may seem fanciful to describe these three groups as the natural development of the Vaisyas, Sudras, and Brahmans, but it is difficult to exaggerate the pervasive endurance of the Hindu social system. Many English people assume that caste and caste observances are disappearing from India, but statements to this effect need very careful examination. If the caste system is to break down, we should expect from analogies with other countries, that this would be due either to a reformist movement inside Hinduism, or to disputes amongst the castes and a rebellion of the lower castes, or to the impracticability of adhering to caste rules in our modern industrial towns. All three influences are at work in India, but their result has been limited. The earliest reformist movements, such as the Brahmo Samaj and the Prarthana Samaj, were frankly opposed to caste, and so also have been the small group of social reformers, men like Ranade, Gokhale, and Mr. K. Natarajan, but the revival of Hinduism during the last fifty years, its defence by Theosophists and others, and above all the connection between nationalism and orthodox Hinduism, of which Bal Gangadhar Tilak was a notable example, all reacted in the other direction. There seems to be now a tendency back towards the old reformist ideas; Mr. Gandhi, at the expense of much popularity, has always been an opponent of caste, and the one important proselytising Hindu sect, the Arya Samaj, after adopting for a time an ambiguous position, has now thrown its influence more definitely on the same side, and its half-million adherents contain many members of the lowest castes.

The tendency of inferior castes to claim a higher status is a very important development, but its outcome is doubtful. During the last thirty years many castes have formed *sabhas* or associations, and these like to justify their existence by trying to enhance the importance and position of their members. This works both for and against the caste system. In the case of the Dhanuks and Kahars the *sabha* insists that their members are 'twice-born', and must wear the sacred thread and follow all the strict Brahman observances. The *sabhas* also form convenient political units, and in the South of India have taken an active part in affairs under the new Reform Scheme. This has helped to keep the caste system alive, and 'the census enumeration made it clear that there was in South India no sign of a weakening of caste feeling'.[1]

[1] *Census of India*, 1921, Vol. I, p. 231.

On the other hand, the claim to Brahman status now being made by larger groups of cultivators, such as the Goalas of Bihar, will tend to make the pretensions of the 'twice-born' seem ridiculous, just as the creation of a large number of peers must inevitably reduce the prestige of the House of Lords.

The third way in which it seems probable that the caste system will be weakened is from the enforced mixing of all castes in the large cities and industrial centres. The rules which deal with feeding have already been relaxed in most modern towns, or they are only observed in a perfunctory manner. All castes mingle freely on railway platforms, and all except the highest will sit side by side in factories, but inter-caste marriages are still rare, and are usually the subject of special mention in journals devoted to social reform. The next twenty years will show whether the Hindu system can adapt itself to modern city life, but caste will exercise a strong influence, even in towns, so long as there is no inter-marriage, and no member of one caste can possibly have a relation belonging to any other caste. Over most of India it is probably true, as Mr. S. C. Dutt affirms, 'those who kick against caste are such as it has virtually repudiated'. It is harder to accept his cynical view about the modification of caste that 'this as a rule has not been the work of the schoolmaster. A love of food and drink proscribed by the *Shastras*, and a morbid craving for promiscuous intercourse with females of all orders, have been the chief accelerators of improvement.'[1]

Not only is caste likely to remain a powerful factor in village life for some generations, but for many other

[1] S. C. Dutt, *India, Past and Present*, p. 131.

reasons a classification into three groups, along the lines we have suggested, has more meaning in the East than it would have in Western Europe or America. There are a number of influences besides the caste system which combine to keep both elder and younger children in their father's way of life. The joint family system, the law of inheritance which divides up land and property equally amongst the children, the lack of business openings, the pressure on the land which will be discussed in the next chapter, the difficulty of emigration, village illiteracy, all tend to prevent a man from rising high, while the first two prevent him from falling altogether. The peasant's youngest son will wait to get his share of the paternal acres, partly because he is by caste a cultivator, but also because no other land is available, and the towns have little to offer. The craftsman's son can only escape from his father's calling by sinking into the coolie or factory-hand class, or by rising through a college education into the ranks of the one or two overcrowded professions which are open to him. The effect of the joint family system can be best seen in the professional classes. The rising lawyer has to drag along with him an army of cousins and nephews. The failure can always find a place at some relation's table. Also Brahmanism encourages an exaggerated respect for literary attainment and a contempt for manual work, and as the latter is for purely physical reasons less attractive in India than in more temperate climes, it is not surprising that the poorest member of the third group, those who do not work with their hands, will spend years living on a miserable pittance from some distant relative, rather than join the ranks of craftsmen or cultivators.

A Hindu is not taught to look upon the world as his oyster. Few of them would appreciate the typical American career in which a professional or business man may spend part of his life in manual work without degradation, and can pass easily from one social sphere to another. The Moslems and the Parsi community are more open-minded, but the latter seldom condescend to manual work, and the very low standard of Mohammadan education makes it hard for their young men to fight their way up the social ladder. One sometimes comes across an Indian counterpart to that immortal adventurer Hajji Baba, and Pathans and Punjabi Mussulmans are found scattered about the world, taking their opportunities where they find them, but fatalism and a hot climate combine with religion and custom to keep the ordinary Indian tied to the class into which he is born. Throughout most of India, the real India of the villages and small country towns, a competent observer could probably place at sight nearly every human being into the group to which they belong.

There is, of course, some movement between the three main groups. The richer agricultural families become small landlords, or send their brighter sons to the University in order to make them clerks, or Government servants. The poorest cultivators sink into the farm-servant class, or move into the factory towns. In some parts of eastern India the craftsmen, whose business was being hard hit by manufactured goods, bought land and their families have become cultivators, but this was not common. The most enterprising traders and craftsmen – in India the maker or producer is usually the seller as well – may rise into the third group by becoming successful business men, and most of their relations will follow them into the ranks of the sedentary class. Once Indians have become *bhadralok* and joined the middle classes only starvation will drive them back again. The structure of Indian Society is essentially rigid, except for these small movements.

## CHAPTER II

# THE CULTIVATORS

THE agricultural families – the Vaisyas of the old Aryan village – still form the great bulk of the Indian people. In some areas they have been converted to Mohammadanism, and in others they have been reinforced by aboriginal tribes, like the Santals, Khands, and Bhils, but in every province the typical Indian family lives in a village, jointly cultivates a small area of land, and keeps a few head of cattle. Their tenure of the land varies. The old communal system has mostly disappeared, though in some backward areas villagers still raise crops by the simple method of burning down successive patches of jungle, and planting their seed in the ashes. In the west and north of India land is generally owned by the peasants themselves, as 'ryots' paying land revenue to the Government. In the east, and especially in the fertile valley of the Ganges, they are usually tenants paying rent to a private 'zemindar'. There are also a large number of more complicated tenures, due very often to the richer villagers letting out part of their land to their neighbours on some basis of sharing the produce, corresponding to the *métayage* system in South Europe, but sometimes practically reducing the tenant to the level of a farm servant.

In every case the working members of these families are officially given the cumbrous title of 'cultivators', and it will be best to use this word rather than 'farmer' or 'small holder'. The farmer conjures up a picture of the English tenant farmer, who is an employer of labour, and a business man on a small scale. The latter has, in

England, a special legal meaning. For centuries the Indian cultivators have, as the Australians say, 'carried' the rest of the population. They have lived in their isolated villages, ploughing and sowing, propitiating their innumerable gods, cursing impartially the dacoit and the tax-gatherer, marketing part of their produce, and providing that small surplus which enabled their rulers to uphold the legend of the gorgeous East. No one can understand India or her history unless they are always conscious of this silent immovable audience before whom captains and kings, governors and politicians, have played their parts, strutted or capered, and passed away forgotten. The modern leader, Indian or European, is perhaps less certain of himself than his predecessor, and more apt to look to his audience for a little applause. Viceroys vie with extreme Nationalists in laying down 'what the ryot really wants', and proclaiming their ability to satisfy him. In theory everybody agrees that our rule in India, and all future changes, must be judged chiefly by their effect upon the cultivators, but in practice there is nothing so easy to forget. Writers and politicians refer continually to the silent masses of India, but their interest often goes no further, a proof of this being the lack of accurate information about village life. Even upon such important questions as agricultural indebtedness, and recent alterations in the standard of living, we have to rely upon rather meagre official statistics, and a few detailed inquiries about specific areas.

To give in a broad outline the position of the cultivating class it will be safest to use round numbers only. To quote exact totals suggests an accuracy which is deceptive. The census of 1921, for example, differentiates between 'actual workers' and their 'dependents', but, as the compilers themselves recognise, there is no standard which could be applied both to the industrious Jat and the shiftless Meos of the Punjab, to the hard-working Lingaiyat and the lazy Bhil. Anyone acquainted with the poorer lands of the Deccan must realise that no exact line can be drawn between what is known as 'culturable waste', and 'land not available for cultivation'. One can, however, say that there are roughly 55 million cultivators in British India and the Indian States. They have another 123 million persons dependent upon them, but dependency is a relative word, for many of the women help in the fields, and the children take the cattle to graze in the 'jungal' or amongst the stubble. Altogether the 178 million cultivators and their families total well over half of the 319 million inhabitants of India. With the help of another 20 million farm servants, the men and women employed on the larger holdings, these cultivators plough and sow India's 250 million acres of arable land, leave another 50 million fallow, and keep 150 million head of horned cattle.

These figures suggest immediately that most cultivators have only a very small acreage from which to support themselves and their families. This is clearly seen if the millions are omitted from the figures given in the last paragraph. An English farmer who had to employ over fifty men and nearly half as many women upon a three-hundred acre farm would be driven to the most intensive market-gardening, and almost inevitably to bankruptcy. Fifteen to twenty men would be the utmost for whom he could find work on a well-managed 'mixed' farm. Perhaps South Africa would be a more suitable area for comparison, with its thirteen million acres of arable land, and a very large extent of pasture. All the work is done by 350,000 Europeans, natives, and Asiatics. On an Indian basis it would require ten times as many men to cultivate the area. Undoubtedly there is a very large population on the available arable land, and taking province by province we find that, though there is comparatively little migration from one part of agricultural India to another, the pressure on the soil is fairly even. Further examination shows, however, that within each area the smallest holdings are always the most numerous, and we may say that roughly throughout India half the holdings are under five acres, and three-quarters are under fifteen acres.[1] Some of these small plots represent parcels of land attached to temples, but nearly all of them would be the only means of subsistence of the men who own or rent them. Few Indians take up land as a spare-time occupation, like the European townsman's allotment, or the English village shopkeeper's 'accommodation acres'. On the other hand, there are many Indians entered for census purposes as factory workers, who return each year to help on their family holdings during the busy seasons. These add to the pressure on the land rather than diminish it.

One of the oldest problems in the world is the amount of land which a man needs. Tolstoy makes this question the title of a story in which he takes a Russian peasant through every stage until he finally earns the six feet by two which brought him peace at last. Even if we take a less gloomy view, we find a great divergence of opinion as to the acreage

[1] Bombay Presidency, 47 per cent. under 5 acres; 75 per cent. under 15 acres. Punjab, 58 per cent. under 5 acres; 84 per cent. under 15 acres.

upon which a man may live in comfort, bring up a family, and have a balance from which to save a little money and pay his taxes. No exact figures are possible, for the man with irrigated land wants less than a 'dry' farmer, and the market-gardener less than either. There seems, however, to be a consensus of opinion that for growing the ordinary grain crops fifteen acres of dry land is about the minimum upon which a man can live decently unless he has some secondary occupation, like sericulture in Japan and Italy, or toy-making in Germany.

The question of village industries will be discussed later; at present we may say that the ordinary Indian cultivator must look to his land for support, and that dairying, pig-feeding, and poultry-keeping, which are the European smallholder's salvation, help him very little. On this assumption Dr. Keatinge has given fifteen acres as the least upon which a man can live and raise a family, but elsewhere he describes an economic holding as

> 'a holding which allows a man a chance of producing sufficient to support himself and his family in reasonable comfort after paying necessary expenses. In the Deccan an ideal economic holding would consist of forty or fifty acres of fair land in one block, with at least one good irrigation well.'[1]

Dr. Mann, writing of the same part of India, takes 'thirteen acres of dry and garden land as being an economic holding . . . and this is the minimum'.[2] Professor Stanley Jevons thought that between twenty and thirty acres was the ideal holding, and a special committee

[1] *Rural Economy in the Bombay Deccan*, p. 52.
[2] *Land and Labour in a Deccan Village*, Vol. II, p. 43.

appointed recently in Baroda reported in much the same strain as Dr. Keatinge. Mr. Darling, writing of the Punjab, says that

'where, as in India, rural industries are relegated to the menial castes, and market-gardening considered polluting, and scientific stock-breeding impossible to anyone but a Mohammadan, the economic holding is likely to be larger than where these restraints are absent. Nor after examining the conditions in different parts of the Punjab, can we doubt that the eight or ten acres which he commonly cultivates are wholly insufficient, under present conditions, to maintain him in decency, independence, and comfort.'[1]

In England it has been found that, where smallholders go in for arable cultivation only, they need at least twenty-five acres if they are to be better off than a farm labourer. In areas of good land where it is possible to grow vegetables or fruit, ten acres will provide a man with an economic holding.

It is clear that only an insignificant proportion of Indian cultivators have an economic holding. The Punjab is perhaps the most prosperous agricultural province, because of the large areas of virgin desert which have been recently brought under irrigation. These new areas are divided into 'squares' of about twenty-six acres, and in a district like Lyallpur the proportion of owners with twenty-five acres or more is nearly 35 per cent.[2] In spite of this only one in seven of the Punjab cultivators farms

[1] M. L. Darling, *The Punjab Peasant*, p. 281.

[2] H. Calvert, *Size and Distribution of Agricultural Holdings in the Punjab*, pp. 3 *et seq.*

the fifteen acres which are considered the minimum for a decent life. There are also a number of other influences which fasten the peasant down to his little plot of land, and make it difficult for him to escape from the methods and limitations of his forefathers. The cultivator's son is cribb'd, cabin'd and confin'd from the day of his birth. The smallness and inconvenience of his father's holding, the impossibility of getting more land, lack of capital, debt, marketing difficulties, illiteracy, religious restrictions, and the absence of secondary occupations, all combine with a fatalistic philosophy to kill incentive and keep down the standard of living. These factors are bound up with each other, and form a vicious circle through which it is almost impossible to break. We shall have to discuss them in more detail, for India's future depends on solving the cultivator's problems, and it matters little where in this circle we begin. The destruction of the poor is their poverty, and it would perhaps be most logical to start with the smallness of the holdings.

Throughout the last century a steadily increasing rural population has pushed arable cultivation back on to those 'starvation acres' which in many parts of the world would be left for rough grazing. Only in areas where irrigation has brought new land under cultivation has there been any relief from this pressure, and even in the Punjab this relief has only been temporary. In the Deccan there has long been a shortage of land, and the cultivation line has spread from the comparatively fertile valley into the stony barren hills, while the holdings have become smaller, and the evil known as 'fragmentation' has increased. This last term is applied to the dividing up of small plots of land until they become unworkable.

Custom and law of inheritance have led to each separate plot belonging to a deceased cultivator being divided amongst his heirs, so that there is a tendency for fields to become smaller and smaller, and for every ryot's holding to be scattered over the village in tiny fragments. It is an evil common to many countries where peasant proprietors own most of the land, and in France action has had to be taken against 'morcellement'. In the typical Deccan village which Dr. Mann surveyed, he noted that

'in the last sixty or seventy years the character of the land holding has altogether changed. In the pre-British days, and in the early days of British rule, the holdings were usually of a fair size, most frequently more than nine or ten acres, while individual holdings of less than two acres were hardly known. Now the number of holdings is more than doubled, and 81 per cent. of these holdings are under ten acres in size, while no less than 60 per cent. are under five acres.' [1]

At the same time the process of fragmentation has continued until 611 out of the 729 plots of land were under two acres, and there were hardly any fields on which modern farming methods would be practicable.

The small peasant proprietor nearly always suffers from land hunger. Politicians and professors urge him to cultivate his few acres more intensively, but nearly every one who has actually farmed for a living, or farmed as the phrase goes 'against his cheque book', has the same instinctive feeling that broad acres alone can save a man and his family from a life of incessant toil. Hunger may be a healthy symptom, or it may be the cause of inertia and a

[1] *Land and Labour in a Deccan Village*, p. 46.

prelude to collapse. In Europe land hunger often encourages enterprise. Most English smallholders work partly with an eye to extending their holdings. Few would deny that the Green Revolution, which swept across Europe after the War, had brought new life to these areas, however much one may deplore its excesses. With most Indian cultivators, unfortunately, land hunger has become so chronic, and the chances of obtaining more land are so remote, that it merely encourages their natural tendency to fatalism.

In every country the peasant's tragedy is his small yearly 'turn-over'. It puts a limit on his ambition and makes it difficult for him to weather the least financial storm. The Indian ryot, who cultivates a few awkwardly situated plots of ground, may be able to get enough food from them to feed his family moderately well, but looked upon as a business man on a very small scale he is in a miserably weak position. It is, of course, very hard to estimate the income of a man working as his own master, but however the problem is approached it is clear that the cash balance at the end of each year must be negligible. Many people, with little practical experience of farming, have curiously exaggerated ideas about the produce of arable farming. A few figures may help to correct this tendency. Nearly the whole of India's arable land is under food crops, such as rice, wheat and *jawar*, oil-crops like linseed, or cotton. The area under expensive special crops, such as jute, tobacco, sugar-cane, opium, tea, and coffee, is under 4 per cent. of the total, and these are crops which require considerable expenditure, and often yield only a small net profit. The gross value of the other crops is seldom more than Rs.60 per acre, which means that if the cultivator sold everything off his field, including the straw which he usually gives to his bullocks, he would get £4 an acre. In practice he has, of course, to feed himself, his family, and his bullocks, and either retain or purchase seed. He is seldom a free agent when selling, and often gets well below the market price. If we estimate his net cash balance per acre at £1 we shall certainly be overestimating. An English smallholder, engaged in arable farming only, considers he has done well to make as much. Even on the small farms of Denmark and Switzerland, which are well equipped and heavily stocked, the net balance per acre is under £3 and £4 respectively and in neither case has interest been deducted on the value of the live stock which contribute so much to the result.[1]

The typical Indian cultivator with his three, five, or even ten acres can only hope to accumulate a few pounds a year from his land, even if everything goes well. He may get a little extra food by fishing or hunting, but he can seldom make any more cash. His field work does not of course take him his whole time. Anyone acquainted with village life in India knows that there is much under-employment, and that a considerable part of a cultivator's time is spent sitting and talking, or walking miles into a market where the whole of the business he has to transact could be covered by two or three annas. Mr. Calvert, writing of the Punjab, estimates that the work done by an ordinary cultivator does not represent 150 full days' work a year.[2] In the dry belts of the Deccan, where only one crop a year is attempted, and especially on holdings

[1] *Journal of the Ministry of Agriculture*, July and August, 1925.
[2] H. Calvert, *The Wealth and Welfare of the Punjab*.

where there is no well irrigation, the time spent in field work is much less. Arable farming must be seasonal, and in every country the small farmer is always looking for some means of making a little extra money. In England he depends chiefly on dairying, pig-feeding, poultry, and calf-raising. Many also keep their horses busy by doing a little carting under contract. In Japan, where the acreage is as small as India, the peasant cultivates silk-worms. In Central Europe and Russia they do all kinds of woodwork, and many are employed in forestry.

The Indian cultivator engages in hardly any of these secondary industries. Religion and the climate help to make mixed farming on European lines quite impracticable. The basis of all such farming is the fattening of cattle, sheep and pigs for slaughter, or the keeping of milch cows and goats. No Moslem and no Hindu, except a few of the very lowest castes, will touch a pig, so the 'cottager's friend' must be ruled out. Most Hindus are vegetarian, so there is a very limited market for meat, and fattening cattle or even sheep on European lines would never pay. The question of milch cattle in India has aroused considerable controversy. Over most of India the cows are looked upon as breeders of working bullocks. Dr. Mann, describing the stock of a Deccan village, writes:

'the average amount obtained from the buffaloes was only four pounds a day. Among the cows the quantity was still smaller, the maximum being three pounds, and the average only two pounds a day. No wonder, if these figures are common, that the cow is hardly considered as a commercial milk-yielding animal.' [1]

[1] *Land and Labour in a Deccan Village*, p. 117.

On an English commercial dairy farm a cow is expected to give over forty pounds a day for some weeks, and to average over 7,500 pounds yearly, otherwise she will go to the butcher. An Indian cultivator who had a cow giving a tenth of this would consider himself fortunate, and an ordinary English five-gallon Shorthorn would seem like the mythical 'cow of plenty' for which Visvamitra fought the Brahman, Vashishtha.

There are better breeds of cattle in certain parts of India, but it is only on a few special farms, and those usually not run on business lines, that the cows are fed in such a manner that they can produce a gallon or so per day without putting such a strain on their constitutions that they must inevitably become tuberculous. *Ex nihilo nihil fit.* No cow can produce more than a few cupfuls of milk from rough grazing on untreated grass land and from straw. There are several reasons why improvement is difficult. It appears impossible to acclimatise the heavy milking breeds from temperate climes. The villager also has no conception of feeding cattle for milk, and if he is a Hindu his religion places obstacles in the way of breeding and selecting. It is essential for practical dairying to kill cows before they are old, diseased, and unthrifty. The Hindu cannot slaughter his cows, and lets them linger on to die of disease and semi-starvation. It is equally essential to control all breeding, but in most villages the cattle all run together, young bulls are not castrated, and every heifer is bred before she is mature. Custom prevents the weaning of calves on European lines, and the pressure of population on the land discourages the growing of fodder crops. During a recent tour in India, which included visiting one or two experimental farms and a model dairy, the writer never saw a cow which from conformation, condition, and milk yield would have been retained in a well-managed English herd.

Keeping stock is, of course, the best side-line for the small arable farmer, for he will get the manure for his land. 'Muck is the mother of money', and there is considerable evidence to show that the land of India has steadily deteriorated through starvation. The average yield per acre is exceedingly low. The rice yield is less than half that of Japan, and about half that of Egypt. The wheat yield in England is three times that in India, and in Egypt and Japan about double. A few years ago it was authoritatively stated 'evidence of soil exhaustion in various parts of India and Burma has been adduced by many experts and must be accepted as final'.[1] The evidence produced before the Linlithgow Commission led them to assume that the process had now reached its limit and that there was no further robbing of the soil. The question is very obscure, but the impoverished state of the soil in all the older parts of India is obvious.

There are only four practical methods of restoring this fertility, and none of these is being used to any large extent. Artificial manures could be used, but the price of these is prohibitive, especially the nitrogenous manures. Green crops could be grown either for ploughing in, or for feeding sheep on the land. Both are done in certain areas, but sheep farming is difficult to manage on a small scale, and green manuring has not become popular. The two other methods are the use of farmyard manure, and

[1] H. A. F. Lindsay, 'Note on the Export of Indian Manures', *Proceedings of Board of Agriculture in India*, 1922.

of night-soil and village rubbish. There is too little of the first for reasons which we have just discussed, and large quantities of cow-dung are being made into *upla* or fuel cakes, which the housewife either uses herself or takes into the towns. This is a most unfortunate practice, because the price obtained is often less than the value of the dung as manure, and making the cakes is a filthy and degrading job for the women.

Religious scruples – religion plays a considerable part in Indian farming – prevent most cultivators from using night-soil and other village rubbish. This has two unfortunate results. It almost entirely confines market-gardening to a few lowly castes, for some manure of this kind is essential for their work. It means also that village land is losing one of the best forms of compost which can be made. Chinese farming, which is the finest small scale 'conservative' farming in the world, is based on the intelligent use of such composts. In this respect the English connection has been unfortunate, for there is no European country so wasteful of natural manures as England, but the English farmer can, or at any rate could, afford to import cake for his cattle and use artificial manures.

The Indian cultivator makes little use of the other methods by which small arable farmers throughout the world increase their scanty cash earnings. There is still some carting which has to be done by contract, but the railways have killed the long cross-country transport which, a generation or two ago, employed millions of cultivators and their bullocks during the slack seasons. Hand-weaving is another traditional peasant occupation, and a very convenient one. It requires practically no capital, and the work can be taken up or left off at any time. During recent years there has been an immense amount of propaganda, connected chiefly with the name of Mr. Gandhi, to persuade villagers to adopt this work. It seems, unfortunately, to have had little effect. According to the census figures for the United Provinces only 24 cultivators per 10,000 were also weavers in 1911, and the number had dropped to 18 in 1921. Almost the only way in which cultivators can obtain money apart from their field crops is by sending some members of their family to work in factories or coal-fields, returning home to help in the busy season. This practice is increasing in certain areas. Though evidence on this point is difficult to obtain, the amount remitted would not seem to be very great as the total number employed in factories is well under 3 per cent. of the cultivators.

We must picture, then, the ordinary cultivator as living chiefly on the cereals and pulses which he grows, and having each year only a small surplus which he has to convert into cash. Under such circumstances one expects and finds the inevitable corollaries, debt and financial dependence on middlemen. To some extent agricultural debt is inevitable, and not unhealthy. It is the capital which every farmer needs for buying live and dead stock, and for carrying him over the many months between the sowing and harvesting of his crops. If he cannot find the money himself, he is not likely to get outsiders to advance it as an ordinary business venture. The only alternative is to borrow at some fixed rate of interest. If farming is in a healthy condition this debt is more than covered by the buildings, cattle, implements, and growing crops for which the farmer borrowed the money. Nearly all the £377 millions which were owed by Prussian landowners in 1902 was probably productive debt. Unfortunately in India every authority agrees that the debt, amounting to between four and five hundred million pounds, is almost entirely unproductive. The sum per head is not large, but less than 5 per cent. of it has been spent on permanent improvements, and only a small proportion upon cattle and implements. Nearly all of it is personal debt, needed to meet some financial call, and not borrowed to invest in farm stock. Also it is borrowed not from banks but from professional moneylenders who often combine their business with that of agricultural middlemen. The evil is worse in some parts of India than others. Probably 80 per cent. of the cultivators in the Bombay Presidency and the Punjab are in debt. In other areas the proportion is rather smaller. Investigations in selected districts give about 63 per cent. in Mysore, and 45 per cent. in Bengal.[1] It is no exaggeration to say that most cultivators are born in debt, live in debt, and die in debt.

There is little mystery about the financial calls which drive the cultivator to borrow from his *sowkar* or *bunniah*. Most of his needs can, of course, be satisfied by barter, either in his own village, or by taking a headload of straw, vegetables, or dung-cakes to the nearest market. The only regular demand for which cash is essential is land revenue or rent. Unfortunately there has been much political controversy on the extent to which land revenue is a cause of debt. Many statements have been made which are clearly exaggerated. The total agricultural debt of India is about Rs.30 per acre, and this amount is spread fairly evenly throughout the different Provinces. The interest

[1] On this subject see the works of Mr. Darling and Dr. Mann, and Major Jack's *The Economic Life of a Bengal District*.

charges are about Rs.3 per acre yearly. The average interest charges alone come to more than the Land Revenue, which is in the nature of one and a half or two rupees an acre. In the Punjab, where debt is heavy, the interest charges on debt are reckoned to be three times the Land Revenue. In the examination made by Major Jack at Faridpur, the proportion of cultivators in debt was less than in many parts of India, but the total debt was over twenty times the Land Revenue. It would show a lack of proportion to argue that Land Revenue is the chief cause of debt, but there is another aspect of the question. This revenue is, of course, demanded on an acreage basis. It falls heaviest on the very poor. There is also no doubt that a general demand for cash payments from an agricultural community always helps the middleman, for numbers of small farmers have to unload their grain on an overcrowded market, and are at his mercy. The process can be seen after Michaelmas in any arable county in England. The Land Revenue is therefore responsible, if only indirectly, for part of the *bunniah's* power, and it is probable that after a bad year some at least of the Government's dues are paid from borrowed money. Rent in the *zemindari* areas is a heavier charge on the small cultivator, for owing to the pressure on land he is in no position to bargain, but payment is probably less precise.

Occasional heavy expenditure is undoubtedly the origin of most of the cultivator's debt, and nearly all can be ascribed to three causes – the purchase of bullocks, litigation, and family or religious celebrations. The first is of great importance, especially in areas where the rainfall is precarious, for the cattle are the first to suffer in a bad year, and plough bullocks have to be replaced at any cost before the next season's ploughing. In all parts cattle disease is rife, and runs unchecked through the half-starved village herds, leaving a small cultivator no alternative except a visit to the *bunniah*. In the 1899–1900 famine, when the Bombay Presidency is reckoned to have lost 2,000,000 cattle, most of the replacement must have been done on borrowed money.

There are, unfortunately, few reliable figures about the money spent on litigation, though the cultivator's weakness for going to law is proverbial. Some of his expenses under this head are not such as can appear in statistics, and we must also remember that many criminal cases are really due to disputes about land. A conservative estimate would be about £70 millions yearly as the amount wasted in litigation, and most of this falls ultimately on the cultivators. A considerable proportion of the money spent on litigation, criminal and civil, is borrowed, for the smallest case costs over Rs.100. There are also no reliable figures about the cost of marriages, of *Shradd*, and other rites for the dead. In some parts a man will spend twenty years' rental on marrying his son or daughter, and it would be safe to say that almost every cultivator spends at some time in his life many times his rental on such celebrations, and that in nearly every case he borrows the money.

The trials of the illiterate peasant who goes to borrow from a moneylender, or get 'accommodation' from a corn-dealer, are a commonplace in every village in Europe. All that need be said about India is that the ignorance of the peasant, and the rapacity of the moneylender, exceed anything which the West can show. Until the Co-operative movement helped to organise and regularise debt, the only European contribution was to establish a complicated and expensive form of civil law, and to cover India with enough police to prevent the *sowkar's* extortion being 'tempered by assassination'. We have, in fact, allowed the *sowkar* to be the medium through which the cultivator has first come into contact with world markets, and it was under his guidance that the villager has changed from a system of barter to one based on cash. The *sowkar* has taken his toll in the process, and has helped to bring about one important change in village life. The cultivator has abandoned his old custom of keeping a reserve of grain and fodder. He prefers, or more often is forced, to change this reserve into money, and also to grow cash crops, like cotton and jute, rather than wheat and rice. If the extra money was being saved or used to pay off debts, or spent in buying manures and building up the fertility of the soil, or in purchasing stock, then there would be little cause for pessimism. Unfortunately there is evidence of a degeneration in Indian farming rather than an improvement.

We have endeavoured to show that the cultivator's troubles come primarily from the smallness of his holdings, but it is also obvious that two important factors are the Hindu religion which forbids many ordinary farming operations, and illiteracy which prevents the spread of farming knowledge and hampers the cultivator in his dealings with moneylenders. In spite of this the ryots in many areas manage by hard work and extreme abstinence to maintain their standard of living, and even to raise it slightly. Competent observers have noticed a recent improvement in the clothing of cultivators' children. Jats, Sikhs, and Marathas send stalwart young men to serve in the army, and it would seem that a life of comparative privation in the country is less harmful to the physique than a generation or two in the slums of European cities. If we may use a curious naval phrase, the ryot undoubtedly 'serves with sobriety'. From his birth to his death his one extravagance is a marriage, his relaxation a pilgrimage, and his vice, and that only in certain areas, a little toddy or country spirit.

We have throughout this chapter treated the millions of cultivators as a unit, because we were dealing with their material position, and economically they have so much in common that this course seemed justified. It would be absurd to write so dogmatically about them in any other capacity, but it may be worth returning to a famous generalisation which appeared in the Report upon which the present scheme of Reforms was founded. Mr. Montagu referred to the 'placid contentment' of the Indian peasantry. It was a dangerous phrase for 'the Devil alone knoweth the heart of man', and to discover whether the cultivators were contented would entail prying into the strange mental hinterland of the uneducated Hindu, and of the even less educated Moslem whose family was originally Hindu. One would certainly find much which was hardly consistent with happiness. There would be fear of the unseen universe, of the *bhuts* or ghosts which lurk in the fields and woods, and of the whole concourse of Gods, mostly unknown and malignant, who pervade the upper air.

'Here, in this mystical India, the deities hover and swarm,
Like the wild bees heard in the tree-tops, or the gusts of a gathering storm;
In the air men hear their voices, their feet on the rock are seen.'

One would find the effects of continual under-feeding, which tends to make a man think too much or too little of his body, and either become a sensual worshipper of 'Potoba', his stomach, or drift listlessly through life. The long idle days, which the cultivator spends squatting in the narrow village street, lead inevitably to quarrelling and scandalmongering which fill his mind with envy, hatred, and malice. On the other hand, if it is true that 'he alone is truly happy who can sit in the sun in front of his house, and watch his little children playing naked in the dust', then the cultivator has much cause for happiness, and in this matter it would not be wise to draw up a balance-sheet. About his placidity it is easier to form an opinion.

There is an old Indian saying that the bullock spends his life looking for a place to die, and when he finds it he dies. There are parts of India where this might be applied to the peasant. Something of the Brahman philosophy has filtered down into his mind, and made him see the whole world 'like a dancing girl, dancing before a king and deceiving him and beguiling him'.[1] Long centuries of alien rule have merely confirmed this attitude to life, the centuries in which they have watched one ruler follow another, and known little of their coming and going except that some have chastised with whips and some with scorpions.

> 'And is it a god or a king that comes,
> Both are evil, both are strong,
> With women and worshipping, dancing and drums,
> Carry your gods and kings along.'

There are other parts of India where this would not be true, where the villagers retain memories, half real and

[1] Macnicol, *The Making of Modern India*, p. 125.

half mythical, of events which can still stir their blood. In such districts the peasant has shown himself far from placid. The Sikhs who took part in the Akali movement a few years ago must have had very definite traditions of the time, less than a century ago, when one of their sect was the free and independent ruler of the Punjab. The Moplahs, who rose in 1921, had not forgotten the fierce proselytising tradition of their race and religion. The Marathas, who supported Tilak and the revival of the Sivaji cult, might never have done so if they had had no memories of the time when their great-grandfathers watered their horses in the Indus, and caused the timorous folk of Calcutta to dig their famous 'ditch'.

There is another sentiment which makes the cultivator a willing listener to nationalist leaders. He has undoubtedly a vague belief in a golden age, in a prosperous peaceful era when, as the late Mr. C. R. Das said of Bengal,

'we had corn in our granaries, our tanks supplied us with fish; and the eye was soothed and refreshed by the limpid blue of the sky and the green foliage of the trees. All day long the peasant toiled in the fields; and at eve, returning to his lamp-lit home, he sang the song of his heart.'

The countryman is always inclined to be *laudator temporis acti*, but part of this idea may be true, and true of a more recent time than our historians would have us believe. There is much evidence to show that a larger population is now living on a poorer soil than in the old days when no food was exported, and cotton did not take the place of wheat, or jute or rice. It is possible that in India a slow process has been going on, of which we have seen the exact reverse in Russia. An indirect result of the

Revolution and the breakdown of the Russian railway and taxation system was that the peasants in the villages began to eat their own butter, fowls and eggs, and have quite altered their food habits. It is possible that two centuries ago life in an Indian village was easier, and food more abundant than it is to-day. There is a suggestive passage in Tavernier's *Travels in India*, written in the seventeenth century:

'It is not necessary that those who travel in India should provide themselves with food beforehand – especially is this the case with the idolaters who do not eat anything which has had life – because even in the smallest villages rice, flour, butter, milk, beans and other vegetables, sugar and other sweetmeats, dry and liquid, can be procured in abundance.'

This is hardly the impression which a modern traveller would receive if he went by road from Surat to Delhi. We shall have to return in a later chapter to this belief in a Golden Age; we note it here because vague memories of days when life was easier do survive in the villages, and will become more important as the cultivator is gradually drawn into the Western political system which our Government is initiating.

## CHAPTER III

# THE LANDLESS POOR

FROM the earliest days of the Aryan invasion there were village servants working for the husbandmen. They were paid, of course, in grain, for very little money changes hands even in a modern Indian village. They were probably in a dependent position, and partly recruited from the non-Aryan tribes.[1] The descendants of the casteless tribes and of the landless Sudras form the nucleus of the second large group of Indians. There has been from the first a tradition of lowliness about them. The Sudras, according to the legend, proceeded from the feet of the Creator, just as the Brahmans came from the head, the Kshattriyas from the shoulders, and the Vaisyas or cultivators from the thighs. Although there have been periods when Indian craftsmen enjoyed great prosperity, and though the group which is now being considered contains in modern times a large number of Moslems and some of the higher castes, yet its members have much in common. They neither own nor rent any land in a country where this is almost the only form of property which until recent years was understood or recognised. They work with their hands under a religious system which makes such work hereditary, and which marks them off definitely from the clerical professions. Finally they have been exposed, for nearly a century, to certain forces continually tending to lower their

[1] See Alberuni's *India*, written about A.D. 1030. Chapter IX describes the Sudras, below them Antyaja working as fullers, etc., and finally the casteless Domas and others, 'occupied with dirty work'.

standard of living to the dead level of the unskilled manual worker.

The first group, the Vaisyas or cultivators, numbered with their children and dependents about 178 millions. The second group is smaller, but also very numerous. It includes craftsmen and village servants, factory hands and coolies, farm servants and plantation workers, and finally the whole unhappy army of casual labourers, of unsettled and criminal aboriginal tribes, and of beggars. Altogether they number, with their dependents, at least 125 millions, and form nearly two-fifths of the population. Shopkeepers are also included in this group. Many of the smaller craftsmen work in the bazaar, and conditions, especially in the east of India, are very like mediæval Europe where the craftsmen sold their own wares, and villagers brought their vegetables and other foodstuffs to the weekly markets. Shopkeeping on modern European lines is only seen in a few large cities, and trade generally is in the hands of two classes. The middlemen, like the Marwaris, Parsis, Mohammadan Kachchis, and others are dealers and business men rather than shopkeepers, and many of them will be found in our third and last group. The ordinary retailer, however, and even the *bepari* who deals in foodstuffs is a very lowly type of man, and may well be included with the potters, leather-workers, and tailors who sell or barter their own manufactures.

The craftsmen of India have played a very important part in the world's history. Although their origin may have been lowly, and their future is uncertain, for centuries they set a standard of good workmanship which profoundly influenced Western civilisation. The earliest crafts were probably those needed in every village, like the carpenter, and the potter. These became hereditary callings, separate castes in the Hindu hierarchy, while below them would be the village scavengers, and those who removed and treated the skins of cattle and sheep. These last would probably be recruited from the aboriginal tribes hanging round the outskirts of the village, and who were hardly considered worthy to belong to even the lowest of the castes. As the standard of comfort rose we find new castes supplying less essential services, like the barber, the washerman and the tailor. The goldsmith taught the richer husbandmen a convenient way of hoarding wealth in the form of ornaments. The dancing girls – another caste – taught them an even easier way of spending it. In the Ramayana there is a description of the craftsmen who went out to meet Rama, and it would seem that in the very earliest years of Hindu civilisation there were jewellers, potters, ivory-workers, perfumers, goldsmiths, weavers, carpenters, braziers, painters, armourers, coppersmiths, and others all organised in their guilds. The institution of caste, which made each calling hereditary and gave it a religious significance, encouraged amongst the craftsmen a pride in their work and a level of artistic skill which would be impossible to obtain under ordinary competitive business methods. Before Brahmanism had learnt to use caste to emphasise the social superiority of the twice-born, and while India was a mediæval agricultural country untouched by Western industrialism, the system may well have deserved the tribute paid by Sir George Birdwood in describing the life of the village potter:

'To the Indian land and village system we owe entirely the hereditary cunning of Hindu handicraftsman. It has created for him simple plenty, and a scheme of democratic life in which all are co-ordinate parts of one undivided and indivisible whole, the provision and respect due to every man being enforced under the highest religious sanctions, and every calling perpetuated from father to son by those cardinal obligations on which the whole hierarchy of Hinduism hinges.'[1]

Certain crafts have remained scattered through the villages, but others have become localized. Schools for sculpture and architecture were established, often under the ægis of a ruler or chieftain. Such was the school of Ajanta, which was founded two centuries before Christ, and survived for 900 years, leaving as a memorial the wonderful paintings of the cave-temples. The tradition of craftsmanship and the subordination of the individual gave a continuity to the craftsmen's work which makes European commerce seem like a mushroom growth. The weaving industry at Dacca is much older than European civilisation. The Pharaohs of Egypt wrapped their mummies in muslin from Dacca, and the ancient Greeks knew its products as Gangetika. Dacca muslins were sold, together with Indian gold and silver work, in the markets of Rome,[2] and through the Dark Ages still found their way into Europe through Persia, Syria and Amsterdam. Later the finer work of Dacca was familiar in London, Paris, and Amsterdam, and a century ago the commerce of the city was still estimated at a crore of rupees yearly, and supported thousands of weavers.

[1] Birdwood, *Industrial Arts of India*, p. 319.

[2] E. H. Warrington, *The Commerce Between the Roman Empire and India*.

Indian art owed much to its princes. The institution of 'royal craftsmen' made it possible to select and endow the best builders, sculptors, goldsmiths, and embroiderers, and give them the scope and leisure to do that finished and exquisite work which we find in Hindu and Jain temples, in Moghul architecture, and in the best products of the loom and workshop, in the delicate woven fabrics, and in the working of metal and cutting of gems which are typical of Indian art. Mediæval literature, both Indian and European, is full of stories showing the high regard in which these craftsmen were held, and the coming of the Mohammadans did nothing to lower their status. The old Eastern tradition which St. Paul followed, made every one, from the King downwards, learn and practise a handicraft. In ages when book-learning was confined to a few religious bodies, and power was in the hands of the strong and merciless, the craftsmen were the real saviours of society, preventing the wisdom of their forefathers being lost in the recurring periods of anarchy.

'Even at the present day the Indian craftsman deeply versed in his *silpa-Sastras*, learned in folk-lore and in national epic literature, is, though excluded from universities – or rather on that account – far more highly cultured, intellectually and spiritually, than the average Indian graduate. In mediæval times the craftsman's intellectual influence, being creative and not merely assimilative, was at least as great as that of the priest and bookman.' [1]

If the troubles of the cultivators are chiefly due to the pressure on land, those of the Indian craftsman can be traced to the clash of Western industrialism with the

[1] Havell, *Indian Sculpture and Painting*, p. 183.

mediæval craft system. Such craftsmanship can never be competitive. It is based on the idea of a definite standard of quality, and of personal service by the craftsman who has his fixed remuneration and his settled position in society. How long this system might have survived in India, or whether some compromise with European methods might not have been evolved, are questions which have now little more than an academic interest. The coming of the British to India coincided with the beginning of the industrial era, and both our national interests and the political ideas ruling in England during the nineteenth century combined to make us sweep aside the old restrictions, and expose the craftsmen of India to the full blast of European competition. The first effect was to lower standards, and destroy the strict discipline which each caste imposed upon its members. To quote again from Sir George Birdwood, who is the best authority for this transition period: 'A great industry in gold-embroidered shoes flourished in Lucknow. They were in demand all over India, for the native kings of Oudh would not allow the shoemakers to use anything but pure gold wire on them. But when we annexed the kingdom, all such restrictions were removed and the bazaars of Oudh were at once flooded with the pinchbeck embroidered shoes of Delhi, and the Lucknow shoemakers were swept away for ever by the besom of free trade.' In every centre where craftsmen lived together and did fine work this process of disintegration followed the British occupation, but usually it was the imports from abroad which killed the trade. A kind of commercial Gresham's law operates very rapidly in the East, the shoddy cheap article always displacing the finer and better. Just as the products of Manchester ousted the finer work of Dacca, so British goods are being rapidly beaten by the shoddier merchandise with which the Japanese and Germans flood the Indian bazaars, the 'Kram, Tand, Imitation, Novitäten, Galanterie-, Scherz-, Mode und Special-artikel', the manufacture of which Rathenau deplored as the curse of modern civilisation.[1] Even the Indian princes have dropped their patronage of the craftsmen, and prefer to spend their revenues on motor-cars and race-horses, although in some Indian States we may still find groups of craftsmen, living poverty-stricken and forgotten, but carrying on the traditions of their forefathers. In Gwalior and elsewhere there are towns where magnificent embroideries and metal work are produced by castec raftsmen who earn less than half the wages of a dock coolie.

The typical and perhaps the worst example of the effect of Western industrialism can be found in the cotton- and silk-weaving trades, always the most important of Indian handicrafts. The decadence of handloom weaving began during the eighteenth century. Under the earlier Moghuls the weavers supplied the whole Indian market, the cultivator's *dhoti* and embroideries for the *bunniah's* wife. There were also agents from the chief European capitals continually buying the finer work for export. The anarchy which followed Aurangzeb's reign must have reacted on the weavers just when they were first coming into contact through the English with machine-made goods, and Western tariff methods. First the export of the finer cotton and silk fabrics was discouraged by the heavy duties on imports to England, and then, according to a report by an East India Company Director in 1823,

[1] W. Rathenau, *Von Kommenden Dingen*, p. 118.

'partly from the operation of a duty of 67 per cent., but chiefly from the effect of superior machinery, the cotton fabrics which heretofore constituted the staple of India have not only been displaced in this country (England) but we actually export our cotton manufactures to supply part of the consumption of our Asiatic possessions. India is thus reduced from the state of a manufacturing to that of an agricultural country.'[1]

Throughout the nineteenth century the position of the millions of caste weavers grew steadily worse. The finer crafts were the first to suffer, and by 1840 the better muslins were no longer made at Dacca. In some areas, especially in Bengal, weavers bought plots of land and became cultivators, while others degenerated into farm servants. Starvation drove the townsmen to agriculture, as it did in Russia after the Revolution, but this was only possible in certain areas where land was available. Most of the caste weavers continued at their trade. Their standard of living soon sank to about the level of the casual labourer, and they were always the first and worst sufferers in times of famine. The dignity and security of their calling were lost, but they were naturally a patient race, and were satisfied if, by working all day, they could gain a bare living. Although hand-spinning has died out, and is not likely to be revived even by the efforts of Mr. Gandhi, handloom weaving is still an important industry, and where the weavers have learnt the use of the flying shuttle, as at Serampore, they make a livelihood which compares favourably with that of the small cultivator.

[1] Report by Henry St. G. Tucker, quoted by R. C. Dutt, *Economic History of British India*, p. 262.

There are still nearly 3 million men and women weaving cotton by hand as their chief occupation, and it is remarkable that in 1920 they were producing over a quarter of the total cotton goods consumed in India, and that the proportion of hand-made goods had slightly increased since before the War.

Most of the other handicrafts have, like weaving, survived painfully into the twentieth century. There are over 10 million men and perhaps half that number of women who are engaged in various forms of industry, and only about one in seven is employed in a factory employing more than twenty persons. The remainder are either working alone, or in those small family shops which are so characteristic of India. Unfortunately these craftsmen are nearly all handicapped, just as the cultivators are handicapped, by debt and dependence on the middlemen who sell some of their wares. If the strict discipline of the caste system had not been broken down during the last century the craftsmen would have made admirable co-operators, but this type of organisation never works very easily in an industry which is on the verge of being uneconomic. The weavers and many other craftsmen have also suffered from that neglect of Indian art and ideas which has been a feature of British rule. It is a painful thought that the craft of the Hindu builder and sculptor could flourish under the most puritanical Moslem government, but has degenerated at the first contact with the West; that it survived the iconoclast Aurangzeb but wilted under the touch of the Public Works Department. Apart from the clash of interests England was, of all European countries, the least likely to help the Indian craftsman through the difficult period when he first came into competition with machine-made goods. In England no attempt was made to keep alive the cottage industries, and generations of Englishmen went to India convinced that village craftsmen were bound to disappear, and that it was useless being sentimental about their troubles. With a few honourable exceptions the leading Anglo-Indians despised all forms of Indian art, and either held that it was almost entirely derived from European sources, or that its interest was merely archæological. The establishment of four art schools was the Government's only contribution to keeping intact the craftsman's knowledge and culture which they saw decaying before their eyes. District officers, often the younger sons of country squires, understood something of farming and could see that the ryot's methods were often unsound. Though provincial governments have been parsimonious, yet considerable work has been done in agricultural research and propaganda. There has been no corresponding interest in the craftsman's work. Only of recent years has such an elementary improvement as the flying shuttle been adopted to any large extent, and its use is still confined to certain localities. Perhaps the Indian weavers would not have been so neglected if the Civil Service had been recruited from the sons of Manchester cotton spinners.

It was commonly held, especially when cotton and jute factories began to increase rapidly in India, that the craftsmen would be absorbed into large-scale industry as they were in the North of England. It was a false analogy, for the labour required was mostly unskilled, and many factors discourage migration from one part of India to another. The mill-owners, not being prepared to build *bastis* for their men to occupy, took their labour where they could get it easiest and cheapest. In many places they employed men, women and children belonging to the wandering aboriginal tribes, and in no part of India was there any large movement of caste craftsmen to the mills which were competing against them. From a report on the first 'steam factories' at Ahmedabad we learn that 'the class which has benefited most from these mills is not the caste of local weavers, but the Vaghris, who formerly supported themselves by begging. Now whole families of these outcasts take employment at the mills, and become well off.' Many of the present-day mill-hands of Bombay are either the low-caste Mahars or else Kolis, who are fishermen, or Chamars, who are hereditary leather workers. In other areas criminal tribes, such as the Harin Shikaris, Chapparbands and others, have been settled near factories, either by the Salvation Army, or by officers like Mr. Starte. The caste craftsmen have usually continued at their old calling, but the cheapness and servility of the type of labour employed in the factories and mills helped to make the competition against them more severe, and to press their earnings down to that of the unskilled coolies.

There are other caste occupations which have been little affected by Western industrialism. The washerman, the barber, and the tailor are to be found in most villages, and take their share of the scanty harvest. Village servants are given *baluta*, receiving a fixed proportion of sheaves on the threshing floor, very much as the old-time parson collected his tithe. In these days when life in the villages is slowly changing to a cash basis, the system has many practical disadvantages, and the village servants have a considerable struggle to maintain their old standard.

Even worse is the plight of the many castes doing work such as tanning hides, and scavenging, all of which is ceremonially 'unclean'. Most of them are the descendants of non-Aryan tribes, and they have behind them many generations of servitude and ill-treatment, living in miserable quarters, and excluded from the life of the village. There have been various estimates of the population included in the term 'depressed classes'. No exact figures are possible. At census times certain lowly castes are apt to claim a higher status, and also there is no strict dividing line between the touchable and untouchable castes. There are, however, probably 60 million Indians who are living on the outskirts of Hindu society, against whom nearly every means of livelihood and all opportunities of advance are firmly barred, and who from their earliest years are taught that they are physically repulsive to most of the community, and that their evil plight is due to wickedness in some former existence.

The degradation of life amongst these people has often been described, partly because they have provided the chief field for Christian missionary enterprise, and also because the imagination of Europeans has always been struck by the absurd lengths to which the idea of untouchability is carried in many parts of Southern India. The caste system was originally a method of solving the race problem, and was preferable to the wholesale extermination which followed the European migrations to America and Australia. Unfortunately it has developed until it has turned Hindu India into 'a magnificent cage with countless compartments', and because it has left so many millions without any compartment worthy of the name it has become a dead instead of a living organism.

It is true that in some of the industrial centres caste has lost much of its force, but it would be a mistake to imagine that the system has appreciably weakened in the villages. Not only are the old regulations about inter-marriage and inter-dining kept as strictly as ever, but there seems to have been little 'rationalisation' of the system so as to make it less cruel in times of stress. During the famine of 1919–20 the Deccan Mahrattas still refused to allow the Mahars to use the village wells, although the latter's own well, being usually small and *kacha*, had run dry. The writer has watched the Mahars wait and collect such liquid as trickled past the cattle when they had been watered.

Of late years the depressed classes have begun to organise and defend themselves. They have an overwhelmingly strong case, and can often interpose effectually in modern politics. Whenever the nationalist movement is orthodox and Brahman, as for example it was under Tilak's influence, the spokesman of the depressed classes can deny their leaders' claim to speak for the Indian people, or to stand for freedom. Many liberal-minded Indian leaders, notably the late Mr. Gokhale and Mr. Gandhi, have urged the abolition of caste regulations and especially of those which enforce untouchability. The two great modernist Hindu movements, the Arya Samaj of recent years, the Brahmo Samaj from its inception, have spread this idea, and both Christianity and the Arya Samaj have raised the status of outcasts by taking them into their folds. They are supported by many educated Indians, especially those who have had a Western education. Thus Dr. Rabendranath Tagore, when discussing nationalism, says frankly:

'In India there is no common birthright. When we talk of Western nationality we forget that the nations there do not have the physical repulsion, one for the other, that we have between different castes. Have we an instance in the whole world where a people who are not allowed to mingle their blood have shed their blood for one another without coercion or for mercenary purposes?' [1]

So far, however, missionaries and social reformers have only touched the fringe of the problem. The 'pariahs' continue to live their ghetto-like existence, have the same difficulty in getting their children taken into any school, and are still despised and rejected. The British might perhaps have abolished 'untouchability' as they abolished Suttee [2]; but they have never attempted to alter the caste system, and it looks as if it must, being now morally dead, be allowed to decay slowly.

Industrial development might seem the best solution to this problem of the lower castes, besides affording some relief to the pressure on the land. This question will be discussed later.[3] For the present it is enough to say that the influence of factories is only local, and affects a very small proportion of the population, well under 2 per cent. On the other hand, although the factory workers are few in number, they are likely to become an increasingly important factor in Indian politics, and in those social changes which must precede the breakdown of the caste system. Living huddled together in *bastis* or 'chawls', usually under the most filthy and unhealthy conditions, they are removed from all the restraints of village life

[1] Tagore, *Nationalism*, p. 123. [2] See p. 234.
[3] See Part IV, Chapter II.

and the Hindu system. They become susceptible to new influences, which may in time produce a corporate feeling, a class consciousness of which we already see signs among the lower castes. Though only a few are literate they come much more under the influence of the vernacular press than they would in a village, and they are easily approached by the politician.

At present labcur is only strong politically through the pressure which the workers bring indirectly upon their employers. Although wages are very low, the factory workers are not very docile, especially since the War. Strikes are frequent, though they are too often the prelude to the formation of an ill-regulated union rather than the last weapon to be used after negotiations through an established union have failed. Only in the railway work-shops and at Ahmedabad have unions been organised on anything approaching European lines. Where unions do exist they have too often been used partly for political purposes, being captured by nationalist leaders, many of whom are closely bound by financial and personal ties to the Indian employers of labour. Few social workers have cared to undertake the difficult and thankless task of industrial organisation. Where the status of trade unions is good this can usually be traced to a body like the Servants of India Society or to some individual worker, like Ansuya-bai Sarabhai at Ahmedabad, who is prepared to work without reward and without any political ambition. The weakness of the movement is partly due to the mill-hand's habit of absenting himself from work, either because he has some wages in hand, or wants to help his family who have retained a piece of land. This is unfortunate, for without such organisation neither a British nor a *swaraj*

Government are likely to do much to improve their condition, and yet these industrial areas are the parts to which one naturally looks for the beginning of democracy and the raising of the general standard of living.

If the caste craftsmen had entered the factories in sufficient numbers, the old discipline would have been easily enforced. The castes of Ahmedabad were making rules about overtime and hours of work centuries ago, and the regulation of wages by groups of workers was common in India when similar action would have been a criminal conspiracy in England. The owners, however, have sought their labour elsewhere and town-bred Moslems and outcasts are almost impossible to organise. They are easy to call out on strike, and being used to short commons will stay out for long periods, but otherwise they will not work together. There have been many stoppages of work since the War, but most of them fruitless. In 1925 there were thirty-three strikes at Ahmedabad, none of which were authorised by the Union interested. Too often they have been the work of irresponsible individuals who gamble on a successful strike as being the easiest way to win their political spurs.

Without organisation the workers can do little to raise their wages. Much of the labour is still recruited by 'sirdars' who collect men and women from the villages and outskirts of the towns like the 'gang-men' in eighteenth-century England. They are brought long distances to towns, where they have to face a different climate and environment, and often learn something of a new language. Conditions resemble those in the North of England a century ago. There are great differences between the wages paid for similar work in different mills, and these have little or no relation to the cost of production. It is also difficult to gauge the amount taken by the sirdars as their perquisite or *dasturi*. Miss Kelman, who made a careful study of conditions in the textile works after the War, writes that:

'a rough generalisation for the years 1920–1 would group the wages paid to the larger number of women in jute mills in Bengal between nine rupees and thirty rupees a month; those in factories in Bombay between thirteen and thirty-four rupees a month, and those in Ahmedabad between twelve rupees and thirty rupees.' [1]

The wages of the men vary in the same way, but it would probably be fair to say that an Indian textile mill-hand, male or female, gets about one-sixth of the amount paid for similar work in England. Their work is usually reckoned as being between a half and a third as efficient. These very rough figures show that from a producer's point of view Indian labour is cheap, and the difficulty of obtaining satisfactory data regarding wages is evidence of the disorganised conditions under which most factory work is done. In Ahmedabad, where trade-union influence is strong, wages are paid on a more systematic basis, but through most of India the only factors which tend to improve conditions are the difficulty of recruiting labour, the competition for workmen between the different mills, the poor work done if hours are too long and conditions too bad, and finally some pressure from Government inspectors.

The difficulty which is often experienced in getting labour is one of the many paradoxes of industrial India. According to European standards and ideas there should

[1] *Labour in India*, p. 118.

be an immense reserve of labour upon which factory owners and plantation owners could draw. There are 39 millions classed as farm labourers and servants, many of whom are casually employed. There is another group of 9 millions living on various forms of unskilled labour mostly unspecified. Probably a third of these 48 millions are working-men. There must be an equally large number of men who are for census purposes described under the head of cultivators, plantation workers, scavengers, etc., who are prepared to do other labour for a whole or part of the year. A number of reasons, however, prevent Indian labour from being 'fluid', especially that group of farm labourers who are few compared with the cultivators, but who form a population as large as that of England. In many parts of India they are little better than serfs, and are practically bound to the soil.

'Casual agricultural labour is generally paid in grain, at the rate of 5 to 8 annas a day for a man or 3 to 4 annas for a woman. The farm servant is paid in a variety of ways; his condition varies from practical slavery to comparative independence; but such is the custom of the country that the master nearly always contrives to get his servant into debt, and thus obtain a powerful hold over him in case he thinks of leaving his service.' [1]

The plantation workers are generally recruited from this farm servant type, and they also emigrate from the Madras Presidency to Ceylon and the Straits, but most of them do not like to go far from their homes, and at present industry is very much localised, either in the big cities like Agra, Cawnpore, Ahmedabad and Bombay, or else in areas

[1] Census Report of 1921, Vol. I, p. 275.

like the banks of the Hooghly. The foundation of Tata's works at Jamshedpur in the middle of a scrub jungle was a new and very important departure.

The housing shortage is partly responsible for the scarcity of labour. Even when the owners have built *bastis* or chawls they are seldom of the type to which a mill-hand would care to bring his family, while in many parts the living conditions are indescribably filthy. The factory hands do not look upon such quarters as their home, and in the United Provinces it was reckoned that only a very small proportion, considerably less than 100,000 workers, are permanently attached to organised industries. The Bombay Government, when it decided after the War to build 'model' chawls, still held that a single room in a block three stories high is a proper habitation for a man and his family. The long lines of single-storied *bastis* which surround the better type of jute mills on the Hooghly are probably more suitable for rearing a family, but even the best of Indian employers have only reached the stage of a benevolently paternal attitude towards their workers. This applies equally to the jute mills of the East, which are almost all managed by Europeans, and to the cotton mills of the West, which are usually owned and frequently managed by Indians. Neither group have succeeded in collecting round them settled and contented colonies of mill-hands who are prepared to work steadily through the year.

It is important to remember that the men employed in factories are an insignificant proportion even of the 'landless proletariat'. Nearly all the 125 millions comprised in this term are working either as craftsmen, servants, or farm labourers. Perhaps there are 40 million men in this group, and of these about one in every hundred works in the tea gardens, and about four are attached in a somewhat casual manner to the factories and mines. Most of these 5 per cent., who are thus employed by companies or capitalists, either belong to the lower Hindu castes or are urban Moslems. The remainder, whether Hindu or Mohammadan, are still under the influence of the caste system. They have, as it were, their compartments in the 'magnificent cage' and most of them show little inclination to escape. Their inertia may seem remarkable, and their lack of enterprise deplorable. It is partly due to the climate and partly to a religion which exalts the *faqir* and the *saddhu* and other mendicants rather than the honest and skilled workman. Only amongst certain craftsmen is there any real tradition enforcing a high standard of work, and even amongst them the ordinary avenues for a healthy ambition are closed. It would seem that a change in outlook and in the social system is an essential prelude to any advance.

## CHAPTER IV

# THE UPPER CLASSES

INDIA has been likened to a primeval monster with an enormous body and a small and inadequate head. The comparison is not inapt. The cultivators, the landless workers, the aboriginal tribes, and the indigent form a vast unwieldy body of people, mostly illiterate and narrow-minded, over which the small group of educated Indians has little influence. It is, however, a mistake to consider this group as negligible, or to exaggerate its numerical weakness. The proportion which the so-called upper classes bear to the population would not have seemed remarkable to an eighteenth-century European, or a nineteenth-century Russian. Not one in twenty of Napoleon's *vieux grognards* could read, and Russia is still predominantly a country of illiterate peasants. The modern Western state with its wide diffusion of wealth and education is a new phenomenon. According to the standards of a century ago India has a comparatively large aristocracy, partly intellectual and partly hereditary, and an immensely old tradition of civilisation and abstract learning.

In the early years of the Aryan migration only the priestly castes could have enjoyed the literary education and the opportunities for a comfortable sedentary life which are, perhaps, the chief characteristics of the third and final group which we have to consider. The development of organised government, and the growth of cities brought political power as well as religious distinction to the bookmen. The priestly Brahmans as well as the warrior Kshattriyas became the natural leaders of society.

With the advance of civilisation the leisured life and social amenities, which the Brahmans enjoyed, became the object of nearly every wealthy man's ambition. The rich and well-educated, whether Moslem or Hindu, began to form a class as separate and distinct from the cultivators and craftsmen as the Brahmans. During the last centuries the so-called 'respectable classes' have been joined by an increasing number of lawyers and schoolmasters, by many landowners, and by a new middle class founded on commerce and moneylending. The very favourable terms which the East India Company offered to landlords and tax-collectors in Bengal and elsewhere turned them into mere recipients of rent, and encouraged them to lead easy if not very cultured lives. The legal system and the administrative machinery for which British rule was responsible has brought into existence a new class of educated officials and lawyers, many of whom were Mohammadans or belonged to non-Brahman castes. Internal peace and modern commercial methods have also encouraged the moneylender and the middleman, whose sons become landlords or join one of the professions. The last hundred years has seen the growth, in India as in Europe, of a new class with pretension to culture and a leisured style of life, but belonging neither to the priestly nor to the older landowning classes.

It should not be difficult to define our third group, for in some parts of India they already have a separate designation. The *bhadralok* of Bengal correspond almost exactly to what the Victorian era called the 'respectable classes', and the very sharp line which divides them from their neighbours is apparent in other provinces. Major Jack describes them as landlords, clerks, and professional men. 'The *bhadralok* is a very important class in Eastern Bengal, containing every man of education and influence and nearly every man of wealth in the district along with a considerable substratum of excessive poverty.' Our third group may be considered as the *bhadralok* of India. No exact definition is possible or desirable, but the continuity of caste distinctions helps to keep the groups separate. To return again to Bengal –

'The respectable classes belong almost entirely to the three highest Hindu castes – Brahman, Kayasth, and Baidya – with a few Mohammadans of birth, breeding, or education. Nearly one-half are landlords who support themselves partly or wholly upon the rents paid by their tenants, another quarter are maintained by the professions, law, medicine, or the priesthood, and the remainder are clerks either in Government employ or in the employ of landlords or traders.' [1]

Taking India as a whole there would seem to be about 16 million people who can be included in this group, and these with the 178 million cultivators and their families, and the 125 million landless workers and dependents, make up the population of India. If the number of *bhadralok* – 5 per cent. of the population – seems excessive it must be remembered that either 'birth, breeding, or education' brings them into this class. Many of the women, especially the wives of landlords, are totally illiterate, and many families poverty-stricken. The proportion of the so-called respectable classes to the rest of the population varies in different parts of India. It is highest in the *zemindari* areas, where the permanent

[1] Major Jack, *Economic Life of a Bengal District*, p. 89.

settlement of the land revenue has encouraged the landlord system. In Faridpur Major Jack estimates the *bhadralok* as 27,335 families out of 342,108, which suggest that they are more than 5 per cent. of the population in Bengal. The latter figure would seem, however, to be fairly accurate for India. It is important to realise that the total strength of the Indian upper classes is considerable, for there is a tendency amongst Englishmen to overemphasize the fact that they are an 'insignificant minority'. They far outnumber the combined populations of Canada, Australia and New Zealand.

Historically the priests formed the basis of this group, and they are still a large and important section. Their numbers are uncertain, for it is not easy to differentiate between the priest, who is of the leisured class, and the religious mendicants and temple servants who belong to the second group of the landless workers. It would, however, be safe to include in our third group most of the 2½ millions who are dependent upon religion for their livelihood. Hindu priests belong to two types, neither of which has any European equivalent. The *guru* is a teacher, or more accurately he is an intermediary between the worshipper and the elusive deities which can only be approached by men of spiritual eminence. Most of the castes formerly had their special *gurus*, whom they treated with immense respect, and to whom they ascribed powers which were almost divine. On entering a house the *guru* was greeted with a formula which marked his great authority. 'I bow down to the Guru; the Guru is Brahma; the Guru is Vishnu; the Guru is Shiva; verily the Guru is the sublime Brahma.' Secular education has, however, undermined their position, and the far from holy lives which so many led hastened the process. The *gurus* are now more like private chaplains shared by a number of families, whom they visit about once a year. They move round from one place to another, taking care to collect their *dakshina* or fees, and in some parts are mere hangers-on of the rich. The *purohits* are a poorer type and more numerous. Their duties are entirely ceremonial, and a family of *purohits* is to be found in most villages where there are Brahmans. They have taken over many of the duties of the village astrologer. They fix the auspicious days for weddings, preside over marriage and funeral ceremonies, and cast horoscopes. The work of the *purohit* is less individual than that of the *guru*, and when he dies his sons divide up his clients, in the same way as they divide up any land or property he may have owned.

Both kinds of priest seem to be steadily losing ground. They have shed much of their spiritual authority, and the 1921 census shows that their numbers, with those of the temple servants, had decreased during the previous decade. All the characteristic evils of priestcraft are to be found in India.

'The pre-eminence of the Brahman was originally, perhaps, attained because of his superior devotion and the unworldliness of his spirit; but the time when this was true of him, it must be admitted, is wrapped in the mists of antiquity. To-day for the most part the testimony of the low-caste man in regard to him is true: "Brahmans are like palm-trees, very high, but giving little shade to us poor people." '[1]

Some of the ideas which have led to the decline of priest-

[1] Macnicol, *The Making of Modern India*, p. 65.

craft in Europe have filtered down even to the Indian villages. The *purohit*, who practises a religion which has no claim to any altruistic or moral basis, finds it increasingly difficult to justify his existence. A spirit of individualism is spreading, partly due to education and contact with the West, but even more to the decay of the joint family system, and the increased use of money in the villages. The new generation is less patient under the Brahmans' exactions, and their opposition is stiffened by the activities of some of the caste *sabhas* and other organisations. The rapacity of the Brahmans is so great, and their lives are often so little admirable that Europeans must marvel at the patience of the villagers. The extent to which agricultural debt is due to religious observances has already been discussed. Readers of Tagore's remarkable novel, *The Home and the World*, will remember the unhappy fate of Nikhil's most indigent tenant:

'Panchu's wife has just died of a lingering consumption. Panchu must undergo a purification ceremony to cleanse himself of sin and to propitiate his community. The community has calculated and informed him that it will cost one hundred and twenty-three rupees.'

There must be an increasing number of men whose social sense revolts at the waste and brutality involved in these observances and will, like Nikhil, wonder 'when will come the time for the purification of the Brahmans themselves who can accept such offerings?' The importance of reformist movements like the Arya Samaj will be considered later. For the present it is enough to note that the Brahmans who exercise their religious functions are an important section of the educated classes, and one which is opposed not only to British rule, but to most Western innovations. Their position is, however, being constantly assailed, on one side by the lower castes, and on the other by upper-class reformers. Their number and their status are on the decline. The Mohammadan *mullah* does not seem to have suffered to the same extent. The recent increase in Hindu-Moslem tension and the method of communal electorates have placed the Moslem religious leaders in a very strong position. Where religion influences politics to the extent which it does, say, in the Punjab, and so long as parties are based entirely on communal divisions, the *mullah* must be a most important political factor, and his social standing is proportionately enhanced.

The decline in the number of priests has been counterbalanced by an increase in the professional classes, but it is remarkable that neither change has been at all rapid. The Brahman priest does not readily adopt a profession. There is a tradition dating back to the Code of Manu which discourages the 'twice-born' from accepting a 'dog livelihood' in the form of wages. The 'professions and liberal arts', though extended to include actors and itinerant musicians, support less than 1 per cent. of the population. We hear much of the 'vakil ka raj' or lawyers' rule in India, but it is important to realise that though their numbers are excessive compared with those of the doctors, engineers, and schoolmasters, yet they are no longer increasing at all rapidly, and that taken as a whole the professional classes are few in number and almost stationary. The increase, about 10 per cent. in ten years, in people supported by the law was almost entirely confined to the Indian States, and so was the rise in the teaching profession, which between 1911 and 1921 was 50 per cent. in the Indian States, but only 10 per cent. in British India. Actors and musicians, as well as some other professions, such as journalism, show a distinct decline, and the medical profession has only risen 5 per cent. during the last census decade. This whole group, with the possible exception of the lawyers, are much too few for a country which claims to be civilised, and it is distressing to find that it shows little signs of increasing, and that, again excepting the lawyers, they neither receive the emoluments nor the consideration which they deserve.

Litigation has always possessed a peculiar fascination to the Indian mind. The quarrelsomeness of the peasant proprietor, the Asiatic love of forensic eloquence, the absence of other forms of competitive sport or outlets for combativeness, all combine to fill the civil courts with suits over minute divisions of land, and the criminal courts with cases arising out of the most trumpery disputes. Most of the amount wasted on such disputes does not, of course, go into the lawyer's pocket. Mr. Calvert has recently estimated that 40 per cent. of the adult male population of the Punjab attend the courts every year, either as parties or witnesses, and that three or four million pounds are wasted in the process. The Punjab, where the moneylender flourishes more than in most areas, may possibly spend more on litigation, but £70 million would probably be an under-estimate of the yearly waste due to India's two million civil suits and the innumerable criminal cases which are really of a civil nature. Much of this money goes in court fees, but there is a considerable balance from which the hundred thousand lawyers, petition writers, and legal agents and clerks, make sums varying between a few rupees a month and the income of a leader of the English Bar. The enormous prizes which it offers, and its close connection with nationalist politics make the legal profession the natural choice of most educated and ambitious young men, nor do they seem to be deterred by the fierce competition amongst the lower grades of *vakils*. India suffers both from this competition and also from the excessive prestige attaching to what must always be a parasitic profession. In many districts the *vakils* find it necessary to organise a system of agents who tout for work in the country areas, and whose object is to foment disputes, and encourage litigation. Indian lawyers combine the work of solicitor and barrister, so they have to keep in close touch with landlords in the *zemindari* areas, and with moneylenders everywhere. In some parts they are superseding the latter, and have obtained a hold upon the cultivators as drastic and more effective than that of the old-time *sowkar*. All these reasons make the continued predominance of lawyers in politics most undesirable, but they are at present almost the only class who can compete with the landowners in the new assemblies.

In 1921 there were 335,000 teachers in India, of whom only 35,000 were women, and about three-quarters were Government servants. The figures suggest an educational system which is unlike that of any Western country, but one which has also developed a long way from the old Hindu ideal of the *guru*, to whom the eight-year-old *chela* or disciple repaired and spent the next fourteen years of his life. There are still many private schools, in most of which a religious training is given, and in Burma a large part of the population passes through the Buddhist monastic institutions. Both their numbers and their pupils are declining, and India is being gradually covered by a network of primary and secondary schools, all of which are definitely under State control. About one boy in every three passes through the hands of the primary school teacher, about one girl in thirteen, so that even if we allow that the number of villagers who retain any literary education is small, the influence of the schoolmasters on the population must be very great. Unfortunately village teachers, practically all of whom are men, do not usually play a large or sympathetic part in the life of the little communities to which they are sent. Many of them are 'failed matriculates' who have been forced, disillusioned and disheartened, to take a poorly paid mastership in very uncongenial surroundings. Life in a small Indian village is intolerably dull for an educated man with urban interests. Most Englishmen who have worked in Indian districts retain a picture of the village schoolmaster as an unhappy and ill-nourished person, hardly ever taking any great interest either in his work or in the village. The experience of most Western countries is that it is hopeless to expect men to teach in small villages, where the school is usually treated as a *crèche*, and where it is impossible to give proper attention to the elder children. Unfortunately Indian conditions make it impossible to employ married women, or even the innumerable widows whom the Hindu religion forbids to re-marry, and the staffing of the smaller village schools is only possible because of the severe unemployment amongst the middle classes. Education is now under the charge of Indian Ministers, and in each Province they are faced with the same problem, how to pay their masters something more than the coolie's twenty-five rupees a month which they often receive at present, and at the same time build and staff new schools. As less than one Indian in ten is literate, and three-quarters of India's innumerable villages and hamlets have no school, there is an almost unlimited field for extending primary education, but the authorities are hampered by trying to work a voluntary system under a very difficult circumstance. The general question of allotting more money to education will be considered later. The present position is that most primary schoolmasters are very badly paid, and spend much of their time in the undignified work of keeping up their school attendance in areas where they receive little help from the parents. From experience obtained in other countries it would seem that the only way to raise their status would be to have central schools in the larger villages, infant schools with women teachers in the smaller villages and arrangements for collecting the elder children at the central schools. Reforms on these lines are being carried on in many rural areas of England, but are hampered in India by innumerable practical and economic difficulties.

The position of the schoolmaster in the larger towns and in the secondary schools is much better. Primary education in India is carried on painfully and inefficiently in the face of continual opposition from the cultivators, but India's ten thousand secondary schools cater chiefly for the middle classes who have a traditional keenness for a literary education. While there are under 8 million pupils in primary schools, over a million and three-quarters are undergoing secondary education. On a population basis the first figure is less than a fifth of what it should be in a country with compulsory education, but the proportion of children in secondary schools is higher than it was in England just before the War. It would seem that there is not a very great field for the further expansion of secondary education unless it can be made vocational, a conclusion borne out by the excessive competition for Government and clerical posts. Unfortunately there are no signs that the parents are growing more far-sighted, for in 1926 over 8,000 out of 87,000 attending Universities and colleges were studying law, and only 9,000 were taking special subjects such as engineering, commerce, medicine, and the profession of teaching. Agriculture could only attract 641 students, and two subjects most essential to India's future, forestry and veterinary work, only 119 and 272 respectively.[1] The teacher's position cannot be satisfactory while the system is so top-heavy. Another weakness is the growing dependence upon Government. Probably the old ideal of *guru* and *chela* is bound to disappear, in spite of such isolated attempts to revive and modernise it as Rabindranath Tagore's famous institution at Bolpur.[2] One cannot, however, fail to deplore the rapid decadence, probably more rapid than the official figures show, of independent educational institutions, especially those which teach oriental subjects. The teachers are tending to become primarily Government servants, belonging to a cadre which is inferior because its members are worse paid than administrative officials. The evil is being partly met by the 'formation of separate University cadres of academic, not official,

[1] *India in* 1926–7, p. 316.

[2] See W. W. Pearson's *Shantiniketan.*

status,' and Mr. Mayhew hopes that 'forces have been released which may in time restore the ancient sanctity and repute of the *guru*.'[1] It will, however, be more difficult to work such a reform in secondary education and there are no signs that the Indian Ministers of Education are more inclined than their Civilian predecessors to relax control of the schools. There is little agreement about the type of secondary education which is needed. The Pandit and the Moulvi are losing their place in Indian education, but the present system does not seem likely to produce men like 'Sanderson of Oundle' who will lead enthusiastic pupils along the new and untried paths of scientific technical education.

The slow progress of the medical services is due to similar causes. India has three indigenous systems of medicine; the Ayurvedic is Hindu, while *tibbi* and *unani* are usually practised by Mohammadans. In all three there is much traditional wisdom, but they have no modern scientific basis, and much Hindu medicine is closely connected with religious formalities and rites. This has made India the happy hunting-ground for the quack doctor, and the Hindu belief in the religious uncleanness of women at child-birth, has left the whole field of obstetrics to a lowly and ignorant caste. Under these circumstances it was, perhaps, inevitable that British administrators should repudiate the indigenous medical systems even more decisively than Macaulay and Ram Mohun Roy had previously discarded the oriental basis of education. Indian private practitioners, the *Hakim*, the *Vaidya*, and the *Kabiraj*, still do much work in the towns and larger villages, but they have suffered some-

[1] Mayhew, *The Education of India*, p. 205.

thing of the same eclipse as the *Moulvi* and the *Pandit*. Indigenous medicine instead of spreading to the smaller villages is losing ground in the larger ones, and there are not sufficient men with Western training to fill the gap.

During the last twenty years there has undoubtedly been an improvement in the work and scope of the Government Health Officers, but they can only hope to cover a small proportion of the villages, and are scarcely able to hold in check such endemic diseases as plague and *Kala-azar*. A new epidemic must sweep uncontrolled through the country, and in 1918 influenza was responsible for over 7 million deaths.[1] Few Indians who have undergone the necessary European medical training would care to risk a private practice amongst a population chiefly composed of peasants. They prefer to wait for an appointment either under the Government or under some municipality. It may ultimately be possible to divide India into a number of health areas small enough for a single doctor to reach every village when needed. In the Punjab a five-year scheme has been adopted for building 375 dispensaries, and in other Provinces Health Officers are being appointed to new specified areas. Western medicine under State or municipal control would seem to have won the day. A few *unani* institutions, like that admirable hospital founded at Delhi by the late Hakim Azmul Khan, still manage to survive, but not many Indians seem willing to subscribe to private hospitals.

There are two disadvantages in the present system. It is entirely Western in organisation and methods, and

[1] Census Report, 1921, Vol. I, p. 13. It states that seven million is 'a substantial under-estimate.'

may degenerate when not under European control. Public Health is now a 'transferred subject', which means that in every Province it is under the charge of an Indian Minister. Already there have been signs of a political revolt against Western medicine, for which Mr. Gandhi is partly responsible. Disputes have also occurred about the salary to be paid to English doctors, and for some time India was practically boycotted by the British Medical Association. The other danger has its counterpart in the educational services. It is easy to organise urban areas, but the law of diminishing returns operates very rapidly when any system has to be extended to the villages. It was calculated that a recent extension of primary education in the United Provinces had taught only 25,000 more people to read, but had cost ten million rupees.[1] Literacy at Rs4,000 a head becomes something of a luxury. The development of the medical services may be checked in the same way. Bursts of enthusiasm in the Assemblies are liable to be quenched by the production of estimates, and followed by periods of stagnation. Medical students are almost entirely dependent on Government for their career. They never know if they are going to end their long and specialised training at a time of restriction or expansion. The very small increase in the medical profession, and the paucity of medical students suggest that these fears are not unjustified nor has Western medicine succeeded in ousting the enormous army of charlatans, unlicensed accoucheurs, untrained *dhais* and others who assist most Indians into and out of the world.

Clerks are an important and numerous section of

[1] Census Report, 1921, Vol. I, p. 185.

India's *bhadralok*. At least 2 millions are supported by this ill-paid and unhealthy profession. For many years one of the most noticeable features of Indian life has been the large floating population of men who have received some kind of literary education, and after failing to obtain Government employment are forced either to work as agents, clerks, rent-collectors, or else help some little shopkeeper with his accounts. The amount of unemployment in this class is unbelievable. Each year thousands of 'failed matriculates' with no commercial training of any kind are thrown upon the labour market. Most of them marry as students, so they have to leave their wives and children with their parents, and seek such work as may be available for a man with no qualifications except an ability to read and write, and perhaps a smattering of English. Owing to the relatively small industrial development of India, the demand for clerical labour is insufficient even to absorb a reasonable number of those young men who take the University examinations each year. Bengal, for example, has a population only slightly larger than England and Wales, and perhaps one in ten of its people are literate, yet each year over 16,000 young men take the University matriculation examination, and only a very small proportion have any vocational training or are able to obtain Government posts. In 1926 and 1927 a Commission on Unemployment sat in Madras, and found that some 14,000 educated and partially educated young men were being thrown each year on a labour market which could not absorb half of them. A trial advertisement for a clerk on Rs35 a month (say 13*s*. a week) produced over 600 answers. They also noted that while the number of students had increased there was a steady reduction since the War in Government posts, in municipal clerkships, and other openings. The Committee could suggest nothing but the appointment of more school teachers, and a return to agriculture.[1] Our system of secondary education has produced an immense reserve of clerical labour, a real 'landless proletariat', which, as was seen in the last chapter, is foreign to the whole structure of Hindu society, and hardly exists amongst the manual working classes. Though these clerks are politically united, because they are mostly keen nationalists, they are completely unorganised industrially, and their wages often fall well below those of the coolie. Some of them are the children of small landowners or fairly prosperous cultivators, but they can seldom go back to the land even if they have any inclination to work with their hands. The University student of this class is usually one of the younger sons of a large family, which is already weighing too heavily on the paternal acres. His brothers would not relish the return of the *babu* brother who would add his inefficient help in cultivating the few fields, and would claim his share of the land on the father's death. They prefer to look after his wife and family, and trust him to remit some money home when he has any work.

Middle-class unemployment is not due to any temporary disturbance. It is, at least, as permanent as unemployment in the mining industry in England. It is closely connected with two problems for which no easy solution exists, India's small industrial development, and the pressure on her agricultural land. The position grows worse rather than better, and it is impossible to under-

[1] See report by Prof. A. J. Saunders, *Economic Journal*, March, 1928.

stand the attitude of the average educated Indian of to-day without realising that somewhere in the background of his life there are nearly always several hungry nephews and cousins continually drifting into and out of badly paid clerkships.

We have dealt up to the present with those members of the upper classes who either work or wish to work. There is, however, a large section of this group, something over 8 millions, who merely live on their rents. They range from the very wealthy *zemindar*, who dreams of keeping a racing stud in England, to the indigent children of the small landowners. The family system has much to commend it amongst cultivators and craftsmen, but it is disastrous to the *rentier* class.

'Landowners are accustomed to spend an idle life in their village homes, not only the father but all the sons together. The result is that idle men are found in many villages who have no possible means of spending their days profitably, and who not unnaturally devote themselves to intrigue or to fomenting strife between their neighbours; wherever villagers quarrel or are at loggerheads with their neighbours there is usually some idle *bhadralok* who acts as the agent-provocateur.' [1]

The very large numbers of landowners is partly due to the fact that land has been for centuries almost the only form of productive investment. Until the last fifty years the man who made money had either to lock it up in the form of bullion and jewellery or else buy land. Banking has had a somewhat chequered history, the field of industrial investment in India has never been very large or

[1] Major Jack, *Economic Life of a Bengal District*, p. 33.

safe, and most of the Government and railway loans at fixed interest were floated abroad. Religious scruples prevent most Moslems and many Hindus from lending money, and even to-day it is clear from recent transactions in the Punjab that men will pay prices for land which cannot possibly bring them in more than a very small return, considerably less than an investment in Government stock. There is also, of course, some social prestige connected with landowning, but this unfortunately depends little on the well-being of the estate. In a country where farm buildings play only a small part in the economy of the farm, where there is usually no homestead, no indoor feeding, no fencing and gates, and no pipe-draining, it is clear that an agricultural landowner has little to do except collect his rents. In India he seldom even does this, for nearly all estates in the *zemindari* areas are under the management of poorly paid clerks, a swindling and rapacious class. The landlord has little direct connection with his tenants, nor is he expected to exercise the benevolent paternalism of the old-time country squire and Justice of the Peace. He does not even feel called upon to send out his younger sons to fight for their country or earn their living. No large class could stand the temptation of such a lazy and irresponsible life. In areas where the estates are large, such as Oudh, they form a society not unlike the serf-owning landlords of Tsarist Russia. Anyone who reads Gogol's *Dead Souls* must be continually reminded of certain sides of Indian life, and must wonder if any class so lacking in public spirit as the Indian *zemindars* are likely to reform themselves, or whether they will be finally engulfed in some social upheaval.

Although the ownership of land is still much the most important form of investment, it would be a mistake to ignore the growth of a new capitalist class in India. There are many Indians, notably the Parsis and Marwaris, who take quite naturally to the development of industry along modern lines. No section of the population increased so rapidly between 1911 and 1921 as the 'manufacturers and business men', whose numbers trebled during the ten years. Even if we allow for some alteration in the method of enumeration the figures are remarkable. The change is partly due to the development of new industries by Indian enterprise. This was responsible for nearly all the new cotton and flour mills, the brick and lime works, and printing presses which came into existence during the period. Another factor has been the displacement of Europeans by companies with an Indian directorship. This has happened in the tea industry. In Bengal nearly all the new gardens are owned by Indians, and in ten years companies with Indian directors increased from 18 to 82, while the number of gardens privately owned by Europeans fell from 46 to 36. Other Indians, inspired, perhaps, by Messrs. Tata's works at Jamshedpur, have launched out into engineering and mining enterprises. This new and rapidly increasing class is bound to play an important part in the future of India. They already number, with their dependents, nearly half a million. They are more intelligent and open-minded than the landowners, and in much closer contact with Western ideas.

Political activity in India, as in nearly every country until the last few years, has been almost entirely confined to the educated and wealthy classes. The Mutiny, so far as it was political, originated amongst landlords. The Congress was founded by a few members of the professional classes, and the part played by lawyers, journalists, and doctors in its subsequent history is well known. The nationalist movement in the Deccan which was organised by Bal Gangadhar Tilak owed all its strength to the Brahmans. The agitation against the partition of Bengal was almost confined to the Hindu *bhadralok*. The protectionist manufacturers and mill-owners have taken a large share in the financing of the *swaraj* party. The indirect effect of the British occupation has been to bring the upper classes together. It has given them English as a common language, and nationalism as a common ideal. To some extent it has prevented them breaking up into parties along the lines of their natural and economic interests. The professional classes include a number of social reformers who would normally be opposed to the conservative landlords as well as to the orthodox religious leaders. The landowners might well object to the heavy tariffs demanded by the industrialists which must ultimately bear heavily on their tenants. It is not difficult to see the lines of future cleavage quite apart from communal disputes and local jealousies. Nationalism has brought the educated classes together, and given them an opportunity of leading their fellow-countrymen. The history of the next century will depend upon the extent to which this cohesion is real.

# PART II

# INDIANS AND ENGLISH

## CHAPTER I

# THE BRITISH IN INDIA

THE French draw a useful distinction between *colonies de peuplement*, in which their own countrymen are likely to settle permanently, and *colonies d'exploitation*, where the conditions and climate do not attract Europeans, and they only go for part of their lives as soldiers, traders, and administrators. India would undoubtedly come into the second category. Of its 318 millions about 163,000 are English, a small proportion compared with Java, where there are 70,000 Dutch as against 28 million inhabitants, or Indo-China with over 10,000 Frenchmen out of 20 millions. The East India Company discouraged European settlers, and the policy has been continued since 1858. About half the British in India are soldiers and officials, most of the remainder are planters or business men, and there are no European agriculturists as in Algiers, Java, or even Tonkin. One result of this policy has been that the English have from the first kept themselves as a race apart. There is no large intermediary population, like the French and Spanish colonists in Morocco, working as small farmers, mechanics, impecunious traders, and innkeepers, scattered about the country and forming a link between the races. The only Indian equivalent is the Eurasian community, but almost all of the 113,000 'Anglo-Indians' are concentrated in a few large cities and railway centres. Many of them are not really of mixed blood, but are Indian Christians who have taken to wearing a 'topi'. If the English, following the custom of the country, have made themselves into a new caste, the 'Anglo-Indians' are merely a sub-caste.

The history of the last century might have been very different if the English, like former conquerors, had entered India from the North, instead of making their way slowly inland from the low-lying unhealthy delta of the Ganges or the poverty-stricken Konkan. They naturally got a very unflattering impression of the inhabitants. Those who remained in Bengal were brought into contact with decadent landlords, dishonest traders, and clerkly effeminate *babus*. Those who went into the Mofussil found a country ravaged by dacoits, thugs, and robber bands. The old civilisation was in the last stages of disintegration after the breakdown of the Moghul Empire. Gradually the few Englishmen in administration learnt to take the same kind of interest in their charge as a country squire in his villagers, but it would be a sheer anachronism to expect these early pioneers to have had a social conscience in advance of ideas current in Georgian England, or to have seen Hinduism with the eyes of a modern student of comparative religions. It was some time before they passed the first stage of realising that, though they might 'shake the pagoda tree' themselves, it was their duty to prevent unauthorised exploitation by others. It must be placed to the credit of our administrators in all parts of the Empire that they do usually adopt this attitude towards the 'natives', and in India there was a long and bitter feud between the 'civilians' and the 'interlopers', the latter being the private planters and traders. A similar feud has recently developed in Kenya, but there the 'interlopers' are in a much stronger position.

As India grew more settled, and officials were given fixed salaries, they acquired a pride in their districts, but they never got over their original contempt for the 'idolators', and remained socially aloof from all Indians, except a few wealthy landowners who shared their interest in sport. At no period did the British officers spend their spare time living on equal terms amongst upper-class Indians, as Russian officials have always done in Turkestan, or the Turks did in Mesopotamia. There does, however, seem to have been a tradition of greater friendliness before the Mutiny, and possibly the earlier official found certain sides of Indian life more familiar than does his successor to-day, and the customary liaisons with Indian women gave him a more intimate knowledge of the language and the people. This, however, was only true of the isolated officials and regimental officers. The colour bar in the cities and larger stations would seem to have been as strong under the Company as it ever was afterwards.

The Mutiny changed a feeling of contempt into one of active hatred, but it made little difference to the habits of the English, to the 'solemn etiquette, the visits to the Brigadier and the General *en grande tenue*, the invitations to dinner, the white kid-gloves, the balls, the liveries, the affectations of the *plus haut tons des haut tons*, the millinery anxiety of the ladies, the ices and champagne, and supper, the golden-robed Nana Sahib, moving about amid haughty stares and ill-concealed dislike. "What the deuce does the General ask that nigger here for?"' Cawnpore might be reduced to ashes and Nana Sahib revenge himself for those sneers, but in ten years' time the cantonment was rebuilt, and life went on as before, but was even more divorced from that of the country. Only a few men would come to India and feel

'the grave unhappy doubt whether India is the better

for our rule, so far as regards the social condition of the great mass of the people. We have put down widow-burning, we have sought to check infanticide; but I have travelled hundreds of miles through a country peopled with beggars and covered with wigwam villages.'[1]

Wherever the English came into contact with really primitive peoples, like Outram amongst his Bhils, or the missionaries with their outcastes, and whenever they had definite constructive work to do, making canals or training recruits, then they were happy, both in their lives and in their relations with the Indians. But even these men failed in the much harder task of putting India on the right path for self-development. They lacked the finer wisdom of Mother Carey in *The Water Babies*; 'anyone can make things if they take time and trouble enough: but it is not every one who, like me, can make things make themselves.' Reading the lives and writings of those Victorian soldiers and statesmen who fashioned modern India, it is clear that they despised too heartily the material with which they had to work. Men like Charles Grant, Bentinck, Macaulay, Edwardes, the Lawrences, Outram, and Aitchison were clean-living Englishmen or Scotsmen, mostly keen and rather narrow Christians, with memories of a peaceful countryside, somewhat idealised, ruled patriarchially by its squires. They found India in the throes of dissolution, having apparently earned the righteous displeasure of the Almighty. They saw Hinduism in its greatest degeneracy, sprawling across the land 'naked and gross like the red-painted stones that represent its gods'. They knew of suttee, either at first hand or as

[1] Russell, *My Diary in India*, Vol. I, p. 195.

a practice recently repressed, of infanticide, of the evils of child marriage and enforced widowhood, of the religious basis of Thagi, of idolatrous and obscene rites, and of a worship the visible symbols of which appeared to be

'The organs of birth and circlet of bones,
And the light loves carved on the temple stones.'

It would have seemed incredible to them that such a religion could survive. Macaulay wrote in 1836 that

'it is my firm belief that if our plans of education are followed up, there will not be a single idolater among the respectable classes in Bengal thirty years hence. And this will be effected without any effort to proselytise; without the smallest interference in the religious liberty; merely by the natural operation of knowledge and reflection.'

Edwardes, when Commissioner of Peshawar in 1853, stated his belief that

'the reason why India has been given to England is because England has made the greatest efforts to preserve the Christian religion in its purest apostolic form, has most stoutly protested against idolatry in any shape, and sought no other mediator than the One revealed in the Bible.'

The comparative ease with which the Mutiny was suppressed tended to confirm this idea. Edwardes himself wrote home, shortly after the fall of Delhi,

'the natives are confounded. They don't know what to attribute it to. They say it is our unanimity, our extraordinary resolution, our individual devotion to the public service, our good destiny, and so on; and I then wind up by saying, "Yes, it is all these, no doubt. But who gave these virtues to us rather than to you? Why, God. And those who counted the English as few at the beginning of the war forgot to ask on which side God was to be counted." '[1]

The England from which these early administrators came was far more interested in religious than social questions. They held that the duty of the Government was to keep the peace, and provide a few public services. The idea that it should interfere continually and actively in the economic life of the people is comparatively modern. Like John Lawrence they looked forward to seeing the Punjab 'thickly cultivated by a fat contented yeomanry, each man riding his own horse, sitting under his own fig-tree, and enjoying his rude family comforts'. With a somewhat superficial knowledge of their own country they believed these conditions existed in England, and were the direct result of a stable Government and a people sound at heart. Naturally they thought more about converting India to Christianity, and training her youth in European ways, than about preparing the upper classes to take over the work of Government. The views of Sir Donald M'Leod, Lieutenant-Governor of the Punjab in 1865, explain the attitude of many English officials before the rise of nationalism.

'If we have any regard to the security of our dominion in India, it is indispensable that we do our utmost to make it a Christian country. We are raising up a large number of intellectual youths, and if these youths are not imbued

[1] G. Smith, *Twelve Indian Statesmen* p. 216.

with Christianity, they will prove, I believe, to be the most dangerous part of the population.'

Only a few men were sufficiently far-sighted to realise that a paternal Government must contain within itself the seeds of its own decay. Of these the most remarkable was Sir Thomas Munro, the Governor of Madras, who as early as 1827, wrote that

'we ought to look forward to a time when natives may be employed in almost every office, however high, and we ought to prepare them gradually for such a change by entrusting them with higher duties from time to time, in proportion as experience may prove their being qualified to discharge them. The employment of natives in high offices will be as much for our own advantage as for theirs: it will tend both to the economy and efficiency of the administration of public affairs.'

Lord Bentinck a year or two later gave a number of responsible executive and judicial appointments to Indians and laid the foundation of the 'Provincial Service'. The Charter Act of 1833 declared that no native of India 'shall by reason of his religion, place of birth, descent, colour, or any of them, be disabled from holding any place, office or employment under the Company', and another Charter Act in 1853 allowed Indians to appear for the Civil Service examination in London. The principle was reaffirmed in 1858, but the process of 'Indianising' the administration, which in the earlier years was held up by the lack of suitable candidates, received a much greater check from the ill-feeling and distrust aroused during the years which followed the Mutiny.

Indian Nationalists often confuse two quite distinct methods by which the English have from time to time transferred some of their authority and responsibilities. From the earliest days of the Company's rule many Indians have been enlisted and trained in the Government service, and the simplest form of 'Indianisation' is to allow these officials to be promoted into the highest and most responsible positions. Up to the end of the nineteenth century this was the only kind of devolution seriously considered in British India. The more important stage of associating non-official Indians, elected or nominated, with the Central Government and with local administration has only begun during the last generation. The demand for some control of the bureaucratic machine from within is much older and was originally much more insistent than the claim to direct it from without. The earlier struggle was, of course, only for the appointment of Indians to a relatively small number of well-paid posts. The English have never flooded India, or any of their dependencies, with the hordes of petty European officials who are such a notable feature of the French colonies. Although there are nearly four and a half million people supported by Government employment in India, the European staff in civil administration has seldom exceeded six thousand. The Government of India has, however, always fought to retain a majority of Englishmen in the highest appointments, and in this they succeeded so well that in 1913 Europeans still held 2,153 of the 2,501 posts carrying a salary of over 800 rupees a month, though only 4,898 of the 11,064 with salaries of over 200 rupees. This marked the culmination of a long struggle which had begun a century before, and had been characterised by a complete lack of any considered and settled policy. The bureaucratic machine of to-day is the result of a series of compromises and concessions, most of which were granted unwillingly and never honestly enforced.

The first effect of the European foreign occupation of an Eastern country is that a certain class is suddenly brought into prominence. There is an immediate demand for clerks, who must be bilingual, and be prepared to learn new ways. Usually they have to be recruited from a rather lowly type of man, the drudges of the old society. The natural leaders generally retire in dudgeon to such estates as the fortunes of war may have left them. The system is inclined to produce a bad type of official, subservient to his new foreign masters, but tending to domineer over his own countrymen. The process may be seen in operation over most of North Africa, especially in Egypt where British occupation displaced the Pashas by the Effendi class. What Lord Milner wrote of the latter might be applied to certain types amongst the Indian official classes:

'Anybody who knows the social life of modern Egypt is well acquainted with the Effendi class. Their familiar characteristics, the obsequious manner, the slouching gait, the short-sightedness which is often so extreme as to amount almost to blindness, the worn frock-coat buttoned up to the chin, the general air of dinginess and servility – all these are calculated to make the most unfavourable impression upon the typical Briton.'[1]

Other classes are gradually attracted into the public

[1] *England and Egypt*, p. 325.

service, but in India as in many Eastern countries, the coming of the European turned the lowly scribe into 'the petty tyrant of the fields' through whom the handful of foreign administrators gave their orders. Despised by their employers and often socially ostracised, Indian officials have never been a very happy class, and they have been inclined to vent their displeasure on the poorer classes with whom they had to deal. This may help to explain two facts which have often been noticed by Europeans. There is little popular demand for the promotion of Indian officials to posts of greater responsibility, and amongst the ryots a preference is sometimes expressed for justice administered by an Englishman rather than an Indian. There is no evidence, however, of any general dislike to being dealt with by their own compatriots, but only a very special objection to certain officials whom they know. The feeling has grown less during recent years, and it dates back to times when Indian officials were very badly paid and often extremely corrupt. The same distrust can be noticed in the Indian Army. The older men do not appear to want their own Indian officers, most of whom have worked their way up from the ranks, to be given the King's Commission, and replace British officers, but they do not object to Indians of a different class being brought in to command them.

Self-interest as well as a natural pride in the machine which they had evolved encouraged the English in India to resist, sometimes actively but usually passively, the introduction of Indians into the higher administration. The unanswered letter is a very potent weapon in the East, and the Government of India used it effectively whenever pressure from Liberals at home became troublesome. The most remarkable instance was after 1870 when an Act was passed in Parliament requiring the Governor-General to frame regulations for admitting Indians into the Covenanted Service although they had not passed an examination. For four years nothing was done, and after another four years of desultory correspondence the Government of India sent a dispatch proposing to close the Covenanted Service to Indians. This evoked the following bitter comment from Lord Lytton in his reply of May 30th, 1878:

'Since I am writing confidentially I do not hesitate to say that both the Government of England and India appear to me, up to the present moment, unable to answer satisfactorily the charge of having taken every means in their power of breaking to the heart the words of promise they had uttered to the ear.' [1]

For fifty years after the Mutiny vague half-hearted attempts were made to 'Indianise' the administration. The motive force came from the upper classes of India, whose children were going into Government service in increasing numbers. It was transmitted to Parliament through a few Liberal Members of Parliament who occasionally obtained the ear of a listless but not unsympathetic House of Commons. Only a few statesmen, like Lord Lytton, seem to have realised that there was an opportunity of enlisting the help of new classes, socially and intellectually superior to the older clerks, and that the proper utilisation of these new forces was more important than anything else.

[1] J. Ramsay Macdonald, *The Government of India*, p. 104.

'The fundamental mistake,' wrote Lord Lytton, 'of able and experienced Indian officials is a belief that we can hold India securely by what they call good government; that is to say, by improving the condition of the ryot, strictly administering justice, spending immense sums on irrigation works, etc. Politically speaking, the Indian peasantry is an inert mass. If it ever moves at all it will move in obedience, not to its British benefactors, but to its native chiefs and princes, however tyrannical they may be. . . . The Indian chiefs and princes are not a mere *noblesse*. They are a powerful aristocracy. To secure completely and efficiently utilise the Indian aristocracy is, I am convinced, the most important problem now before us.' [1]

This was written in the 'seventies when no one seems to have realised the immense social prestige which our legal system was to give to Indian lawyers, or the opportunities which the vernacular Press would bring to Indian publicists. The history of the Roman Empire might have suggested the power which clients, dependent for legal advice and often for loans, would bring to their patrons even if they were a new group of educated men who could scarcely be described as an aristocracy. The failure to associate either the old landowners or the new professional classes with the Government, or to provide suitable openings for their sons in the administration, brought into the Nationalist movement nearly all Indians who were either influential or articulate.

It is important to realise the effect of the Mutiny upon the attitude of the English in India. Although few of the

[1] W. S. Lilly, *India and its Problems*, p. 248.

earlier officials were as anxious for Indian co-operation as Sir Thomas Munro, they pictured a much smaller English staff working on cordial terms with local Indian authorities. Men like Frederick John Shore, Sir John Malcolm, Mountstuart Elphinstone, and Sir Robert Hamilton had none of the contempt for the inhabitants of the country, for their customs and privileges, which was so common in the cantonment towns. Many of the junior civilians must have shared that more statesmanlike attitude, but the effect of the change is described by a contemporary writer:

'The new order of things is not as the old. The children of the soil are no longer regarded with the lively interest, the credulous partiality of yore. Those are plants which do not flourish amid the rank weeds and rushes, the sand and rubble that overspread the land which was lately submerged by the deluge of civil strife. Men cannot at will cast aside the recollection of those times when all was doubt and confusion and dismay: when a great fear was their companion, day and night: when the mother and child were in sanctuary at the headquarters of the Division: when the husband worked with a loaded revolver among his papers, a horse standing saddled in the stable, his feet resting on a pair of saddle-bags crammed with his most valuable property. The distrust and dislike engendered by such an experience are too deeply rooted to be plucked out by an act of volition.' [1]

The bitterness of the feeling can be illustrated by a quotation from the diary of Raikes, an experienced

[1] G. O. Trevelyan, *The Competition Wallah*, p. 304.

civilian, who in his younger days had been known as a friend of the Indian people:

'We went to see the Jumma Masjid which is now held by a battalion of Beloochees. I sincerely hope that the plan proposed by Mr. Philip Egerton, the magistrate of Delhi, may be carried out. He suggests that the Mosque be used henceforth as a Christian Church, and on each of the thousand compartments of the marble floor, the name of one of our Christian Martyrs be inscribed. It is the general opinion that it would be madness to restore this noble building to the Mohammadans.'

The Indian Empire was founded with its principal servants in this bitter frame of mind. Inevitably the administrative machine, which they began to build up after 1858, was based on the subordination and not on the co-operation of Indians. Men of the school and time of Sir John Strachey held that 'our Governors of provinces, the chief officers of the army, our district officers, and their principal executive subordinates, must be Englishmen under all circumstances that we can foresee, and in all departments of essential importance there must be selected Englishmen to maintain a standard of efficiency'. They built their machine, as Englishmen will, heavy, durable, and efficient, fit to last a hundred years but not much suited to the country. They looked at their work, and thought it was good. No Indian would be able to understand it, appreciate it, or handle it properly. Undoubtedly self-interest played its part, consciously or unconsciously, in this argument, but the feeling was perfectly genuine. The Indian, however, was in no mood to accept such a permanent arrangement. He felt, if interested in politics, that 'this world has been harsh and strange; something is wrong; there needeth a change'. He was not much inclined to admire the machine merely because it was durable, especially as it seemed to leave a great part of its work undone. He felt that he was living in an age of transition, and would have preferred a machine, fashioned more on American lines, light and suited for a hot climate, and which could be 'scrapped' after twenty years. The solid drabness of Indian bureaucracy invited a bomb.

If the English are inclined to under-estimate the indirect results of the Mutiny, educated Indians are equally prone to forget the effect of the Nationalist movement upon the British who were resident in India. From the early 'eighties' they have been subjected to a continual flow of abuse, both in the Press and from the platform. To Lord Morley, living in England, this somewhat hysterical vituperation seemed to be 'froth', but because of the murders which followed from it, he qualified this into 'froth flecked with blood'. The English in India, especially the army officers who make up such a large proportion of the small ruling class, did not take the matter so seriously. To them it seemed more like the continual whimpering of a fretful and peevish child, and confirmed their contemptuous attitude towards the town-bred Indian. The educated classes of the towns had no real personal contact with the English. The civilians were busy officials at headquarters, or district officers with the instincts and interests of country landlords. Only a few men like 'Pandit' Jackson, who was murdered at Nasik, had some special interest such as a love of Sanskrit which brought them into touch with the studious high-caste Indian. The missionaries worked entirely amongst the lower castes, from whom alone they had any real prospect of winning converts. Schoolmasters had perhaps the best opportunities, but they were few in numbers and hampered by their close connection with the Government. None of them wielded an influence approaching that of earlier teachers like the famous Dr. Miller, of the Madras Christian College, whose students went through life content to describe themselves as his pupils. The Nationalist movement roused the Government to the need of getting into touch with the educated classes, but made it difficult for the individual Englishman to do so with a good will. From the rise of Tilak we can date those totally artificial social relations between English and Indians, which are such a strain upon the sense of humour.

There is no evidence to support the idea that English manners towards Indians have grown worse. They were always bad, and have probably improved. The following extract from a book written at the time of the Mutiny may help to make this clear, as well as being a very fair attempt to see the Indian point of view:

'I could not help thinking as we drove home how harsh the reins of our rule must feel to the soft skin of the natives. The smallest English official treats their prejudices with contempt, and thinks he has a right to visit them just as he would call on a gamekeeper in his cottage. Lord Clyde and others have said they were often pained by the insolence and rudeness of some of the civilians to the sirdars and chiefs in the north-west after the old war. Some of the best of our rulers administer justice in their shirt-sleeves (which, by the way, are used as a substitute for blotting-paper all over India), cock up their heels in the tribunal, and smoke cheroots to assist them in the Council; and I have seen one eminent public servant, with his braces hanging at his heels, his bare feet in slippers, and his shirt open at the breast just as he came from the bath, give audience to a great chieftain on a matter of considerable State importance. The natives see that we treat each other far differently, and draw their inferences accordingly. As we were driving home this evening Mr. Melville told me that some time ago the Rajah of Puttiala came to visit Sir John Lawrence, who was encamped near Umballa, and that he entered the camp with his band playing and his zomboruks firing: but as it happened to be Sunday Mr. Melville desired him to desist. The Rajah was much humbled and annoyed.'[1]

Comparing modern conditions with those of seventy years ago, it would seem that our officials are more formally correct, and our attitude towards wealthy ruling princes has become almost obsequious. There is, however, throughout most of India a painful absence of any cordial relationship between the English and the educated Indians. The trouble lies to a great extent in the artificial and pretentious life of the larger stations. Most Western nations have ceased to take what the Americans call 'this king business' very seriously, and it was a thousand pities that India, which has always suffered from too much of it, should have fallen into the power of those English upper middle classes who still retain such a fondness for it. The setting of false standards begins with the Viceroy, and the wasteful extravagance of his two palaces and two seats of Government. It extends rapidly to the Provincial

[1] Russell, *My Diary in India*, Vol. II, p 255.

Governors with their ludicrous travesty of royal pomp and procedure. It fastens like a blight upon the higher officials and the chief military officers, and tempts every Indian Prince, as well as every Indian landowner and cotton spinner, to find some new value and justification in ostentatious display. In this respect those colonies are more fortunate which have come under the control of republics or of countries with little *bourgeois* monarchies.

Relations are much better in the Indian States and in the very small stations where there are only two or three English officials. The few Europeans soon find some Indians with whom they can be sincere friends, and whom they can meet without that attitude, *de haut en bas*, which makes social relations such a hollow and ridiculous sham. Much ill-feeling is aroused over the question of the admission of Indians into clubs, but this again only arises in the larger stations, and usually those where there are British regiments. There is no objection amongst Indians to races living apart, to the Japanese having their own club in Bombay, or the Parsis their own gymkhana, and the trouble about the English clubs is that somehow they have acquired a semi-official status, or else they have occupied a site which is obviously too advantageous.

The present English attitude might be described as correct but unfriendly, and every nation in the world will testify to the fact that it is one which we can carry off with an air. It has spread down to many circles which formerly had a reputation for the roughness of their methods. The modern English soldier is a very different type from his predecessor, and the number of violent and unpunished crimes against Indians has now become insignificant. There is, however, little desire for intimacy between the races, and perhaps the most hopeful sign is the 'fraternisation' which occurs amongst those officials and politicians who are members of the new Legislatures. Much of their work is of such a farcical character that they are united by the same bond as the Roman Augurs, who are reputed not to have been able to pass each other without a sly wink.

## CHAPTER II

# THE ORIGIN OF NATIONALISM

THE Indian nationalist movement is older than its nationalism. Opposition to British rule has smouldered like an underground fire throughout the last century. Every year or two it would break into violent flame whenever some body of individuals chafed under restraint, or if the English pressed too heavily on religious susceptibilities or territorial loyalty. At no point is it possible to say that here was the first outbreak which was not local, or that this particular agitation was the first to be based on the idea of a free India. Many writers claim that the 'eighties', which saw the rise of Bal Gangadhar Tilak and the founding of the National Congress, mark the beginning of nationalism, but the succession of outbreaks and waves of agitation can be traced back to the Mutiny and beyond. In 1875 the Bengal paper, the *Amrita Bazar Patrika*, was commenting upon the attempted murder of Colonel Phayre at Baroda according to the recognised nationalist tradition: 'To emasculate a nation that the Government may rule without trouble. Surely to poison an obscure Colonel is by far a lighter crime.'[1] Three years previously the Moslem Wahabi movement had claimed a victim in the Earl of Mayo, who was then Viceroy. Towards the end of the 'sixties' the 'seditious' tone of the vernacular Press had already begun to disturb the Governors of Bengal. Certain changes, however, can be noticed. In very early days the opposition was either religious or local, and during the first half of the century

[1] Parliamentary Returns, C. 2040 of 1878, p. 41. Quoted in S. M. Mitra's *Anglo-Indian Studies*.

a large body of educated Indians were keen 'Anglicists'. The reformers, Ram Mohun Roy, Dr. Tagore, and their followers were often *plus royaliste que le roi*, and continually pressing for the introduction of Western methods. They were the forerunners of men like Ranade, Kashab Chandra Sen, and Gokhale, who admired European civilisation, and wished to bring Hinduism more into line with Western ideas.

From the Mutiny onwards a double tendency can be noted. The sporadic outbursts of political and religious excitement become more national in character, and the reformist element amongst the educated classes grows more critical of England while it loses ground steadily to the leaders of orthodox Hinduism. The importance of the Mutiny itself is often absurdly under-estimated. Most standard English histories treat it as a military rising which only affected a small proportion of the civil population. They dwell upon the many undoubted acts of bravery which characterised the small bodies of Englishmen who were isolated at Lucknow, Delhi and elsewhere. They recount the heroic stories of the Lawrences, John Nicholson, and other leaders. Emphasis is laid upon a few acts of great brutality committed by sepoys and others against English civilians and their families. They describe how these were duly avenged, Lord Canning magnanimously checking any tendency to excessive severity, and the episode is then considered ended. 'Justice was done, mercy shown to all who were not guilty of deliberate murder, the land cleansed of blood.'[1]

It is impossible to understand certain aspects of Indian

[1] Sir George Forrest, *History of the Indian Mutiny*, Vol. III, p. 623.

nationalism unless it is realised that this reading of history is not accepted by any intelligent Indian, and that the Mutiny was followed by punitive measures, which most Englishmen at home have forgotten, but which are still remembered in India and which have influenced successive generations of English officers and officials. There is little need to discuss here the extent to which the Mutiny was a popular rising. The civilian revolt certainly extended far outside Oudh, and included the Mahrattas who followed Nana Sahib, and also such a host of Mussulmans that some competent observers thought they formed the backbone of the rebellion. The facts that are pertinent to this question of modern Indian nationalism are that after a war, which in retrospect seemed a war for freedom, the English killed their prisoners without trial and in a manner held by all Indians to be the height of barbarity, – 'sewing Mohammadans in pig-skins, smearing them with pork-fat before execution, and burning their bodies, and forcing Hindoos to defile themselves'.[1] They also massacred thousands of the civilian population, not only in Delhi, but in the countryside. General Neill, whose statue in Madras has still to have a special guard, gave orders to his lieutenants that 'certain guilty villages were marked out for destruction and all the men inhabiting them were to be slaughtered',[2] and the indiscriminate burning of villages and killing of their inhabitants occurred wherever our armies moved.

'When Neill marched from Allahabad, his executions

[1] Russell, *Diary*, II, 43. The author was *The Times* correspondent.

[2] Kaye, *History of the Sepoy War*, V, Chap. II.

were so numerous and so indiscriminate, that one of the officers attached to his column had to remonstrate with him on the ground that if he depopulated the country he could get no supplies for the men.'[1]

The same seems to have been true of Havelock's advance guard:

'The officer in command was emulous of Neill, and thought he could show equal vigour. In two days forty-two men were hanged on the roadside, and a batch of twelve men were executed because their faces were "turned the wrong way" when they were met on the march. All the villages in his front were burned when he halted. These "severities" could not have been justified by the Cawnpore massacre because they took place before that diabolical act.'[2]

The rank and file were naturally even less particular. The following is a contemporary account of a little trouble amongst the drivers attached to a newly-landed regiment:

'On inquiry it appeared that the hero of the affair was an honest fellow who had disembarked with his head full of the Nana and the fatal well. His story was simple – "I seed two Moors talking in a cart. Presently I heard one of 'em say 'Cawnpore'. I knowed what that meant; so I fetched Tom Walker, and he heard 'em say 'Cawnpore', and he knowed what that meant. So we polished 'em both off."'[3]

Many occurrences during those fatal months were the

[1] Russell, *Diary*, I, p. 222. [2] *Ibid.*, p. 402.
[3] Trevelyan, *The Competition Wallah*, p. 284.

inevitable consequences of a war fought in a strange and backward country. Those who were with the army in Mesopotamia may remember not dissimilar incidents connected with the 'buddhus' – the wandering Arabs who hung about the flank of our forces. The reason why it is necessary to recall a period so discreditable to all concerned is that the effect of this period of repression has survived till to-day. The evil that men do lives after them in the minds of their companions as well as of those they have wronged. An admirable attempt has been made recently to present the Indian side of the Mutiny,[1] but it is probably impossible for a European to imagine the effect which stories of the Martial Law period would have upon an educated Indian. Previous to the Mutiny the English must have appeared as strange exotic creatures with unpleasant habits but possessing certain martial and other virtues which put them considerably above the Moghuls. The Mutiny confirmed the idea of European bravery, but showed that in times of stress we were no better than our predecessors. Nadir Shah sacked Delhi, and so did the English. The Moghuls enforced their will by burning villages, and killing indiscriminately the innocent and the guilty. The British carried on the tradition. Henceforward the English became the secret enemy, the more hateful because they were invincible. The English *raj* seemed established for ever just when India saw its worst side. The Mutiny marked the beginning of that inferiority complex which attacks all who hate what they cannot alter.

The effect of the Mutiny upon the English was equally disastrous. The news from India caused an excitement

[1] Edward Thompson, *The Other Side of the Medal.*

which can hardly be appreciated by a generation which has supped its fill of horrors. Countless middle-class Englishmen learnt to look upon Indians as the creatures, half gorilla, half negro, who appeared in the contemporary *Punch* cartoons. They were usually depicted standing over a murdered woman but cowering before an avenging Britannia who is praying to the God of Battles to 'steel our soldiers' hearts'. For another generation their children learnt of India from the same source. The young men who went out East during and after the Mutiny left a country where

'every one chuckled to hear how General Neill had forced high Brahmins to sweep up the blood of the Europeans murdered at Cawnpore, and then strung them in a row, without giving them the time requisite for the rites of purification'.

They found in India that

'this hatred was shared by the entire mass of our countrymen. Invectives against the treacherous bloodthirsty Mussulmans, ironical sneers about the "mild Hindoo", were nuts alike to the civilian and the planter. The latter rejoiced to hear the world acknowledge that his estimate of the native had been correct throughout.'

These two quotations are from that most amusing book, *The Competition Wallah*, by G. O. Trevelyan, a series of letters purporting to be written from India some six years after the Mutiny. Few Englishmen now read these contemporary works which show vividly the effect of the hatred and fear engendered by those troubled years upon the small colony of Englishmen who were then living entirely estranged from the Indians. Certain Anglo-Indian ideas were evolved during that period. The first was that the life of one European was worth those of many Indians. The second was that 'the only thing an oriental understood was fear'. The third was that England had been forced to lose many lives and spend many millions to hold India, and 'did she not merit some more substantial recompense than the privilege of governing India in a spirit of wisdom and unselfishness?'

The Nationalist movement must be traced back to this period which followed the Mutiny, when both Indians and English retained a feeling of bitterness which only the latter could have cured. Samuel Butler left amongst his notes a very wise remark about reconciliation:

'We all like to forgive, and we all like best not those who offend us least, nor those who have done most for us, but those who make it easy for us to forgive them. So a man may lose both his legs and live for years if his amputation has been clean and skilful, whereas a pea in his boot may set up irritation which must last as long as the pea is there and may in the end kill him.'

The English have never attempted to remove the irritation caused by their behaviour after the Mutiny, and from that time we must date the long and bitter estrangement between the two races. Born of hatred and fear it was nourished on a series of unfortunate incidents, most of which were the direct result of the new spirit which the Mutiny encouraged amongst Europeans.

One potent factor was the long succession of murders and brutalities perpetrated by Englishmen upon Indians which either went unpunished or for which, at the demand of the whole European community, only a small penalty was exacted. This scandal, of which there were many flagrant instances in the 'sixties, has continued till recent times. Sir Theodore Morison, a member of the Indian Council, wrote in 1898,

'it is an ugly fact which it is no use to disguise that the murder of natives by Englishmen is no infrequent occurrence. In one issue of the *Amrita Bazar Patrika* of this month three contemporary cases are dealt with, in none of which have the prisoners paid the full penalty for murder.'[1]

Lord Curzon caused much ill-feeling amongst his compatriots by driving home upon a British regiment its responsibility for a wrong done by a soldier to an Indian woman. At the Durbar in 1903, when he had completely estranged most Indians in Bengal, there was a remarkable and typical incident. The offending regiment marched past, and was the subject of a special demonstration from the Anglo-Indian crowd. As a reply to this the Indian multitude gave Lord Curzon a most unexpected ovation. The importance of this question is often overlooked. A very clever Indian writer goes so far as to make it the chief cause of sedition:

'The unrest, then, sprang some decades ago, from the personal ill-treatment of the natives by Englishmen, who ought to have been deported from the country; this was utilised, probably magnified, by the Vernacular Press, and from such beginnings unrest has developed into seditions, bomb-throwing, and violence.'[2]

[1] Sir Theodore Morison, *Imperial Rule in India*, p. 27.
[2] S. M. Mitra, *Anglo-Indian Studies*, p. 382.

If European life was considered sacrosanct the obvious corollary was that in times of danger Indian lives should be of little account. The Maler Kotla case of 1872 was an instance of this new attitude. A hundred Sikh fanatics attacked a Punjab town and were repulsed. The sixty-six survivors fled into Patiala State where they surrendered themselves. They were handed over to the nearest Deputy Commissioner, Mr. Cowan, who had them sent to Maler Kotla, and wrote to his official superior, Mr. Forsyth, 'The entire gang has been nearly destroyed. I purpose blowing away from guns or hanging the prisoners to-morrow morning at daybreak.' Although two letters reached Cowan from Forsyth telling him to keep the prisoners for trial, he carried out his intention, and this action was condoned by Forsyth. The Government afterwards censured Forsyth and dismissed Cowan, but the entire Anglo-Indian Press was on the latter's side. Forsyth had a prosperous career and became Sir Douglas Forsyth. In his autobiography he wrote of the incident: 'I did my utmost to help him (Cowan) when he was turned out of the service by procuring him a very good appointment in India.' [1]

The same tradition has survived till to-day. General Dyer's action at Amritsar in April, 1919, is too recent to need recalling. The fact which links up the Jallianwalla-bagh massacre with the Mutiny tradition is that the purpose of opening fire upon the mob was to teach it a lesson. It was never contended that there was any military necessity, for General Dyer's small escort fired away all its ammunition into a crowd which had no fire-arms though some

[1] *Autobiography and Reminiscences of Sir Douglas Forsyth*. See also Edward Thompson, *op. cit.*

were carrying the peasant's *lathi* or heavy club. Anyone who has seen the enclosed garden in which several hundreds were killed and wounded must realise that there was no possibility of dispersing the crowd by fire, because the place is closed in on all sides. General Dyer's action is still justified in every Indian station and regimental mess on the grounds that in times of danger and popular excitement it is permissible and right to kill Indians merely for terrorist purposes, and to use methods which no military officer or magistrate would think of employing in England. Indian nationalism is, of course, wider and deeper than the antagonism which has grown from the feeling that as between Englishmen and Indians there is neither justice nor the will to do justice, but the Mutiny and the obsessions which it caused in men's minds are always in the background of Indian politics, darkening counsel and inciting to violence.

The interest of the educated classes in nationalism has always been partly economic and partly religious. Unemployment is a canker which has eaten into Indian social life for generations, and has brought about an alliance between the classes, which would usually do clerical work, and the small but influential group of manufacturers who are interested in India's industrial development. The less extreme sections of the movement have, from the first, received financial and moral support from the mill-owners, who are keen protectionists, and India's fiscal independence has always figured amongst the Congress demands. This side of nationalism received a great impetus in 1894, when at the demand of Lancashire exporters the cotton duty was lowered to 3½ per cent. and a countervailing excise duty imposed on Indian products.

For twenty-three years this grievance ensured the cause, support and sympathy from a class which has usually little liking for revolutionary methods. The industrialists, however, have always worked behind the scenes, and in the earlier days of the movement the influence of religion was far stronger than any other.

Hinduism had reached its nadir by the middle of the last century. The old *gurus* were discredited, and the purely secular teaching introduced into the colleges after 1835 was having its effect.

> 'The ancient scriptures of the country, the famous records of numerous Hindu sects, had long since been discredited. The Vedas and Upanishads were sealed books. All that we knew of the immortal Mahabharata, Ramayana, or the Bhagavad Gita, was from the execrable translations into popular Bengali, which no respectable young man was supposed to read. The whole religious literature of ancient India represented an endless void. Our young reformers studied Paine's "Age of Reason" to get fresh ideas on the subject of religion.' [1]

If the Gods had willed otherwise, educated India might well have become Westernised, but the bitterness and estrangement of the 'sixties had a remarkable tonic effect, and about 1870 a great change began to show itself in the Hindu spirit. One form in which this change manifested itself was a zealous defence of the old religions. Sometimes, as in the case of Arya Samaj, the return to the Vedas

[1] See Lord Ronaldshay, *The Heart of Aryavarta*, Chap. V. The quotation is from P. C. Mazumdar's *Life and Teachings of Kashab Chandra Sen*.

was accompanied by a strong movement for reform. The founder of this sect, Dayananda, lived until 1872 as a *sannyasi*, wearing the minimum of clothing, and arguing against the orthodox leaders of Hinduism that idolatry had no sanction in the Vedas. His new society began as a religious and reformist body in Bombay. It failed at first but became a great success when in 1877 Dayananda moved to the Punjab. The Arya Samaj soon developed into a powerful force combining education based on the Vedas with opposition to child marriage, idolatry, and the existing caste system. In Bengal Ramakrishna Parahamsa and his better known follower, Swami Vivekananda, were much less critical of the old Hinduism. It is unfortunate that the enthusiastic but irresponsible support which the leaders of this religious revival received from certain European Theosophists like Colonel Olcott, Madame Blavatsky, and Mrs. Besant undoubtedly encouraged a tendency to defend the old religion in every particular.

Although the various religious leaders of this period had only a limited following, the general effect of their teaching upon the educated classes was enormous. The close connection between politics and this revival was speedily established. The campaign against killing cows which Dayananda started in 1882 was taken up with enthusiasm by Bal Gangadhar Tilak in the Deccan, and the Arya Samaj soon fell under the influence of keen politicians like Lajpat Rai. The religious revival has left its influence upon the whole nationalist movement. It encouraged the glorification of India's past, and the blind acceptance of the most exaggerated interpretations of the Vedas. Max Muller writes of Dayananda:

'he succeeded in persuading himself and others that everything worth knowing, even in the most recent inventions of modern science, were alluded to in the Vedas. Steam-engines, railways, and steam-boats, all were shown to have been known, at least in their germs, to the poets of the Vedas.'

Since those days the list would have to be extended to include aeroplanes and anæsthetics, and doubtless the Mahabharata will provide texts to cover all future developments.

From this uncritical treatment of the sacred books there follows inevitably a belief in a Hindu Golden Age, and equally inevitably a contempt for Western ideas and culture. Hindu civilisation, springing from the oldest and finest of religions, must be spiritual and beautiful in every particular.

'The old ideas may be all superstition, but within these masses of superstition are nuggets of gold and truth. Have you discovered means by which to keep the gold alone, without any of the dross?' [1]

This spiritual gold is known to the Hindu teachers alone, and the hard-won science of the West has for centuries been the heritage of the Indian. European nations are gross, selfish, and sensual, and their civilisation purely material. Whatever parody of civilisation they may possess is based, ultimately, on Hinduism. It is impossible to imagine a more flattering unction to be applied to the souls of the disillusioned and bitter young men

[1] Vivekananda, *My Master*.

who grew up in the evil atmosphere which followed the Mutiny. Supply will follow demand, and Vivekananda

'has no historical conscience whatsoever. He is ready to re-write the whole history of antiquity in a paragraph, to demonstrate in a sentence that China, in the East, and Greece and Rome, in the West, owed all their philosophical acumen and every spiritual thought they had to the teachers of ancient India.' [1]

A good idea of the lengths to which this kind of argument was carried can be seen in the work of his English disciple, Sister Nivedita, whose book, *The Web of Indian Life*, won immense popularity amongst the younger generation of Indian students.

Many English writers, like Sir Valentine Chirol,[2] treat Indian nationalism as if it was the result of a deliberate conspiracy on the part of the orthodox Hindu leaders to recapture the supremacy which they had lost owing to British rule. It is undoubtedly true that the memories of the high status enjoyed, say, by the Chitpavan Brahmans under the Peshwas may have helped to mould the opinions of Tilak and his chief supporters in the Deccan, but in other parts of India, and notably in Bengal and the Punjab, the leaders of the political nationalism were not Brahmans. The *Amrita Bazar Patrika*, edited by the non-Brahman family of the Ghoses, was busy converting religious nationalism into practical politics some years before Tilak began his fiery career. In the Punjab Ajit Singh and Lajpat Rai, who were the first to be deported

[1] Farquhar, *Modern Religious Movements in India*, p. 190.
[2] See especially his *Indian Unrest*.

under the old Regulation III of 1818, were neither of them Brahmans, nor were the two foremost leaders of the agitation against the partition of Bengal, Bepin Chandra Pal and Arabinda Ghose. A movement which has spread so rapidly as Indian nationalism could not be created by a group of individuals, it can only be led and directed by them. It would be more logical to consider the political unrest which has been endemic in India since the 'eighties' as the natural and inevitable result of the religious revival of the previous decade, and the form which this revival took was influenced by those unhappy years which followed the Mutiny.

To orthodox Hinduism and also to the memories of the Mutiny must be ascribed much of the violence and the justification of murder which have been such a marked feature of the nationalist movement. The train of argument is clear. Indian civilisation is healthy, spiritual, and in every way admirable. Any corruption is due first to Moslem, and subsequently to British aggression. Western civilisation, lacking all spiritual significance, is rotten at the core. Superficially, however, it is attractive and powerful. This deceived many Indians during the early part of the nineteenth century, but they learnt after the Mutiny that this civilisation was only a thin veneer. The Indian who loves his country must therefore fight against every element of Western influence, and try to expel not only the English, but all their works. This is a religious duty, and the whole hierarchy of militant deities, of heroes real and mythical, can be evoked to prove that in such a cause killing is no murder. As Krishna slew Kamsa, so the Indian must slay the European demons. As Sivaji disembowelled the Moghul Governor Afzul Khan when paying homage to him, so the Indian must use craft and relentless cunning. It was only a short step from the *vagnak*, which Sivaji concealed in his hand, to the pistol and bomb of the young Hindu student. If the English did not like murder and suggested that killing for political purposes is not justified, the Hindu had only to recall the massacres ordered by General Neill, the defence advanced by Cowan and later by General Dyer, or even the long line of low-grade murderers whose crimes have been justified in the Anglo-Indian Press.

Political nationalism of the most bitter and intransigent kind was the inevitable consequence of the complete disillusionment about Western civilisation which followed the period of the Mutiny. It began with a religious revival amongst the educated classes, and a revulsion against the secular education which had been forced upon India by Macaulay and the Indian 'Anglicists'. It found thousands of ready disciples amongst the unemployed and unemployable clerks whom the new colleges were yearly sending out into an unsympathetic world. By 1857 some reaction was already overdue. The form which it was to take was decided by those crucial years when 'cantonments and arsenals, field batteries and breach batteries, seemed more essential to the Government of the country than courts of law, normal schools, and agricultural exhibitions'.

## CHAPTER III

# THE GROWTH OF NATIONALISM

THE opponents of any movement which they consider subversive invariably ascribe its growth to the work of individuals. This is a commonplace in the history of all agitations which precede social and religious reforms. It is equally true of the Indian and other nationalist movements. The origin of an idea is generally too subtle to be widely appreciated, and its comprehension often involves a degree of self-criticism of which few are capable. If Tilak, Arabinda and Barendra Ghose, B. C. Pal, C. R. Das, Lala Lajpat Rai, the Ali brothers, and the Mahatma Gandhi had all suffered the untimely fate of most children born in India, and had died as infants, there would undoubtedly have still been a nationalist movement attracting most of the educated classes. It would have been marked by the occasional murder of Europeans, but more generally by an extreme ferocity in the written and spoken word. It would have tended to be realist in the Deccan, and idealist in Bengal. In the North there would have been religious revivals and sectarian attacks upon the Government. The Punjab and the West of India would have felt bitterly about the restrictions on emigration, and the South African and Kenya questions. The business men would have agitated against the Cotton Excise, and townsmen generally have discovered leaders to fight against a system of justice too partial to the European. The *bhadralok* and the *bazars* alike would have been equally thrilled by the defeat of Italy by Abyssinia and Russia by Japan. A Khilafat agitation would have followed the War.

No one, of course, can gauge the effect of the partial successes obtained by those leaders whose names have been mentioned. Did the cult of Sivaji, the agitation against the Bengal Partition, and the Non-Co-operation movement build up and strengthen nationalism, or waste its energies by leading the young men along roads of which no one knew the destination? The importance of the individual leader depends upon his driving force, and his ability to bring new ideas and a new technique into the work of agitation. Judged by these standards there are two names which stand out pre-eminently, Bal Gangadhar Tilak and the Mahatma Gandhi. Although a nationalist movement was inevitable, it might well have been reformist and unsectarian in character, and not come into great prominence till the end of the century. It was chiefly owing to Tilak's personal influence that the revolutionary movement became a real power in the land during the 'eighties', and that it was so closely connected with the revival of orthodox Hinduism after the Mutiny. For many years the inspiration behind Indian nationalism was religious and even obscurantist. It was only towards the end of the War, when Tilak's influence was declining and Gandhi's reputation growing, that the reformist element became prominent, and the movement was sufficiently unsectarian and political to gather Moslems and finally Indian Christians into its fold.

When Tilak first entered public life about 1880 his early struggles were against his own compatriots at Poona, many of them Chitpavan Brahmans like himself. The Deccan had been little affected by the Mutiny, nor was Bombay a political centre like Calcutta. Centred round Poona was a body of very distinguished men who kept alive the Hindu reformist tradition of Ram Mohun Roy, combining social activities with a mild Liberalism and an intelligent criticism of the Government. Their leaders were Ranade, Dr. Bhandarkar, N. G. Chandavarkar, and, above all, Mr. G. K. Gokhale. Their ideals are embodied in the 'Servants of India Society'. They were the type of men, as will be seen, who founded the National Congress, and from 1880 to 1890 Tilak waged ceaseless war against them. Although he suffered an occasional defeat he had far greater resources than his opponents. Taking advantage of the repeal of the Indian Press Law he founded the first successful vernacular newspaper, the *Kesari*, and thus made an invaluable contribution to the technique of nationalism by proving that political invective could make such a paper pay. With the help of those two champions of orthodoxy, the Natu brothers, he helped to revive the ancient gymnastic societies, and then to organise annual festivals in favour of Ganesh, perhaps the most popular deity in the Mahratta villages. When, in 1890, the reformers lent their support to the Age of Consent Bill, which was designed to mitigate the evils of child marriage, Tilak was able to bring popular forces to bear against the measure which completely routed its Liberal backers, although the bill in a modified form was finally passed by the Government.[1]

After Tilak had captured the Poona Sarvajanik Sabha and become the acknowledged leader of the advanced politicians of the West, he began to take more interest in similar movements outside the Province, and his propaganda assumed a definitely anti-British character. There is little to be gained by inquiring into his exact

[1] See p. 237.

motives. No European is likely to recapture the mental processes of an exceedingly astute and learned Chitpavan Brahman, steeped in the Vedas and Hindu literature. There is no need to doubt his sincerity, or to assume, with Sir Valentine Chirol, that he aimed at a Brahman hegemony in India. The Chitpavan Brahmans have always been a race apart. Their blue eyes and the very 'masculine' quality of their intellects give colour to the legend that they have in them the blood of some seafaring race from the North. Tilak, more than most Indians, found delight in what a famous economist calls 'successful energising', and he turned his energies into the most natural field for a man of the educated classes at that epoch. He undoubtedly did desire an India ruled by Indians, and he must have foreseen that in the West of India most authority would fall into the hands of people of his own stamp, and probably of his own caste. But he was always prepared to work with other castes, and most of the men with whom he collaborated in Bengal and the Punjab were non-Brahmans. He did not, however, include Mohammadans as Indians, and the nationalist movement so long as he led it, was strictly Hindu. One of the first All-India organisations with which he identified himself was the Cow Protection Association founded by Dayananda in 1882, and this, like the cult of the Maratha chieftain Sivaji, was used to rouse the Hindus of the Deccan against all *mlencchas* or foreigners, a word which is equally applicable to Moslems and Europeans.

Tilak was a sincere Home Ruler, and possibly correct in his belief that the only way to obtain concessions from the British is to weary them out by incessant agitation, and by keeping the opposition always upon the point of an outbreak. He showed, however, his limitations by his idea that Hinduism was strong enough to alienate both the Mohammadans and the British—to say nothing of such lesser breeds without the law as Indian Christians and the depressed classes. In Bengal or the Punjab, where the Moslems are in a majority, such views would seem absurd, but Tilak's outlook in these earlier years was distinctly provincial. As an All-India politician he showed his usual energy, but much less than his usual acumen. He even attempted to transplant that very local hero Sivaji to Bengal, where unhappy memories still survive of Maratha invasions as ferocious and devastating as any which came from the North.

Tilak's activities, up till the end of the nineteenth century, are important because he taught the educated classes of India the elementary technique of agitation. He proved the value of religious enthusiasm and local patriotism. He explored the possibilities of the vernacular Press. He discovered what invaluable material lay in the college students. He was a born journalist, and organised what can only be described as 'stunts' with much the same genius and success as Lord Northcliffe in his war-time propaganda. Tilak's policy was to keep agitation constantly simmering. Inevitably there were times when popular feeling would boil over. The Hindu-Moslem riots of Bombay in 1893, and the murder of Mr. Rand as the result of Tilak's agitation against the measures taken to deal with plague, were unfortunate incidents which showed the possibilities and dangers of his methods. India learnt much from this first period of Tilak's activities, but the linking up of the various local agitations was not his work.

It will be necessary occasionally to use the expression 'all-India' politicians in order to emphasize the fact that during the last forty years some leaders have tended to confine their activities and influence to their own Provinces while others are more definitely nationalists. When it is remembered that most Provinces are in area and population the equal of great European powers, it will be seen that the first group have a sufficiently large field for their energies, and there are signs, which will be discussed later, that they may ultimately eclipse the second group. For the present it is important to notice that the first nationalists were provincial in their outlook, and that the men from the North and the South, from Bombay and Bengal, only gradually came into personal contact with each other. The great instrument for developing the all-India politician was the Congress.

It is easy to exaggerate the part which the Congress has played in the history of the last forty years. It has never been the motive force behind the agitation against British rule, though its organisation has frequently been captured and used by men of great energy and very extreme views. It has served at some times as a convenient platform, at others as a battle-ground between rival nationalist groups. The first meeting, held in 1885, was not organised by nationalists, but by a small group of Liberals, amongst whom were one or two Englishmen. A retired Civil Servant, A. O. Hume, was partly responsible for its inception, just as a year or two later a chance article by an English antiquary called attention to the forgotten grave of that mountain chief Sivaji, and suggested to Tilak's fertile brain a magnificent opportunity. Mr. Hume, when he looked at the seventy delegates, 'who had to be pressed and entreated to come', may well have wondered if this child of his would survive another year. The delegates were mostly schoolmasters and lawyers, drawn from a small class, and not much touched by the religious revival of the period. The tone of the first meeting was decorous and mild. The President, Mr. Bonerjee, talked about the 'fuller development of those sentiments of national unity that had their origin in our beloved Lord Ripon's memorable reign'. Mr. Subramania Aiyar, who thirty years later was to be a bitter opponent of British rule, spoke to the first resolution: 'By a merciful dispensation of Providence, India, which was for centuries the victim of external aggression and plunder, of internal civil wars and general confusion, has been brought under the dominion of the great British Power.' Certain reforms had been introduced into the Provincial Councils, but no speaker when suggesting the inclusion of some elected members, dared suggest such a radical alteration without first handing out a few compliments to the Viceroy and his government.

A comparison with a recent Congress, held in Madras in 1927, is perhaps inevitable. Some twenty-five thousand delegates and visitors were collected in a huge 'pandal', and listened with the help of 'loud speakers' to the Home Rule leaders. No speaker would have dared to mention either England or the Government without the use of an opprobrious epithet. A speech like that made by Mr. Aiyar would have been received with shouts of laughter, but then Mr. Aiyar himself had recanted some nine years previously when he wrote to President Wilson about the 'officials of an alien nation' who 'refuse us education, they sap us of our wealth, they impose crushing taxes without our consent: they cast thousands of our people into prisons for uttering patriotic sentiments – prisons so filthy that often the inmates die of loathsome diseases'. A few officials had attended the 1885 Congress, but if any retired officials were delegates in the latter year they had probably – like the Ali brothers – purged their offence by some months in jail. An almost unanimous vote decided that the aim of the Congress Party was complete independence, and no single voice opposed a whole-hearted boycott of the Simon Commission.

It would be unwise to emphasise the contrast any further. The Congress is not a difficult organisation to capture, though it remained for some years an essentially Liberal body. Within a year or two it had become popular enough to attract delegates, and soon dropped its apologetic tone. By 1892 the Congress was expressing quite frankly its dissatisfaction with the new Councils, and its leaders, not yet converted to Tilak's new methods of agitation, were starting with the help of some English Liberals a periodical, *India*, to spread their views in England. Even in 1888 it was sufficiently independent for the Government to have become unfavourably aware of its existence, and for Lord Dufferin to throw a little cold water on the 'microscopic minority' who belonged to it. The attendance was usually about a thousand, but there is little evidence about the strength of the Party. A Viceroy with the insight of Lord Ripon would probably have kept in touch with the movement, but the Government of India under Lord Lansdowne took the view that the Congress 'represented the advanced Liberal party, as distinguished from the great body of Conservative opinion which exists side by side with it; they desire therefore to maintain an attitude of neutrality in their relations with both parties'. The English utterly failed to appreciate the strength of the great nationalist movement or to foresee that it was bound to cut right across the ordinary economic interests which divided their own countrymen into two parties. The reformist Liberals were left to be crushed between the fervour of the extremists and the apathy and hostility of the Government. By the end of ten years the Congress had won a definite place in Indian life. Every one who took part in public affairs had to consider his attitude towards it, and most of the younger men joined the party. Then followed a very difficult period of its existence when its activities were doomed to be overshadowed by two revolutionary movements, Tilak's agitation in the Deccan which led up to the Rand murder and his own imprisonment, and the storm over the Bengal partition.

There is no need to discuss the rights and wrongs of Lord Curzon's policy, but undoubtedly the old and evil tradition of disregarding the feelings of educated Indians still influenced the Government of his time. The rout of Italy by Abyssinia is supposed to have added fire to Tilak's agitation in 1897. The defeat of Russia by Japan caused even greater excitement throughout India in 1904, for it seemed that a turning-point had been reached in the aggrandisement of the European races. For years the English had encouraged the idea of a powerful and brutal Russia which was ever ready to fall upon an unprotected India. It was useless after her defeat to suggest the truth, that she was a vast disorganised Empire, administered on semi-oriental lines, and had suffered a deserved defeat from a small compact race deliberately organised on the most efficient European models. Just when the enthusiastic Bengali foresaw the return of the old-time glory of Asia, Lord Curzon instituted a series of unpopular University reforms, and felt constrained, in a Convocation address, to lecture the Indian upper classes on the need for greater truthfulness. Then in 1905 came the Partition of Bengal, a justifiable administrative measure, but planned with little regard for popular sentiment, and supported by Lord Curzon in a series of most provocative speeches. Against him were thousands of educated Bengalis who happened to be 'spoiling for a fight'. Owing to the Permanent Settlement Bengal has an unusually high proportion of the 'respectable classes', and these *bhadralok*, inspired by Tilak's work in the Deccan, were longing to do even better in their own country.

The agitation against the Partition was definitely Hindu, for the proposed division was favourable to the interests of the large Moslem population, but it was not a Brahman movement. Neither of its best known leaders, Bepin Chandra Pal and Arabinda Ghose, belonged to that caste, though they were friends and almost pupils of Tilak. The general methods adopted were those which had been found effective in the Deccan. Most of the educational work was done through that remarkably successful paper, the *Juguntur*, which was edited by Barendra Kumar Ghose, and Bhupendranath Dutt, whose brother, the Swami Vivekananda, had helped so much to revive orthodox Hinduism. In many ways the task of organising the agitation was easier in Bengal than in the West or the Punjab. Not only was there a larger educated class, which was being continually reinforced from Calcutta University, but rhetoric and panegyrics of the past made a greater appeal than to the dour Mahratta. Life in the stony Deccan villages must always have been hard, and the image of the bountiful Motherland despoiled by greedy foreigners would mean less to an inhabitant of those precarious areas which are usually on the verge of famine.

To the Bengal the appeal to his patriotism was irresistible. 'Behold this is our Mother, well-watered, well-fruited, cooled with the southern breeze, green with the growing corn; worship her, and establish her in your homes.'[1] The nationalist leaders wisely combined their political propaganda with mystical teaching. The cult of the bloodthirsty Kali, *Shakti* worship, and the revival of Tantric ritual all awakened a subtle and immediate response in that *terra incognita* the mental hinterland of the educated Hindu. The student was, of course, most impressionable of all.

'To a readiness to become "passion's slave" he adds a capacity for hero-worship which is unparalleled,' writes a very experienced educationalist. 'Give him outside the semi-official world of school a powerful personality with oratorical genius and a reputation for self-sacrifice tested by imprisonment or fine, and he will gladly place his head under the great man's feet.'[2]

The inevitable period of disorder was intensified by the riots which followed the enforced boycott of European goods, and by political dacoities. The assassination of officials, European and Indian, became extremely common, and it is necessary to emphasise the fact that these

[1] For an admirable account of this side of Bengali Nationalism, see Lord Ronaldshay's *The Heart of Aryavarta*, Chapter IX.

[2] A. Mayhew, *The Education of India*, p. 134.

do not and did not appear in the same light to Englishmen and Indians. The former have a peculiar horror of isolated political murders, from which their country has been singularly free, and when these occur they have an effect out of all proportion to their importance. One can instance the Phœnix Park murders, or the bombing of Sir Curzon Wyllie in 1908 which first drew English attention to the state of affairs in Bengal. On the other hand, the English middle classes have never shown any strong repugnance to the indiscriminate slaughter of crowds by Government troops, like the Peterloo massacre or the shooting in the Jallianwallabagh. There is not very much logic in the English attitude, for public men lead fairly safe lives, and in theory one life is as good as another. The English repugnance to political murder is not shared by other European countries, certainly not by the Latin races nor by the Irish. Even in Germany a large part of the public condoned the shooting of Rathenau in 1922, and the murder of Rosa Luxembourg by German officers received as 'good a press' as any assassination of an Indian police officer. The Indian views about the value of an individual life are completely at variance with those held in England, but not with those held by quite intelligent and normal Irishmen. To the Indian student of the Bhagavad Gita, his most sacred of holy songs, there would be nothing abhorrent in the idea that one man should die that a nation should be saved, besides the dead man is but casting off the outward garment, and 'he who regardeth the dweller in the body as a slayer, and he who thinketh he is slain both of them are ignorant'.

Most Indians would view as sheer hypocrisy the special sanctity which the British attach to the lives of Englishwomen, and which in 1919 as well as in 1857 was made the excuse for much retributive brutality. They consider, with much justification, that this sentiment is essentially racial because it does not extend to Indian women, and they can see no logic in the horror aroused by the tragedy of Muzafferpur in 1908, when Mrs. and Miss Kennedy were killed by a bomb intended for a British official. A nation which demands widespread retaliation for an unpremeditated murder, but can approve General Neill's treatment of the Brahmans or General Dyer's action at Amritsar, presents an insoluble problem to the educated Indian.

The imprisonment of Tilak, and the passing of various repressive Acts, such as the Press Act and the Summary Justice Act of 1908, marked the end of an epoch. The extremists had given an immense impetus to the old Hindu religion, and made nationalism into a living issue in every town and nearly every village in India. They had not, however, upset the stability of British rule, and had in some ways done incalculable damage to political nationalism. The methods employed in the Bengal agitation had driven some of the keenest leaders out of the movement, and it had definitely estranged the Moslems. In 1890 a quarter of the delegates to the Congress had been Mohammadans, but at the important Congress held at Benares in 1905 only 17 of the 756 delegates were of that faith. Within the Congress a considerable struggle took place, in which Gopal Krishna Gokhale, himself a Chitpavan Brahman, fought against and finally defeated the extremists under Tilak. The Congress at Surat in the following year ended in riots, but Tilak's trial and the suppression of the revolutionary movement gave Gokhale a supremacy which lasted for many years. He was himself essentially a realist in politics, and many years spent as a college Professor probably accentuated his natural caution. He saw the grave defects in Tilak's theories, and attempted to bring back the Mohammadans into the movement. In 1907 the Muslim League had been founded by Sir Saiyad Ali Iman, and though in 1909 the Congress pledged itself to work with the Government and gave an enthusiastic welcome to the Morley-Minto reforms, it was not found possible before the War to bring in either the more theoretical extremists or the Mohammadans. Until Mr. Gokhale died in 1915 the Congress movement remained predominantly Hindu, advanced but not extremist, critical of Government but not inclined to lead any popular, much less any revolutionary, movement to change the constitution.

# CHAPTER IV

# LATER PHASES OF NATIONALISM

THE news which came from India at the beginning of the last war, undoubtedly stirred the hearts of people in England. At a moment when the bottom seemed to be falling out of the safe and stable world which they knew, they heard about offers of support from Indian Princes, and later about the dispatch of Indian troops to France, the suspension of domestic controversy, and the support given by Indian politicians to a large grant of money for war purposes. Unfortunately these were but small incidents in an immense struggle. The average Englishman, if he thought about the matter at all, felt that India's response to the War was a confirmation of the rather vague ideas which he had gathered from Mr. Kipling and others. India was all right at heart. Disloyalty was confined to a few disgruntled and self-interested individuals, and even they, apparently, knew when to keep quiet. There was no realisation, even amongst the more advanced politicians, that an opportunity was being presented to them which would never return.

There is a Sanskrit word *prayaschitta* which is not infrequently used by educated Hindus to describe the kind of gesture of friendliness and expiation needed from England before there can be any peace and confidence between the two races. In 1915 this gesture might have been made. Europeans were then being rapidly withdrawn from civil posts, and Indians were entrusted with work and responsibility which had previously been reserved for Englishmen. The Congress, in spite of the untimely death of Mr. Gokhale early in 1915, remained friendly and moderate, and the speech of Mr. Sinha (afterwards Lord Sinha) as President of the Bombay Session was almost reminiscent of 1885: 'Princes and people alike had vied with one another to prove to the great British nation their gratitude for peace and blessing of civilisation secured to them under its ægis for the last hundred and fifty years and more.' Even that old warrior, Tilak, who was released from jail in 1914, remained quiet, disclaiming any hostility to the Government, and repudiating the few sporadic outbursts which occurred in Bengal. The only serious danger was an abortive conspiracy in the Punjab, largely due to the return of the Sikh emigrants on the *Komogatu Maru*. They had been refused admittance by Canada, and considered, not unjustifiably, that they had been badly treated. Any forward movement made by the British Government during the first fifteen months of the War would have been accepted as the sign of a new spirit. A constitutional compromise such as the scheme of 1919 would have been worked in the friendly and helpful way which alone could have given it any hope of success. Even the Declaration of 1917, if made two years earlier, would have done much to rally educated opinion to the side of England, and would have saved India many of those calamities which followed the end of the War.

The people waited for a sign, but no sign was given. Lord Hardinge and Mr. Austen Chamberlain were Viceroy and Secretary of State. Both were able men, but tinged with the Foreign Office outlook, and lacking the imagination and force of character to seize an opportunity, and to force their views upon a cabinet distracted by other problems which seemed more urgent. No demand for a new angle of vision came from the English in India. Simla was busy trying to make a totally inefficient machine function, and after a few months was fully involved in the Mesopotamian fiasco. The commercial interests soon settled down to an attitude of benevolent neutrality, and made money so rapidly that they lost interest in the ultimate fate of India. Where the English had worked honestly and with a good heart they reaped their reward in the loyalty of the regiments, and the orderliness of the districts. They failed in the whole field of their social relations with the Indians, for there they had worked unwillingly. Life in the Mofussil stations remained ostentatiously the same as before the War, and the shadow of the Mutiny hung over the clubs where English men and women danced and drank in order to keep up the prestige of their country. Early in 1916 Lord Hardinge sailed for England, and left unfulfilled one of the greatest opportunities which any one of his race has ever been given. Within a few months the tide had definitely turned, and any future experiments would have to be made in an atmosphere of hostility and suspicion.

India was soon weary of a war fought about issues of which she knew nothing. Only a few profited by the sudden rise in prices, and there were many causes of discontent. To the Moslems it was 'a sore point that the Government of our Caliph should be at war with the Government of our King-Emperor'.[1] British support of the Arabs and the revolt in the Sharif did not decrease this feeling, especially when it was widely reported that the Holy places of the Hedjaz were in danger. The methods employed in enlisting men for the Army and Labour Corps often savoured of the press-gang. The

[1] Presidential Address, Muslim League, 1915.

writer remembers the court-martial of a young Mahratta boy for deserting his regiment which was stationed in North India. He pleaded, apparently quite truthfully, that he had never intended to join the army, but had gone to the station with his mother who was travelling by train. As he stood on the platform, waving to her, a recruiting party at the back of the train picked him up by the shoulders, pulled him into a carriage, and took him over a thousand miles to their regiment. Equally objectionable was the collection of money for Red Cross work by subordinate officials who imagined their position depended on the amount they raised.

It is always invidious to discuss war-time activities in times of peace, but the point to be considered is not whether certain activities were justifiable, but how they affected the nationalist movement, especially in the North of India. The reader, for reasons discussed in the Introduction, must be referred to the Hunter Committee, the three Indian members of which emphasise the special incidence of war-time restrictions and demands upon the Punjab. It was here that the inevitable reaction assumed its worst form.

The soldiers, wounded or on leave, who began to drift back to India had tales to tell of prosperous French peasants, of muddle and inefficiency in Mesopotamia. The politicians began to see that their exemplary behaviour was being taken as a sign of weakness. When in 1916 the nationalist leaders again became active they found a great volume of popular support behind them. The Lucknow session of the Congress was dominated by Mr. Tilak and Mrs. Besant, who had little difficulty in carrying the assembly in a demand for 'Home Rule within the

Empire'. From this time forward no politician, however extreme his views, has found the Congress too moderate for him to attend.

In 1917, just two years too late, the Government in India, and a few people at home began to realise that some recognition of India's loyalty and support was necessary. The former started the good work by undoing the fiscal policy of 1894. In order to meet the interest charges on the £100,000,000 war loan the import duty on cotton fabrics was raised to 7½ per cent., but the excise duty remained as formerly at 3½ per cent. In this simple way an old and bitter grievance was removed, though not without strong protests from Lancashire, which were supported by local Members of Parliament belonging to all political persuasions. This action and the abolition of indentured emigration to Fiji showed a new spirit, which helped to conciliate the Legislative Council, even if it had little effect in the country generally. Opinion at home was also being prepared for a fairly drastic change. The report of the Mesopotamian Commission proved that the Indian bureaucracy was not only inelastic – that had always been suspected – but also thoroughly inefficient. Mr. Austen Chamberlain left an office in which his heart had never been set, and was succeeded by Mr. Montagu, who had sufficient imagination and understanding of the East to see that some gesture of friendship was needed. He may also have seen that the right moment had already passed, for he certainly wasted no time, and on August 20th, 1917, two important pronouncements were made by the Secretary of State. The first foreshadowed a new policy of 'the increasing association of Indians in every branch of the administration and the gradual development of self-governing institutions with a view to the progressive realisation of responsible Government in India as an integral part of the British Empire'. The second removed the bar to granting Indians Commissions in the Army. Later in the Autumn, Mr. Montagu set out to India to consult the Viceroy and the leaders of the various political parties. He arrived in time to hear of serious rioting at Arrah in Bihar, which began as an attack on the local Mohammadans and ended by widespread disorder which had to be put down by the military. His cold weather tour was carried out in an atmosphere of veiled hostility from the European population, and of suspicion from the more active nationalists, many of whom were organised in Mrs. Besant's Home Rule League, which captured the Congress that December.

The system of dyarchy which was evolved from the Montagu-Chelmsford Report will be considered in the next chapter. Although it represented a great advance on the existing system it did not have the disruptive effect on the nationalist movement which such an offer would have occasioned ten years previously. In 1909 the Congress had welcomed the Morley-Minto Reforms, but it decisively rejected the much greater measure of autonomy initiated by the Government of India Act in 1919. The former were brought forward when a great anti-British movement had spent itself; they came in, as it were, at slack tide. When Mr. Montagu brought in his scheme the tide was running strongly against the Europeans, and he introduced into a country, afflicted almost with xenophobia, a complicated and delicate piece of constitutional machinery with immense potentialities, but requiring the most considerate and careful treatment.

The wave of unrest, which swept through the country after the War, was totally unlike any of the earlier periods of agitation. It showed itself in many different ways; in the clamour against the Sedition Act which led to the tragedy of Amritsar; in the Khilafat movement which induced hundreds of hard-working Mohammadan ryots to sell all they had and move into Afghanistan; in the recrudescence of political dacoities and murders in Bengal; in the non-co-operation movement led by Mr. Gandhi which caused the partial boycott of the new legislatures, and introduced amongst the educated classes a new ideal and a new method of corporate action; in the widespread release of new forces which resulted in the Moplah rebellion in the South, in the horrors of Chauri-Chaura in the North, and the peasant agitation in Gujerat. Compared with these manifestations the pre-war agitations in Maharashtra and Bengal seem provincial and sectarian. Tilak had never attempted to conciliate the Moslem 'foreigners', he had fought the reformist Hindus with as much zeal as he had harassed the British, he was nothing of a democrat at heart, and was too profoundly contemptuous of Western ideas to hate them. His death in 1919 left the field open to Mr. Gandhi, who promptly captured the Congress, and wrenched the nationalist movement out of its old groove. He had knowledge and ideas, he understood the West enough to fear and dislike it, and above all he was 'Mahatma', and thus linked in the minds of men with those dreams and ideals which are the very essence of the Hindu religion.

This new phase of nationalism was broad enough to include the Moslems, and sufficiently popular to attract the masses. The fear, which spread through the Mohammadan world after the Armistice, that the Christian powers were going to destroy Turkey and the last remaining bulwark of Islam gave Mr. Gandhi, as he himself stated, 'such an opportunity of uniting Hindus and Mohammadans as would not arise in a hundred years'. Here and there, through India and Mesopotamia, men would dream that they had seen the Prophet floating through the air, and weeping because he had no piece of Moslem land on which he could lay his foot. There were all the elements ready for a popular Mohammadan movement, and Mr. Gandhi by fixing his hope on a distant and vague future was able to harness these forces to the Nationalist chariot. 'The end we do not know. For me it is enough to know the means. The means and the end are convertible terms in my philosophy of life.' [1]

The idealist succeeded where the realist Tilak had failed, and by hitching his waggon to a star Mr. Gandhi found himself the acknowledged leader of a vast popular movement which included ryots suffering under the bad harvests of 1919 and 1920, soldiers chafing under the dull and restricted life to which they had returned, Indian Christians who admired his hatred of caste and reformist tendencies, financial magnates who saw visions of India becoming a vast industrial nation, and Moslems who found themselves isolated in an unfriendly world. His methods were not unlike those of an amateur but very successful soldier who commanded a supply column through the worst part of the Mesopotamian campaign. When all his subordinates were running to explain exactly why it would be impossible to start at the appointed time, he would mount his horse and ride slowly off into the

[1] Address to Indian National Congress, December, 1924.

desert, and his motley command would perforce have to follow. Mr. Gandhi similarly led his army from in front. He promised India *swaraj* on December 1st, 1921, and set out to get it. Because of his faith and sincerity men of every creed and kind followed him. 'Shaukat Ali believes in the sword, I condemn all violence; but what do such differences matter between two men in both of whom the heart of India beats in unison.' [1] His idealism 'leaving the earth to lose itself in the sky' recked little of the nature of his followers so long as they shared or seemed to share his views. It was only in later days that disillusionment came, and he looked more critically at the very mixed array of those whom he had collected beneath his banner. There must have been times when he thought 'I'll not march with them to the New India, that's flat'.

One effect of this new leadership was partly to Westernise the nationalist movement. It is a curious paradox that, although Mr. Gandhi looked upon civilisation as a disease with which England was badly afflicted, his followers introduced into India many of the worst features of modern European democracy. Tilak was a born journalist with a genius for political invective, but his rigid Hindu orthodoxy did not allow him to seek popular assistance except on a religious basis. He was essentially an aristocrat. So was the Moderate leader, Mr. Gokhale, who would undoubtedly have gone to the hustings, but with a fine Whig contempt for the verdict and the methods by which it was obtained. Mr. Gandhi is a reformist and a democrat, and in those days which followed the War he was obsessed by the idea of introducing

[1] Valentine Chirol, *India, Old and New*. An account of an interview with Mr. Gandhi.

the reality of religion into everyday life. His followers were soon busy adjusting his lofty teaching to political expediency, and from this developed a flaw which was to ruin the whole structure, 'the one weak place that's stanchioned with a lie'. There is a magnificent courage in the idea of bringing holiness to the market-place, of 'Christ walking on the water, not of Genesareth, but Thames', but it requires courage almost amounting to madness to bring the mediæval concept of saintliness into the world of newspaper reporters, place hunters, and publicity agents. The agitation against the Sedition Act, which had by May, 1919, resulted in the death of 400 Indians and nine Europeans, showed the limitations of Mr. Gandhi's policy and presaged its ultimate failure.

At the instance of the Government of Bengal a Committee was appointed 'to investigate and report on the nature and extent of the criminal conspiracies connected with the revolutionary movement in India' and to advise as to legislation to enable the Government to deal with them. The Committee, under the Presidentship of Mr. Justice Rowlatt, collected evidence about the political crimes which had become endemic in Bengal, and had increased considerably in the Punjab during the War. It elicited, however, little which was not already known, and the only justification for the Committee was the need for further war-time legislation. Unfortunately the Committee's report and recommendations were allowed to appear in the summer of 1918, very shortly after the Montagu-Chelmsford Report of the Reforms. Educated Indians read the two reports together. The first was clear-cut and its recommendations definite. It proposed the establishment in any notified area of special courts, consisting of three judges sitting without juries, with power to try seditious crime, and the investment of provincial governments with powers of internment. The second was vague and doctrinaire. It suggested, somewhat dubiously, a tentative experiment with a new and untried type of government. The effect of both documents upon political India was immediate and inevitable, and their natural suspicion was changed to blind anger when the first report was speedily translated into the Sedition Act, often called the Rowlatt Act, while the Montagu-Chelmsford proposals were being thrashed out before an apathetic and rather hostile House of Commons.

The agitation against the Rowlatt Act was frankly dishonest. Anyone with the least experience of democracy can see that it would not be easy to organise popular opposition to the Act as it stood. The new powers and the new courts were a menace to liberty which the nationalists were right to combat, but they were faced with the same difficulty which Liberals felt when they were opposing the use of Chinese labour in South Africa, or the Conservatives when they wished to call the nation's attention to communist influence in the Labour Party. The work of the successful propagandist is to make the individual think that he is threatened. The Liberals suggested to the working-man that the Chinese were coming to take his job. The Conservatives hinted that the English people's money was going to be collected and used to bolster up the Russian Government. The Indian nationalists, translating liberty into terms which the ryot would understand, spread the idea that under the Rowlatt Act all couples intending to be married were to be medically inspected, and that all assemblies of three or four people, including marriage ceremonies, were to be prohibited. Thus does the East learn and profit from the West. Unfortunately neither Mr. Gandhi nor his followers had realised that Western democracies have, like Mithridates, taken their daily doses of poison, and are now so immune that the fiercest propaganda can only create an atmosphere which will make some small percentage record their votes in a particular way. Similar methods in the East make the ryot take his heaviest *lathi*, and walk to the nearest town to see what is happening. In most parts of India the agitation led to little more than spasmodic violence. At Viramgaum a minor official was attacked and burnt to death, there were disturbances at Calcutta, and in Mr. Gandhi's own city of Ahmedabad. Only in the Punjab was the anti-British feeling sufficiently strong to rouse more than a feeling of vague dissatisfaction.

To most Englishmen in India the Punjab has certain romantic associations. It is near the Frontier which has always exercised their imagination, and its history has the same kind of appeal as that of Rajasthan to a literary Bengali. It is the Province where 'men are men', the land of the Lawrences, of Nicholson, and of Mr. Kipling. It has always been very heavily garrisoned. The idea, for which Lord Roberts was partly responsible, that troops should only be raised from the so-called martial races was found to be quite unsound during the War. This discovery, however, was not made till too late, and the traditions of the virile fighting North lingers on and adds another unnecessary complication to India's confused politics. A very large number of the towns have cantonments, and consequently social relations between the English and the educated Indians are formal and insincere. The old obsessions, dating back to the Mutiny period, survive very strongly in a society which spends much of its time and shapes its opinions in regimental messes.

When Mr. Gandhi's agitation reached the Punjab, the province was full of disillusioned European officers, military and civil, most of whom had just returned from a war where life had been free, promotion rapid, and their actions untrammelled by 'red tape'. They had learnt that in times of danger one must hit hard and think afterwards. Those who had been in Mesopotamia and the Middle East had seen nothing which would alter their prejudices about the sanctity of European life, and the treatment of oriental races. The massacre of Jallianwallabagh, the indiscriminate floggings, the 'crawling orders' and the many subsequent scandals in connection with the administration of martial law were none of them isolated cases for which individuals could be rightly held responsible. They followed inevitably from the Mutiny traditions taught to generations of subalterns, and accepted in the Punjab, but probably only in the Punjab by the civil officers. Looking back at these events many Indians would be inclined to forgive General Dyer's action more easily than the ostentatious approval which it received from the European community.

It is dangerous for a prophet to be too specific. The first and most active phase of Mr. Gandhi's control of the nationalist movement ended on December 31st, 1921, the date by which he had promised India *swaraj*. From that time onwards he remained an archangel, but 'an archangel slightly damaged'. His volcanic activities continued until his arrest and imprisonment. He organised the National

Volunteers, and attempted to win over the Marathas, always his sternest critics, by raising a 'Tilak Swaraj Fund'. He spread the doctrine of *satyagraha* until every educated Indian had to define his attitude towards it. He rushed into the dangerous field of economics, and, blazoning the *charkha* or spinning wheel on his flag, gave a new direction to the idea of India's material advancement. Yet none of these ventures prospered. There were grave scandals about the Tilak Fund, and the National Volunteers were partly responsible for the lamentable rioting at Bombay when the Prince of Wales landed in 1921, and almost entirely responsible for the Chauri-Chaura affair when twenty-one policemen and watchmen were murdered. The latter incident occurred in February, 1922, and immediately afterwards Mr. Gandhi published the Bardoli resolutions which suspended nearly all the activities of his followers, and confined them to ordinary political work on behalf of the Congress and certain social activities. Nothing but his own personal popularity held the party together. His trial and imprisonment, with its obvious Biblical parallel, and poor Mr. Broomfield playing the dignified and unwilling Pilate, ended a situation which was becoming grotesque and impossible.

During the last five years no single leader has attained a position approaching that held by Mr. Gandhi, and the nationalist movement has broken up into a number of political and communal bodies. The Congress was totally incapable of holding it together. The Moplah rising killed the Hindu support of the Khilafat movement. By 1924 Mr. Jinnah had revived the Muslim League and drawn most of the representative Mohammadan leaders from the Congress. In the autumn of 1927 the League itself split over the question of boycotting the Simon Commission, but it remains outside the Congress movement and only a few extremists, like the Ali brothers, troubled to go down to the Congress at Madras at Christmas. The Liberals, the Independents and the non-Brahmans have their separate organisation outside the Congress fold, and the formation of the Swaraj party in 1923 and the growing strength of the Hindu Mahasabha have distracted attention from the old body. The increase in Hindu-Moslem friction during the last four years has added to the importance of the purely communal bodies, but the growing importance of the other organisations is due to a feeling that the Congress has done its work. Those politicians who have entered Provincial or Central Assemblies need a party which will undertake organisation work, and the function of a body, which does little but meet annually and pass resolutions, is not very clear. The Montagu Reforms, which did not directly disrupt the nationalist movement, are now tending to divide political leaders into two groups. The first contains the all-India politicians, who are interested chiefly in the Central Legislature, and the theoretical side of nationalism. The second group is growing in importance. Its members look to the Provincial legislatures as the natural sphere of their activities, and they seem to acquire a practical outlook and knowledge of affairs which is not required at Delhi. Amongst the latter the nationalist movement will become diffused, varying in its form and intensity from province to province, but remaining always a very powerful force.

Meanwhile the Congress still meets yearly, growing larger in numbers while it becomes weaker in influence. The active political leaders are falling away, or, if they attend, they merely go from a sense of duty. It provides, however, a perfect holiday resort for politically-minded young men. Special trains are run from all parts of India, and it is not difficult for anyone who wants to make the trip to become a delegate. The Congress is held at Christmas, when most offices are closed for several days, and European business men and officials retire into camp to shoot duck or else go and lose money at the races. There is plenty to amuse the visitor, and at the Madras Session in 1927 the real business of the Congress was hard to disentangle from the trades exhibition, musical competitions, and the many subsidiary meetings. These give a young man a chance of rubbing shoulders with his fellows from all parts of India, and of catching an occasional glimpse of delightfully celebrated people, Mr. Gandhi talking to Mrs. Besant, and the Ali brothers, large, cheerful, and noisy. There was a flood of talk of which the meeting in the main 'pandal' is only the principal river. It overflows into innumerable demonstrations, committee meetings, Social League Conferences, and private arguments.

The Congress, politically, has shot its bolt. In spite of Mr. Gandhi's opposition it has demanded complete independence, outside the Empire, and has thus played the last chord of the crescendo for which it has been working up since 1884. Its chief interest now lies in the opportunity it gives for noting new tendencies amongst the younger generation of educated young men, the most remarkable being their impatience at the older and more florid type of oratory, and their suspicion of politicians who had not shown their disinterestedness by going to prison. They have, however, an infinite capacity for listening to speeches and arguments, for only a few of the thousands who attended can have understood the speeches, nearly all of which were delivered in English, and many quite inaudible, even with the 'loud-speaker's' doubtful aid. The delegates seemed always asking for more, especially from the younger men, and if two friends stopped and talked in the road, they were liable to find themselves surrounded by a crowd, who, like the Irishman in the story, would ask 'Is this a private disputation, or may any one join in?' From this point of view the Congress undoubtedly fills a real need, but as a political force it is no longer necessary to take it seriously. In future people will look to the Legislatures and the smaller political groups in order to see the ideals of nationalism being worked out in practice. The Congress will probably fall under the control of one of the groups, which will use its name and organisation.

## CHAPTER V

# EXPERIMENTS IN DEMOCRACY

THE War did much to solve the question whether Indians could be trusted to administer the bureaucratic machine from within. From 1914 to 1919 very few recruits came from England, and many British officers from the various services were allowed to join the army or were assigned to special war work. Both in the Provinces and at Simla many of the highest posts were occupied by Indians, and in several districts the only European left would be the Superintendent of Police. Unfortunately there were divided counsels upon this subject in England, and although the Montagu Reforms specified that an increasing proportion of the Indian Civil Service should be Indians, the Government followed its usual policy of taking away with one hand what it gave with the other. Strenuous efforts were made to ensure sufficient candidates to complete the European quota, and several army officers were appointed. The idea that the question of 'Indianising' of the services might solve itself was finally dispelled by an ill-advised speech from Mr. Lloyd George in 1922, when he succeeded in reviving all the old rancour on this subject. Borrowing apparently a metaphor from Mr. Bevan's book on Indian Nationalism, he described the Indian Civil Service as the steel frame of the whole structure, and made it clear to most Indians that the Service and the British element in it were to be maintained on the same footing and in the same numbers indefinitely. 'Whatever may be the success of Indians as Parliamentarians or administrators I can see no period when they can dispense with the guidance and assistance of a small nucleus of British Civil Servants.' 'There is one institution which we will not deprive of its functions and privileges, and that is the institution which built up the British Civil Service in India.' The Indianisation of the Services still remains a live issue, and the amount of the 'ryot's money remitted to England' is a vague but important item in Nationalist propaganda. It tends to obscure the far more important question of the future status of the civil servants, whether English or Indian.

Within the last twenty years two attempts have been made, both by Liberal Statesmen, to give India some measure of self-government on Western lines. The Morley-Minto reforms of 1909 were little more than a development of the old Executive Councils to which were added certain nominated and elected members. In the Imperial Legislative Council 33 were nominated and 27 elected, but in some of the Provinces elected members exceeded the nominated. Lord Morley, however, was a very hesitant reformer. He had publicly expressed his distrust for 'natives in positions of high responsibility', and stated definitely that his reforms would not lead directly or indirectly to the establishment of a Parliamentary system in India. These new members were only 'additional' to the old Executive Councils, and were attached as consultative committees to them. Any resolutions which they might pass were in the nature of recommendations to the Governor in Council. The Budget was not submitted to their vote, and their functions were so strictly limited to the giving of advice, which might or might not be accepted, that it is difficult to understand the very favourable reception which the Reforms had in India. Lord Morley had no faith in the democratic principle as applied to the East, and animadverted somewhat unnecessarily about the unsuitability of a fur coat in a tropical climate. Consequently he introduced a principle which is likely to cause unending trouble to India in the future. His elected members were returned on a basis of communal or economic interests rather than from geographical constituencies. Many of them were elected by Chambers of Commerce, by municipalities and by local boards. Even when geographical constituencies were used the voters were confined to landowners, or to communal groups, such as all Moslems, living within a certain area and holding certain property qualifications. Members came to the Council feeling that it was their duty to fight for a special section, which was often little more than a coterie of wealthy business men. Each man held a 'watching brief' for some group of people, and for the rest it was sufficient if they were general critics of a Government which had for many years shown itself capable of carrying on the administration. The Councils neither taught responsibility nor inculcated any idea of true public service. The Moslem was encouraged in his attitude, often little more than a pose of holding himself as 'a stranger within the gates'. Indians, generally, were tempted to group themselves politically into caste *sabhas*, and communal leagues, instead of dividing according to their ideas on national, social, and economic questions. The initiation of this principle in India was the greatest blunder which the British have ever committed. It had already eaten into the life of the people by 1918, and there was a strong enough body of opinion to insist upon its retention in the Montagu reforms.

There is some mystery about the origin of 'Dyarchy',

or the methods by which it obtained sufficient support to pass through the 'worst Parliament of modern history'. Mr. Lionel Curtis undoubtedly had much to do with popularising the general principle, but not enough to justify the idea held by many English in India, and voiced by Lord Ampthill in the House of Lords.[1]

'The incredible fact is that, but for the chance visit to India of a globe-trotting doctrinaire, with a positive mania for constitution mongering, nobody in the world would ever have thought of so peculiar a notion as that of Dyarchy.'

The Government of India Act was passed through a sceptical House of Commons and received its final sanction in December, 1919. The unfortunate proviso was added that a Statutory Committee was to reconsider the scheme after ten years and Mr. Montagu was left to display before the Indian upper classes, then in their most ungracious mood, a compromise scheme with few really whole-hearted supporters, East or West.

The chief feature of the Government of India Act, 1919, and the rules made under it, was the division of the provincial administration into two parts. The 'reserved' departments remain ultimately amenable to the British Parliament, and are administered by the Governor in Council. The 'transferred' departments are theoretically controlled by Provincial Legislatures with elected majorities, and are in practice administered by the Governor working with his Ministry, the members of which are chosen by himself from the elected members of the Legislature. This necessitated a prior classification of subjects

[1] December 16, 1919.

into Central and Provincial, for the principle of dyarchy is entirely confined to the latter. The Provincial subjects include the administration of justice, police, and prisons, and also most of the so-called 'nation-building' departments which were then 'transferred'. Amongst the most important of the latter are education; agriculture; local self-government; co-operation; medical administration and public health; excise; forests and fisheries; industrial development and much of the public works department. It will be seen that the charge of law and order has been reserved, as well as land revenue and irrigation, but from the standpoint of ministers in charge of spending departments as education and public health the most drastic and important reservation was that of the whole financial system.

Except for two periods of suspension in Bengal and the Central Provinces – when the Legislatures refused to vote the Ministers' salaries – the system has actually been in operation in the nine major Provinces since 1921. Although the ballot became a farce at the height of the non-co-operation movement the Reforms Scheme has been accepted as an experimental measure by the different Legislatures, and except for the two suspensions it has functioned regularly and with moderate success. It may be noted that even in Bengal and the Central Provinces, the new Legislatures elected in November, 1926, passed the ministers' salaries by large majorities, 94 to 36 in the first case, 55 to 16 in the second. They thus endorsed the opinion commonly held amongst educated Indians on the subject of the Montagu Reforms, which is not unlike the soldier's dictum on the last war, 'Dyarchy's the devil, but it's better than no dyarchy at all'. The men, like Mr.

Jinnah and Mr. Jayakar in Bombay, who have helped to keep a system working although they disliked it, have really done a great public service. It was obvious that the present hybrid system of two cabinets could not be permanent, and it says much for the practical ability of the educated classes that they should have kept it functioning at all.

The outstanding weakness in the Montagu scheme was that it gave the ministers responsibility without power, and the Legislatures power without responsibility. The Ministers, appointed separately, and often, as in the Punjab, in order to satisfy two or three opposing communal groups, have no joint responsibility and the only power they possess is the embarrassment caused by a resignation and the influence which they may have upon their fellow-members, an influence which rapidly fades during their term of office. No uniform system was adopted in the different Provinces. The Governor of Madras tried to make the predominant non-Brahman party into the 'Government', and chose all his Ministers from them, but it was more usual to pick rather mediocre and 'safe' men from the different groups, usually on a communal basis. Such men would not even combine on some general financial policy which they could press upon the Governor, and so get duly considered by the Executive Council. Even if they did combine, they had little power to press their claims unless they had also the full support of the Legislature. The same difficulties arose when their department's activities overlapped those of some 'reserved' department. Sir Mohammad Fakruddin, as the senior Minister in Bihar and Orissa, explained this aspect of the case to the Legislative Council.

'The classification of transferred subjects is seriously defective. There is no reason why you should give the Minister, Agriculture without Irrigation. Why should you give him the administration of the spending department without any control over Finance? Without purse others consider me as if I am simply a clerk to prepare a certain scheme, and after the scheme is ready the Finance Department is entitled to knock it down on the ground of want of funds. What happened this year? I had a scheme ready costing several lakhs of rupees for recurring and non-recurring expenditure. But I could not get money.'

All the new Ministers suffered in the same way. On one side they were harassed by their old colleagues in the Legislature asking why they did nothing to introduce the measures and reforms which they had been advocating for years. The Minister finds himself in charge of a very large machine, and his actions guided by a permanent secretary over whom he has no control, perhaps the same European who had previously had charge of the work. In his dealings with the Governor he is at a disadvantage compared with the Executive Councillors, and in popular estimation as well as in actual practice his status is distinctly inferior. The Executive Councillors are servants of the Crown, the Ministers only nominees of the Governor, and the former take official precedence, a formality of immense importance in Indian and Anglo-Indian eyes. The Ministers are also excluded from the Vice-Presidentship, and so are not qualified to succeed a Governor during a period of vacancy. An Education Minister like Dr. Paranjpye in Bombay, who may desire to push through a large and comprehensive scheme, finds himself blocked at every turn. He cannot put his scheme and his estimates before a united cabinet, and after it has been accepted know that he is certain of full financial backing, and that he will also have a majority to help him during the passage of the necessary Bills through the House. He is lucky if he can bring forward a truncated version of his scheme piecemeal, and placate a sufficient number of those Members who demand the whole scheme and nothing else.

It is almost certain that Mr. Montagu contemplated the establishment of joint ministerial responsibility, and did not foresee the extent to which communal electorates would prevent the working of the party system. The following clause in the Government of India Act seems to make this clear. 'In relation to transferred subjects the Governor shall be guided by the advice of his Ministers – unless he sees sufficient reason to dissent from their opinion.' The drafting is unsatisfactory, but Dyarchy would have had a better chance of success if some of the Governors had read it in the same way as do most Indian politicians, that is to say, as implying joint ministerial responsibility for all the transferred subjects. This would have been difficult in the Punjab, but not impracticable elsewhere. Nearly all the Governors have, however, framed Rules of Executive Business, enabling them to deal separately with each Minister, and this arrangement, which has certain obvious practical conveniences, gives a Governor an immense advantage over the men whom he himself nominated, and who are often of mediocre calibre and inexperienced.

There have been many resignations since 1921, and the worst indictment against Dyarchy is the sad falling off in the enterprise and independence of the Ministers.

Too often the only effect of the Reforms has been to add another extremely expensive and dilatory office through which all administrative work has to pass. If the Minister is not prepared to fight, the real control in all minor matters will rest with the Secretary, and on larger issues with the Governor. As was pointed out by the late Sir Surendranath Banerjea, who was a very efficient Minister of Education in Bengal, the system relies for success 'upon the uncertainties of the personal element'. With a tactful Governor it may work for a time, but between a domineering Governor and an irresponsible assembly the position of a Minister becomes impossible. In either case the Minister's position is fundamentally unsound, and we have Sir K. V. Reddy's verdict after being in charge of Departments from 1921 to 1923 that 'even in the Province of Madras where an honest attempt has been made to work out the reforms in the spirit in which they were conceived, Dyarchy has absolutely failed'.

If the Ministers had responsibility without power, the Legislatures equally have a little power and no real responsibility. A Member of the Legislature may have individual ambitions to be nominated a Minister, but he never undergoes the discipline of being a 'back-bencher' supporting a cabinet which has a free hand and can be called upon to redeem its pledges. He can therefore make any promises he likes, and adopt any wrecking tactics which may appeal to him. His constituents do not return him in order to support items of Provincial Legislature, but on some vague national ideal, or more often on personal or caste grounds. The present system discourages discipline or team work, or any feeling of responsibility either to the constituents or the country at large.

It would be difficult to exaggerate the evil effects of the communal electorates upon the personnel of the new Legislatures. The system is based on the idea, which is almost certainly erroneous, that it is better for a small community to be represented by a few members which it chooses rather than to have a voice, albeit a small one, in the choice of all the members. The disadvantages can be seen by imagining communal representation in England. It would give the Roman Catholics, perhaps, forty and the Jews three seats in the House of Commons, and at each election one could be sure that those seats would be filled by religious stalwarts entrusted with the task of fighting to the death for their parties' sectarian interests. Being in a minority they could never get their own way except by intriguing with other dissentient groups, but in the House they would feel it their duty to advertise their faith as loudly and as insistently as possible. Members with a fondness for publicity would eagerly scan each measure and each administrative action in order to detect some slur upon their religion. Can any sane man contend that the system would be other than harmful to Parliament and disastrous alike for the Catholics and the Jews? At present every member being elected on ordinary political grounds takes care not to unite against him a solid block of people voting on some religious question which cuts across the ordinary party divisions.

The most dangerous guides in this matter are the political leaders of the community. It might well be imagined that a fervent Roman Catholic politician would look with sympathy upon a scheme which would ensure him a safe seat in Parliament. This point is sometimes forgotten when it is stated that the Government has yielded to a 'unanimous demand' from some community. In the East this question is also closely connected with the 'spoils system' and public appointments. The individual politician, Mohammadan or Sikh, who clamours for communal representation is not only thinking of his own seat, but also of his ability to press for Government posts. It is unfortunate that in most of India while the predominant religion is Hindu, the Hindus are also better educated than the Mohammadans and have always tended to monopolise the appointments. One can imagine that it would encourage the English Roman Catholics to demand communal representation if their children had to begin their education by learning the Bible by heart, and if for this and other reasons they found the civil services practically closed to them.

There is no doubt that once the communal system has taken hold of political life it completely overwhelms all other party divisions. In the Punjab it has very nearly killed Nationalism. In that Province communalism is seen at its worst, for no question arises of protecting a small and weak minority but rather of making peace between three sturdy groups, Mohammadans, Hindus, and Sikhs, and the last two nearly equal the first. Though the Moslems began the demand for community representation, the Hindus are apt pupils in the areas where they are in a minority. The Hindu Mahasabha, sweeping aside the Congress party, has organised a solid religious block, which, forgetting the 'Motherland in chains', has been able to concentrate on such essentials as the playing of music outside mosques, and the appointment of sub-assistant surgeons on a community rota.

The only possible argument for the introduction of the

communal system is that it has been demanded, and in India the Moslem's claim was supported by the Indian Congress of 1916 in order to give an appearance of national unity. They could have done no greater disservice to the Indian nation or to their creed of nationalism. They forced the late Mr. Montagu, very much against his will, to embody the principle in his scheme, and the principle having been accepted it had to be extended, sometimes in a modified form, so as to include Sikhs, Anglo-Indians and Europeans, Indian Christians in Madras, and non-Brahmans. Future historians will possibly accuse the English of having introduced the system with deliberate malice, like a retreating army poisoning the wells behind it. This will not be true. The churning of the ocean has begun, and one of the first products is certainly not the nectar which is to make India live for ever.

# PART III

# PROBLEMS OF SELF-GOVERNMENT

## CHAPTER I

# COMMUNAL DIVISIONS

THERE are many considerations which make it difficult to forecast the future of a self-governing India. Her long and exposed frontiers, the dubious position of the Indian States, the fear of internal disorders and administrative decay, all these are serious questions, but they suggest dangers less subtle than the fact that India is divided into innumerable groups, based on religious differences, the members of which never intermarry with those outside their group, have no social relations with them, and have learnt, especially during the last few years, to look to their caste fellows or their co-religionists for help in all times of political unrest.

In the first part of this book an attempt was made to divide Indian society into three main groups, defined by their economic position. These divisions exist, and will ultimately, with their subdivisions, tend to reshape India. The individual, however, is little more aware of them than the ocean is conscious of the tides which keep it incessantly moving. The Indian does not visualise society, like the Marxians do, as a Neapolitan ice separated horizontally into neat blocks. The Hindu ryot, when danger threatens, looks to his village caste mates, the Moslem ryot to other Moslem ryots. He does so because he considers them as his friends rather than because he has any lively expectation of religious consolation or assistance. So in nineteenth-century England, any social upheaval would have driven two fellow farm-workers, one to his chapel and the other to his parson. Now, as likely as not, it would send them both to a trades-union organiser for advice. India is undoubtedly in the earlier stage. There is little prospect, within a generation or so, of the Indian peasant seeing himself primarily as a peasant, and recent events have helped to postpone any change.

The division between Hindus and Moslems is only one of these many vertical cleavages in Indian society. It is, however, far the greatest. The quarrel between the two religious groups has become a severe disease of the body politic. It needs to be analysed in the cool and dispassionate way in which scientists approach the similar problem of cancer. Nothing must be taken for granted, and the first point which needs examining is whether it is, as usually assumed, a religious and racial question. There has been a tendency to accept too readily the romantic idea of the Indian Moslem as a stranger keeping his desert faith pure in a land of idolaters. This view has been endorsed, not unnaturally, by the upper-class Mohammadans themselves. It is intensely gratifying to the educated Moslem, as he watches his people being ousted from power and place by the subtler Hindu, to consider himself, in the words of one of their leaders, as 'a member of a universal religious brotherhood, sojourning in a land in which a neutral Government, with a neutral outlook, kept law and order and justice'. [1] It is equally pleasing to the self-esteem of the impoverished Mohammadans, who make up such a large proportion of the *bazar* population of the small towns, to feel that they have some vague connection with the great world outside. They like to think of their co-religionists in Persia, Turkey, and Egypt enjoying an independence and freedom unknown to the Hindu, and especially to that fat and prosperous Hindu

[1] Aga Khan, *India in Transition*, p. 22.

who happens to be living next door. The world is full of groups, like the 'poor whites' of South Africa, relying on their connection with some dominant race elsewhere. The claim is natural enough, but the English, in accepting this picture of the Moslems as a race apart, seem to have been misled by a writer of genius, who had, however, a journalist's *flair* for the picturesque, and who always saw the Peninsula in terms of the Punjab.

The investigations of census officers make it clear that the vast majority of the Mohammadans in India are the descendants of converts from Hinduism. Fifteen per cent. is a very generous estimate of the Punjab Moslems who are really of foreign origin, and in the rest of India – except the extreme North-West – the proportion of foreign stock is insignificant. As the Punjab contains only a fifth of India's 69 million Mohammadans, it is not unfair to consider those of foreign origin as a small and select aristocracy not incomparable with the old British stock in the United States of America. The remainder are only separated by a few generations from the various Hindu castes from whom they were originally converted. Nor have they become, to any great extent, a mixed race, for the old caste distinctions have survived amongst these converted Hindus, just as they have amongst the Southern Indians who have been converted to Christianity. The castes hardly intermarry, and sometimes will not even inter-dine.

'Although the distinction between section and section is much looser than in the case of the Hindu castes, and it is the fashion to deny the existence of rigid partitions between the various groups, yet there is practical endogamy in the sectional and functional divisions, and in Bengal a Sheikh will not marry a Kulu, while in some parts one Muhammadan will not feed with another.'[1]

In Southern India the process of absorbing a particular Hindu caste is still continuing. The Mappillas are the largest Moslem community in Madras.

'Originally descended from Arab sailors who married women of the country, the majority of Mappillas have next to no admixture of foreign blood; except in few cases they are simply out-caste Cherumans who have turned to Islam in the hope of improving their social status, or the descendants of such converts. Their zeal for Muhammadanism is notorious, and their fanatical outbreaks have for years been the only source of disturbance of the West Coast.'[2]

It would be possible to multiply instances throughout India, but it seems clear that the foreign stock amongst the Moslems is very small, that the great bulk are racially indistinguishable from the surrounding Hindus, and that fanaticism is as strongly marked amongst the most recently converted as amongst the 'older' Mohammadans. The last point is common to most religions, for the enthusiasm of the recent convert is proverbial.

The racial distinction of the Moslems is clearly an illusion. They are in no sense foreigners, and Hindu blood runs in the veins even of the Mohammadan aristocracy. Six of the Moghul Emperors, including Jehangir and Shah Jehan, had Hindu mothers, and in the seventeenth cen-

[1] Census Report of 1921, Section 198. [2] *Ibid.*

tury this form of intermarriage seems to have been common. The great mass of middle- and lower-class Moslems are only a few generations removed from their Hindu kinsmen. There are many races in India, well-differentiated stocks of great antiquity, Pathans, Parsis, Marathas, Telugus, Bengalis and Burmans, but it is only in a few parts of Northern India that two different races are brought into contact with each other, and that one of those is Hindu by religion and the other Mohammadan.

The nature of the two religions is such that it is often said to divide the Moslems clearly and irrevocably from the Hindus. At first sight this would appear to be true. Hinduism is the religion of the forest, Mohammadanism that of the desert. The beauty of Hinduism lies in the virtues of submission and dependence, its weakness lies in ignoring the will, its failure in the merging of the individual into a class, so that class consciousness becomes a substitute for conscience and will. It is the religion of men overwhelmed by nature, whose myriad gods swarm in the tree-tops. It tends to inaction, to sitting 'by the Jumna's bank, waiting and musing and longing to die'. Such a religion could have never survived in the desert, where a man is thrown upon his own resources, where independence is the cardinal virtue, and where a man inclines to a simple philosophy and a direct approach to the Deity. The fundamental incompatibility of the two creeds has undoubtedly tended to estrange Hindu and Moslem, and has to some extent thrown the latter on the side of the other 'people of the Book', the British, but it is easy to exaggerate both tendencies.

The pervasiveness of Hinduism has already been discussed, and the desert religion has undoubtedly been considerably modified by contact with it. Many Mohammadan communities retain caste, and also observe Hindu festivals and ceremonies. In some parts of the Deccan the Moslems seem not unlike a Hindu caste. They keep the Moharram, to which they invite certain Hindu castes, but they attend the Divali festivities. There is a famous shrine at Nagore which attracts both Hindus and Moslems, and in Gujerat and Sind there are many borderland sects, like the Matia, Momna, and Sanghar groups who base their creeds on both religions. Nearly every one with Hindu blood in his veins, appears loath to break entirely with the Gods of the country. Some are like the Christian Kolis, who 'combine the worship of idols with the worship of the Christian Trinity, figures of Hindu godlings being kept behind the altar, and covered with a cloth when a priest comes to celebrate Mass'. In many districts the Moslems have modified the simplicity of their marriage ceremonies by introducing the *Shabgasht*, or night procession, and other Hindu rites. Even among the aristocratic Moslem families of Lucknow and Patna certain Hindu customs are found, and the remarriage of widows is uncommon.

Race is clearly not the basis of the Hindu Moslem antagonism, and religion would seem to be only a partial reason for the continual outbreaks between the two communities. If the nature of the Moslem religion was the chief cause there would never be peace in the land, and it would be difficult to explain why the hostility seems to come in waves, why it is much less common in Indian States than in British India, and why, until the Moplah rising, it was almost unknown in many parts of the south and west. Like the doctors in their investigations of cancer, one is driven to the conclusion that the germs of the trouble are nearly always present, but that they only become virulent when there is some other cause of irritation. When this becomes acute the other preliminaries to a quarrel are seldom lacking. The playing of music before mosques and the sacrificial slaughter of cows are little more than the formalities which precede a fracas between two groups 'spoiling for a fight'. The formulæ have only altered a little since the days of Montague and Capulet. 'Do you bite your thumb at us, sir?'

A map, showing the areas where Hindu Moslem outbreaks are most frequent, suggests that this added cause for irritation is really economic. The communities in these districts are divided into distinct economic groups. Thus, in the North-West, Hindus are the moneylenders and the Moslems are peasants; in the North-East they are often landowners, and the Moslems tenants. In the towns, and it is the towns where the feeling is worst, the shopkeepers, professional men, and employers are Hindu, the craftsmen and workers are usually Moslem. So much have the Hindus in the Punjab become identified with landowning and moneylending that the Land Alienation Act, aimed at assisting and protecting peasants of both religions, has now become the basis of a bitter quarrel between the two groups. The introduction of the machinery of democracy, and the institution of the communal electorate have further confused religion and economics. Every politician knows that it is easier to arouse popular feeling upon a simple religious issue than upon a complicated social or economic question. The question of unemployment in England empties the House of Commons as quickly as a debate on the Prayer Book fills it. There is no cry in the world so effective as 'The Church in danger', and in every Indian

Province, where a creed or a caste is in a minority, this cry is being raised. The educated classes, who employ it, have even less cause to divide upon religious questions than the masses. Many of the leading politicians have their full share of Western scepticism, and their European education has rounded off the angularities of the old creeds. It would be ludicrous to consider Mr. Jinnah and Mr. Jayakar as the rival protagonists of the religion of the desert and the religion of the forest. The Hindu-Moslem antagonism in its modern form has nothing to do with race, and very little to do with the tenets of religion. Like the quarrels between 'Church' and 'Chapel' in nineteenth-century England, the real basis is economic and social. Amongst the upper classes of India the fight is for the most part over offices and Government appointments. Amongst the working classes it takes different forms in town and country, and from Province to Province, but whether they appreciate the underlying forces or not, there are always priests and *moulvis*, newspapers and politicians to keep the latent irritation from dying down, and to spread through the *bazar* those rumours which breed fear and distrust. In many northern towns the situation closely resembles our ideas of mediæval Italian cities, with the craftsmen-shopkeepers sitting at their work, but always prepared to put up their shutters at the first sign of a faction fight. During a recent visit to India the writer came across two cases of serious rioting involving the closing of the *bazar*. The first arose from a quarrel between a Sikh soldier and a Moslem shoemaker who had sold him a bad pair of slippers. The second occurred because a Mohammadan boy had stolen a handful of sweets from a Hindu shopkeeper, and slipped and hurt himself when running away from the irate owner. Under-employment is rife in towns as well as villages, and there are always plenty of *badmashes* ready to join in a fight, especially if there are any prospects of loot.

The severity of the outbreaks since the war is chiefly the result of communal electorates, but it owes something to a reaction after the hasty and ill-considered attempts to produce a 'united front' in 1916 and afterwards. The so-called Lucknow pact, which accepted the principle of separate electorates, Moslem and non-Moslem, was made without the slightest thought for consequences, and for two or three years Mr. Gandhi enlisted the most incompatible forces beneath his banner of home rule, and cared little what terms they demanded. The whole *swaraj* movement found itself pledged to support the Khilafat agitation, and shared the odium which followed from well-grounded complaints of mismanagement and peculation. The abandonment by the new Turkish Government of the cherished institution of the Caliphate made much of their propaganda seem ridiculous, and finally the Moplah rising, which began under nationalist inspiration, developed rapidly into an anti-Hindu movement marked by forced conversions and outrages of every kind. The whole movement suffered from the period of disillusionment which followed, and the pact between the two creeds was shown to have been a shoddy piece of work, for which it is impossible not to blame the nationalist leaders. Mr. Gandhi's complete disregard for the means whereby he might attain his end led him into doing his cause a fatal disservice. In order to produce a superficial appearance of unity the Hindu leaders have admitted a principle which they must have known would turn the democratic experiment into a farce, but they have no alternative to offer to democracy.

The British have been frequently accused of fomenting inter-creed and inter-caste antagonism in their own interests. Assertions are made in the Press that district officers have organised the riots which they are called upon to suppress. The crudity of these attacks tends to obscure the important but indirect part which English rule has played in promoting communal feeling. By adopting the position of the impartial arbiter the British have invited every sect and creed to press its claims. By following the line of least resistance they have allowed certain groups, like the Brahmans in Western India, to obtain such a control of the administration that they excite the apprehension of the other communities, and this they have sometimes attempted to appease by speeches and measures which have only added to the general confusion. Finally, by introducing the semblance of democratic government, the British have given the sects and creeds an easy method of pressing their claims. The comparative immunity of the Indian States from communal outbreaks is chiefly due to the uselessness of organising and pressing the rival claims of groups before an autocratic ruler who probably belongs to one of them. Every Hindu in Hyderabad knows that a *sabha* which demanded anything extravagant from the Nizam would merely defeat its object, and the same is true of a Moslem League which became too active in Gwalior or Indore. The community, professing a religion which is not that of the Prince, takes thankfully whatever is given, and usually the Prince can afford to be generous. He is glad to show his impartiality by an appointment or a gesture. Hindu lawyers are to be found in prominent positions at the Nizam's court, and the Holkar's *tazia* takes part in the Moharram celebrations at Indore. The Nizam has had a Hindu Prime Minister, and Kazi Shahabuddin acted as Prime Minister in Baroda. In Gwalior the administration is in the hands of Moslems, Marathas, and Brahmans. Wherever there is little or nothing to be gained by communal agitation there is seldom any agitation, and without agitation there is little feeling. The increasing number of outbreaks which have taken place in recent years within the Indian States can be ascribed partly to repercussions from British India, but also to the belief that effective sectarian pressure could be brought upon the State.

Obviously each individual riot is a symptom and not the disease itself. If this evil is to be cured it will not be as the result of bargains made between religious leaders on such puerile subjects as the playing of music before mosques. An operation is needed to remove the causes of irritation, it is useless to try and reduce the inflammation before this has been done. As the British have been the cause, even if the indirect and unwilling cause, of most of the present friction, it is clearly their duty to apply the knife, rather than leave it to the patient to perform that difficult task. In this matter the ordinary Indian political leaders are the worst guides to follow, for they are themselves often the product of the system. The main principles to be followed are sufficiently clear. There is nothing in the Hindu and Mohammadan religions which prevents their followers living side by side, and any small adjustments which have to be made should be arranged locally and not imposed from above. There is, however, sufficient difference between the two creeds, and similarly between Brahmans and non-Brahmans, Sikhs and Hindus, to threaten a catastrophe whenever the line of religious demarcation coincides with that which divides political parties or conflicting economic interests. The danger is greatest when the groups are sufficiently equal in number or in power to make an active agitation the most effective method of advancing their interests.

The surgeon's knife can be applied in three places. The splitting up of the larger Provinces into smaller units, a step which is essential for democratic reasons, should, and in practice inevitably would, give an opportunity for granting independence to some of the larger minorities, like the Moslems of Sind, or the Ooriyas of Bihar and Orissa. The communal electorates must be abolished and some form of joint electorate substituted. The immediate effect would be to blur the clear religious lines which at present divide the parties, say, in the Punjab. On many subjects the Hindu peasant would begin to range himself with the Moslem ryot rather than the Hindu moneylender. The Mohammadan lawyer, who combines the advancing of mortgages with his professional work, would find himself strangely drawn at times towards the professional *bunniah* class. Finally the 'spoils' system which is eating into Indian public life must be reduced to a minimum. Proper machinery must be evolved for regulating the great bulk of Government and municipal appointments.

None of these three measures would be popular, but in this matter it would be mere folly to imagine that statesmanship consisted merely in listening to those who can make their voice heard. The division and regrouping of existing administrative areas must arouse suspicion, and in most cases would be opposed by a small section of interested people. The politicians who have been successful under the system of communal electorates will fight against their abolition, and they will not lack support from the Press and from authors of scurrilities like the *Rangila Rasul.*[1] Finally, the politicians, who gain so much from their ability to control appointments, will actively and passively resist all attempts to curtail their influence. These difficulties must, however, be faced. Democracy will function in India even if parties are based on religious divisions, but every evil inherent in the system will be intensified a hundredfold. There are two practical disadvantages which must follow the formation of political parties on religious lines. The first is especially applicable to India where, as every one has a religion, there can be no doubtful and hesitant voters to whom the candidate must address himself. This does away with any necessity for a reasoned programme, or for reasoned arguments. The second objection is that the parties must remain approximately at the same strength. Religious apostasy is a much more serious matter than the changing of political views. There can be no healthy swing of the pendulum, and a group, like the Hindus in the Punjab, who are just in a minority, would have no hope of obtaining a majority except by the proselytising work of organisations like the Arya Samaj. It would be difficult to imagine a more effective way of making democracy a byword and a reproach. This is one of the most crucial matters which will be brought before the Simon Commission, and one

[1] A libellous attack upon the Prophet published in 1924. The conviction but subsequent acquittal of the author, as the result of complicated and protracted legal proceedings, have done much to intensify Hindu-Moslem antagonism in the Punjab.

may venture to hope that they will endorse the remarkably definite verdict of the smaller Commission which has reported on the Ceylon constitution.

'In surveying the situation in Ceylon we have come unhesitatingly to the conclusion that communal representation is, as it were, a canker on the body politic, eating deeper and deeper into the vital energies of the people, breeding self-interest, suspicion and animosity, poisoning the new growth of political consciousness, and effectively preventing the development of a national and corporate spirit. . . . There can be no hope of binding together the diverse elements of the population in a realisation of their common kinship and an acknowledgment of common obligations to the country of which all are citizens so long as the system of communal representation, with all its disintegrating influences, remains a distinctive feature of the Constitution.'[1]

[1] Report of the Special Commission on the Constitution, p. 39.

## CHAPTER II

# THE INDIAN STATES

PROBABLY no race except the English would have allowed seventy years to elapse without attempting to regularise and simplify the relations between the Government of India and the Indian States, yet the position remains as complicated and as illogical as in 1858. The British genius for compromise and tolerance for archaic institutions may be admirable traits, but they are not virtues which can be expected from young and struggling democracies, and the Indian States in their present form would constitute a *damnosa hæreditas* sufficient to wreck the future of any autonomous Government. The difficulty lies not only in the immense area, nearly a third of the Peninsula, which is controlled by more or less independent Princes, but also in the lack of clear frontiers. Many of the smaller States are merely the remnants of larger estates which the English forbore to annex. Some, like the State of Savannur, are shapeless areas lying entirely within a district of British India, with 'island' villages separated from the rest of the State. Along the frontier between Hyderabad and the Bombay Presidency are more of these scattered units, British villages in the Indian State, and Hyderabad villages within British India. These and other administrative anomalies could only survive in a country loosely governed by one supreme authority. They would become immediate and fruitful sources of confusion and dispute under any federal Government. Once more a revision of the map of India seems an essential prelude to any advance towards self-government.

Although the seven hundred States have a population of nearly 70 million, and extend over 700,000 square miles, only about a hundred Chiefs rule over territories exceeding 500 square miles. Most of the remainder are mere territorial magnates, left for some historical reason in charge of their small domains. Shortly before the War it was estimated that a third of the Indian Princes were drawing less than Rs.10,000 in income from their States, and many of them are no more than country squires dressed in a little brief authority. Unfortunately no clear line of demarcation has been made between these princelings and, say, the Gaekwar of Baroda or the Nizam of Hyderabad, the latter of whom rules over an area larger than England and Wales, and containing a population of over 12 millions. Lord Chelmsford was once bound to admit that the only official method of classification was according to the number of guns they receive as salutes. Another method of dividing the States would be into those which have separate political relations with the Government of India, those grouped into agencies having relations with the Government of India, and those having political relations with the Provincial Governments. The whole question of the Indian States and their relation to the Government of India is based on ancient treaties, sanads, and usages so complicated and so diverse that each successive Viceroy has shirked the task of reducing them to order. The demand for a clearer definition of their position has come from the Princes themselves who foresee the difficulties which must arise in connection with future schemes of constitutional reform and the appointment of the Butler Commission is the first step towards regularising their position.

The Ruling Chiefs can put forward a very strong claim for special consideration. Although their rule is autocratic they undoubtedly evoke great personal loyalty amongst their own subjects and most of them can honestly say that they speak for their people. Their special powers and privileges have been confirmed on several occasions since the proclamation of 1858, when Queen Victoria promised to 'respect the rights, dignity, and honour of the Native States as our own'. In the Montagu-Chelmsford Report the Princes were assured that no changes which might take place in British India would affect the rights conferred upon them by treaties, sanads, and other engagements. They believe that they already contribute more than their fair share to the Central Government. Some pay a cash tribute, some have ceded territory in lieu of a cash contribution, and several maintain military forces which they are willing to place at the disposal of the State. All of them have to watch their subjects contributing large revenues through the Customs levied at British Indian ports, and the salt tax. In most cases they have had to abandon their special currency from which the States drew considerable profits. Neither the Princes nor their subjects have any voice in the amount of revenue which is collected nor in the manner in which it is spent. The question of the customs is rapidly becoming acute, for India is now a protectionist country, and higher tariffs are part of the nationalist policy. A State which has no steel industry may well object to paying heavily for all imported machinery in order to bolster up a small and localised industry, situated in some distant part of British India.

So long as the Government of India has been predominantly British the Princes have shown little tendency to combine in order to press their claims. They have accepted as final the decision of the Government on any point at issue, whether it was a question of the military forces which they could maintain, of bad administration within their State, of interpreting the sanad or treaty, or even of deciding some purely judicial and technical point like the assessment of income tax on the railways which pass through their territory. From time to time disputes have arisen, and the ultimate authority of the British Government has been called in question by the rulers of the larger States. The Viceroy, who is personally in charge of relations with the States, has, however, always claimed supreme power, and this was emphasised during a recent controversy over the Nizam of Hyderabad's claim to the return of the Berars. Lord Reading made it clear that the British Government was supreme in India, independently of treaties and engagements, and is responsible for the enforcement of good order and for the general welfare of Indian State subjects.

There are two factors which have secured the acquiescence of the Ruling Chiefs, even when the Government has insisted, as in the case of Maharaja Thukoji Rao of Indore, upon their abdication. They have, until recently, shown little desire or ability to work together, and many of them are aware that the considerable powers which they exercise are dependent ultimately upon the strong arm of the British Government. This is equally true of the smaller chiefs, who enjoy little more than minor judicial powers and immunity from taxation, and of those autocratic rulers whose extravagance and maladministration have roused opposition within their States. The attitude of the Princes, especially those conscious of the defects of their rule, is not unlike that of the money-lenders. They owe so much to the establishment of the *pax Britannica*, and to the fact that their despotism is no longer tempered by fear of reprisals, that they are prepared to accept an occasional chastening from the Government. The active and efficient rulers of States like Mysore, Baroda, Travancore, and Gwalior, have shown more independence, but as their administration was satisfactory, and frequently superior to that of British India, they have seldom had to complain of interference. The political Residents have generally appreciated the old saying that 'their principal duty was to reside'. They keep a watchful eye upon the general administration of the State, upon its finances, upon its military forces, and the intrigues amongst the royal family. They do not, however, often interfere on behalf of individuals who may have grievances against the Ruling Chief, and after seventy years there is still no uniformity in the treatment of Indian State subjects. The administration of justice is usually mediæval in its simplicity. In many States men are imprisoned without trial, and their property confiscated. There is no appeal from the Prince's ruling, even on a matter in which he or his family are personally interested. In Bhopal a man may be imprisoned for apostasy from Islam, and in few States is there an independent judiciary or any machinery corresponding to the Habeas Corpus Act whereby each individual case can be brought before a judge. Nearly all the Chiefs still regard their territory as their private domain, there is usually no Privy Purse, and the State revenues are treated as the Ruler's personal property. There is seldom an administrative service with any security of tenure, so officials are tempted to ensure their future by bribery.

The British have accepted the complete autocracy of the Ruling Chiefs without any serious demur. No protests have ever been made against absolutism as such, but only against bad administration or against extravagant and licentious behaviour. Viceroys have contented themselves with pious homilies on the blessings of good Government, with rewards and compliments to efficient rulers, and with good advice. Any experiment in the form of 'constitutional' Government in the States is heralded as a great advance, but the Princes have learnt only too well from the British Government how easy it is to institute Legislative Councils and Assemblies which are merely debating societies. Even those of Travancore and Mysore can do little more than criticise the Budget and the past administration, and in many cases saving clauses are added which curtail still further these limited rights. Thus the Maharajah of Kashmir introduced certain constitutional changes in his State during the spring of 1927, but while he provided that the Budget should be discussed in the Legislative Council, he also stipulated that 'only such cases should be referred to Council as really required collective deliberation'. A similar proviso reduces the Gwalior assembly to a kind of mock parliament, the subjects for debate being carefully censored in advance. The British Government's own policy towards popular control has been so fitful and tentative that a Viceroy's appeal to the Chiefs can only be on personal grounds. Only a few, like Lord Curzon, have ventured to tell them that they are not 'a privileged body to whom God has given a sanad of perpetual idleness. Their States are not their private property; the revenues are not meant to be swallowed up by their privy purse. Providence has destined them to be the working bees, and not the drones of the hive.' Lord Hardinge, however, returned to the old tradition, and when he invested the Maharajah of Jodhpur with ruling powers took care to point out that 'irksome restrictions on the exercise of sovereign powers are apt to chafe and irritate a proud and sensitive spirit, with results disastrous not only to the ruler and his people, but also to the Empire at large'.

Efforts have been made to improve the education of the future ruling chiefs, most of whom still receive much of their early training in the women's quarter of the palace, where high-caste wives and low-caste concubines live together in an atmosphere of intrigue and superstitious gossip. Unfortunately the intense and deep-rooted snobbery of the British in India has converted the Chiefs' Colleges at Ajmer, Rajkot, Indore and Lahore into institutions which faithfully reproduced the worst features of the English Public Schools, and their pupils are turned out into a world of sycophants and courtiers with enthusiasms and ideas which are physically healthier but otherwise almost as limited as those which they would have acquired in the *zenana.* They are apt to fall as easy victims to the European parasite, with his string of third-rate race-horses, as their fathers did to the court astrologer and the pandar. Only a few of the wealthiest Princes can send their sons out of the country to be educated in Europe, where they may have an opportunity of obtaining new ideas and adjusting their values to the modern world in which they will have to play their part.

Although no great improvement can be expected in the actual personnel of the ruling Princes, and the States will be as dependent upon the individual character of the Chief as formerly, there are signs that the recent changes in the Government of India have brought the rulers of the larger States together, and also tended to separate them from those who are merely landlords with judicial powers. There are only 110 Princes qualified by their status for membership of the Chamber of Princes, that somewhat anomalous body which meets periodically at Delhi. Most of the members would appear to have joined a movement to bring their grievances before the Government and before the Commission of three which has been appointed under Sir Harcourt Butler to make recommendations for regularising the relations between the Paramount Power and the States, and also for adjusting the economic relations between British India and the Indian States. Some of them have gone as far as to appoint an English lawyer, Sir Leslie Scott, as their counsel, but the southern States are represented by Sir C. P. Ramaswami Iyer. Even if it is not true that the Nizam of Hyderabad has allied himself to the former group, the movement proves a willingness amongst the Princes to combine together which is an entirely new development in India. They appear to have abandoned their original demand for the transfer of the Political Department from the Government of India, and its establishment as a branch of the British Diplomatic Service. This would have given them direct access to the Government in England, and 'short-circuited' the Government of India, an impracticable suggestion. The fact, however, that it was seriously put forward shows that the

Princes are agreed in considering the Government of India as a new organisation which has taken over the functions of His Majesty, and not as the body to which they are tied by existing treaties. Obviously their future status is not a question which would, as some Indian politicians claim, 'solve itself' under an autonomous Government of India. The problem of the Indian States, like that of communal representation, is one which must be solved by the authority originally responsible for it, and that is the British Government.

The first essential is to simplify the position. The Provinces are often unsuitable administrative units because of their size and diversity. Many of the States are equally unsuitable because of their small area and scanty population. Those Princes who are not qualified to sit in the Chamber of Princes might well be reduced to the rank of noblemen, and their territories absorbed either into the Provinces, or in some cases amalgamated with other larger States. Some financial compensation would be necessary. This would leave only 110 States, and these again might be divided into two groups according to their size and revenue. It would be difficult to deny the claim to full sovereign power of the rulers of Hyderabad, Mysore, Gwalior, Baroda, and Travancore, and a few other of the largest States. At present their sovereignty is only relative, and varies partly according to their original sanads or treaties but also according to the pressure which the Government of India has been able to bring upon them. The members of each group, those with 'sovereign' and those with 'semi-sovereign' powers, would have the same status as others within their group, and the problem would be reduced to settling the relations between the future Government of India and the sovereign States, and between the future Government of India and the semi-sovereign States. The trend of recent events should help to bring the problem within manageable limits. The Princes, who have been joining together to present their case before the Butler Commission, belong for the most part to the second group, those in the first group tend to hold aloof, and the smaller rulers have disappeared out of the picture. Mysore, Baroda, Travancore, and Cochin do not seem willing to subscribe to the scheme which is being brought forward by the majority of the Chamber of Princes, probably because they realise that their size and good administration would entitle them to an independent position in any form of federal government which may ultimately be developed. The proposals put forward by Sir Leslie Scott on behalf of the other Princes suggest that they foresee the weakness of their position if they are left to compete with provincial Governments as members of a federation. They are proposing three new bodies. The Viceroy in Indian States Council would deal exclusively with the affairs of the Indian Princes. The Governor-General in Indian States Council would be a more ambitious innovation, consisting of representatives of the Princes' administration as well as those of British India. Finally, a Union Court would be a kind of arbitration tribunal in the event of disputes between the States themselves, or between the States and the Paramount Power, or the British Indian Government. Such organisations would provide a possible method by which the second group of States, those with semi-sovereign powers, could be brought into contact with the Government of India. They would probably function best if the larger States, those with full sovereign powers, were not brought within their scope.

The problem of the Indian States is bound up with that of the future map of India. The existing map is due to a series of historical accidents. A traveller by road from the west coast to Delhi would pass from village to village, the first occupied by ryots holding their land direct from some British provincial Government, the next by the tenants of some *inamdar*, who owns the village but is under the Provincial Government. A few miles further another exactly similar village will be part of some Indian State, which is smaller perhaps than an English county. England, which is compact, homogeneous, and trained to democracy, may be able to afford anomalies like the dual system in education, but if India is to develop any form of federal government the units on which such government is based must be as clear and simple as possible. The first step would be the absorption of the very small States, and the rectification of the frontiers between the larger States and British India. The problem of the hundred larger States remains, for it would be a mistake to consider them as the moribund relics of a dead past. In education, in the encouragement of Indian art, in commercial development, even in social legislation many of the State Governments have shown enterprise and vitality. It is impossible to pass from most Provinces of British India to a State like Gwalior without being struck by the better relations which exist in the latter between the Government and the people. If a plebiscite could be taken amongst the subjects of the Indian States there is little doubt that the majority would not vote for transference to British India. In the increasing number of decently governed States there is a real pride in the ruling dynasty, and an interest in the fortunes of their realm which few Indians can honestly feel for the country as a whole. In several States loyalty is inextricably bound up with religious sentiment, and this feeling is further strengthened by the pomps and ceremonies of the Court. The Ruling Princes satisfy certain deep-seated instincts which are sadly starved in British India. There is, of course, little definite evidence about this popular feeling. In many of the larger States there is a 'nationalist' party, opposed to the autocracy of the Princes, but their position is less logical than it would be in British India, and the movement is more definitely confined to the upper classes. Shortly before the War negotiations were started to exchange some of the 'island' villages which lie on each side of the boundary between Hyderabad and the Bombay Presidency, but curiously enough both sets of villagers showed a strong disinclination for any change. It seemed that the State officials were more rapacious and high-handed – 'moghali' justice was a local expression for tyranny – but they were also more casual and more human than those from British India. At any rate these outlying villages were little troubled by officials, and wisely opposed any alteration. Hyderabad is a Hindu State governed by a Mohammadan, but in other States, where the ruler has the same religion as most of his subjects, the feeling of personal loyalty is much stronger. It would be unwise to accept too readily the statement often made by Indian politicians, that the Indian State subjects are only waiting for the establishment of a 'free' India to throw off the yoke. The Princes have still several shots left in their lockers, and those among them who choose to govern decently will prove very difficult to dislodge.

It must be assumed, then, that a considerable number of more or less autocratically governed States will have to find a place in the future Government of India. It is impossible to isolate them, for even if the smaller States are absorbed, the territories of the others are scattered over the Peninsula. It is equally impossible for the Central Government to avoid indirectly taxing the Indian State subjects together with those of the rest of India, for both are affected alike by any policy regarding customs, the salt duty, posts and telegraphs, State railways, opium, and other matters. At present the States have no voice in the management of these, and no share in the responsibility. These anomalies could not exist under any form of Federal Government, and ultimately the States must be given some form of representation comparable with their population and importance. This task would be much easier if the British India Provinces were divided into smaller units. The largest, with a population of about 10 million, would then be commensurate with the largest State, and all those States with full sovereign powers would have a standing equal to the smaller Provinces. Even with the present divisions Hyderabad and Kashmir are each larger than the Province of Assam, and the former has considerably more inhabitants. Gwalior and Mysore are little smaller than the North-West Frontier Province, and the latter has a larger population. There should be no insuperable difficulty about a Federal State based on units some of which are 'democracies' – but not very democratic – and others are 'autocracies' – but based on considerable popular support.

More difficult would be the question of these medium-sized States, which are too large and active for absorption, but too small to stand alone as units in a Federal State. There are probably about seventy or eighty which would come into this category, and some method of grouping would have to be adopted. This would be no great innovation, for the Government of India and also the Provincial Governments have never attempted to deal individually with each Ruling Prince, and there are already several groups of States, like those in the Central India Agency, the Rajputana Agency, and in Kathiawar. Of recent years the Ruling Chiefs who would come into this second category have shown that they can work together, and the schemes which they have brought before the Butler Commission could probably be developed into organisations which would enable their subjects' interests to be adequately represented upon the Central Government. The necessary changes could be made while the Indian constitution is in its present elastic and uncertain condition, but the position of the Indian States must be defined by the British Government which was originally responsible for their existence.

Those Indian politicians, who foresee all future changes in terms of a transfer of authority from the British Government to an Imperial Legislature, are apt to talk about the Indian States as a possible 'Ulster'. The analogy is not happy, but it is, of course, probable that the inhabitants of certain areas would, if their opinions could be canvassed now or after a transference such as these politicians suggest, prefer comparative independence under the protection of the British Government to inclusion within an Indian Federation. This would be true of certain Indian

States, for the subjects of many States would follow their Rulers' views in this matter. It might also be true of predominantly Moslem districts within British India, if they felt that the future Central Government either was or was likely to be markedly Hindu in sentiment and policy. For this reason it seems essential that the transference of authority to the Central Legislature, and the defining of the form and exact functions of the Central Government should follow and not precede the building up of autonomous provincial governments. If the number of these provincial governments was also increased so that they did not overshadow the larger States in size and importance, then the main objections to co-operation would vanish. The advantages of a Federation of such Provincial and State Governments would be overwhelming, and the weakness of any recalcitrant State which claimed independence without having any sea-board would be obvious. It might, in fact, be unnecessary to bring anything but economic pressure to bear upon the States to come within the Federation, for these land-locked territories are becoming daily less self-dependent. It would, however, be fatal if such pressure had to be applied by a newly-formed Central Government based upon an untried and disorganised electorate.

## CHAPTER III

# INTERNAL AND EXTERNAL SECURITY

INDIAN politicians are frequently blamed for taking little interest in the future security of their country, and for failing to appreciate the blessings of the *pax Britannica*, and the difficult guardianship of the North-West Frontier. These accusations are perhaps inevitable. They certainly belong to an old historical tradition. Never has one country occupied another without emphasising the resultant stability and security. Never has the subject race shown the least gratitude, or failed to criticise the army of occupation. When the Commander-in-Chief grumbles because the Indian Legislature questions each item of his estimates, he only echoes the complaint of the Spanish Grand Commander in the Netherlands who, whenever he demanded supplies, received from the estates-general a long remonstrance against the conduct of the soldiery. 'Oh, these estates,' cried the Grand Commander, on receiving such vehement reproaches instead of his money; 'may the Lord deliver me from these estates!' [1] When the Governor of Bombay, in 1919, tactfully reminded the Convocation that, but for the British fleet, their University would have equalled 'at least in its ruins' that of Louvain, he was honestly surprised that his remarks were received with so little enthusiasm. The Italians gave the Austrians no credit for the long period of peace which followed the Napoleonic wars. The Irish never appreciated the fact that the British navy may have prevented

[1] Motley, *Rise of Dutch Republic*, Pt. IV, Chapter III.

them from becoming a German province. The German Poles forgot that they might have been absorbed by Russia. No race likes to owe its safety to another country, especially when the motives of that other country are not above suspicion. Mexico and Nicaragua may have benefited by the Monroe doctrine, but they do not rise up to call the United States blessed. The heart of the Bengali does not overflow with gratitude when an Englishman quotes some old Rajput Chief about there not being 'a virgin or a rupee in Bengal' a week after the British have gone.

Apart from the natural susceptibilities of any people who know that they are not really responsible for their own security and independence, there are many old grievances connected with the Indian army and the defence of the country. Like so many other problems of modern India, these date back to the period of reconstruction which followed the Mutiny. The military officers who served under the Company had an implicit belief in the loyalty of their sepoys. Stories of the early days of the Mutiny show that many officers retained up to the last an almost childlike trust in their own regiment, and this confidence was reflected in the general policy of the Company. The Army consisted of under 40,000 Europeans and 215,000 Indians, and the latter were employed in all branches of the service, including the artillery. The Government of India started its work of reconstruction in 1858 at a time when this excessive confidence had been followed by an equally violent reaction.

'The lessons taught by the Mutiny have led to the maintenance of two great principles, of retaining in the country an irresistible force of British troops, and of keeping the artillery in the hands of Europeans.'[1]

These main principles have been adhered to until the present time. The ratio of British to Indian soldiers has been altered from time to time, but it has usually been at about two British to five Indians, a formula which was sanctioned in 1893, and rigidly kept for some years. The proportion of British troops was more than doubled after the Mutiny, and Indians were debarred from serving as gunners in the Horse and Field Artillery. The forces were thus converted definitely into an Army of Occupation, with Englishmen in the key positions, and the Indian troops carefully arranged so as to be unlikely to combine. As the Punjab Committee on Reorganisation advised in their report of 1858,

'next to the grand counterpoise of a sufficient European force, comes the counterpoise of natives against natives. . . . To preserve that distinctiveness which is valuable, and which while it lasts makes the Mohammadan of one country fear or dislike the Mohammadan of another, corps should in future be provincial, and adhere to the geographical limits within which differences and rivalries are strongly marked.'

An army of occupation is bound to be expensive, and is seldom efficient as a fighting force. It must be a mercenary army, with the foreign element highly paid, while its organisation is hampered by the fact that it is being partly used to overawe the civil population. Both these weak-

[1] Report of Commission on Indian Army Reorganisation of 1879.

nesses have been apparent in India. For many years her military organisation has cost the country between a half and a third of her total revenue, the British troops absorbing the greater part of the fifty or sixty crores of rupees which are needed for the peace-time establishment. In spite of this the army has never been brought up to date, and the Mesopotamian campaign showed its deficiencies in equipment and organisation. No one who took part in that campaign is likely to dispute the findings of the Mesopotamian Commission on this point, yet it is extremely doubtful if another war would find the Indian Army much better prepared. It would probably have to set out again with 'its transport carefully modelled on that of Alexander the Great'. A man cannot serve two masters, and an army cannot fulfil two entirely different functions. Since the War an attempt has been made to separate these functions. As Lord Rawlinson explained to the Assembly in 1921, the modern army has been divided into a Field Army, which is organised for foreign service; Covering Troops, which are maintained for keeping order on the Frontier; and Internal Security Troops, which act as a garrison. The last have a majority of British troops, and in the Field Army the proportion is about one to three. The Covering Troops are mostly Indian. This division is more logical than the old arrangement, but it has yet to be seen if it is more efficient, and the expense of the personnel is still so heavy, with 7,000 commissioned officers and 61,500 European troops, that it has been impossible to organise suitable mechanical transport.

While the military organisation of India was based on the idea of an army of occupation under British control no steps could be taken to build up a force which could take its place. Lord Roberts, and others of his school of thought, never seem to have envisaged an India in which the Indians should be other than a subject race.

'It is this consciousness of the inherent superiority of the European which has won for us India. However well educated and clever a native may be, and however brave he may have proved himself, I believe that no rank which we can bestow upon him would cause him to be considered as an equal by the British officer.'[1]

This attitude still survives amongst army officers, and puts the English into the illogical position of saying that India is unfit for self-government because she cannot undertake her own defence, and at the same time taking every precaution to ensure that the army of occupation under British control shall be the only military organisation in the country. Only gradually and cautiously has there been any retreat from this position, and the process adopted has been to draft a few Indians as officers into the present army of occupation, rather than to build up the nucleus of a future Indian army. Ten Indians pass each year through Sandhurst from which they receive the full King's commission, and are eventually drafted to certain selected units. These units will not be completely 'Indianised' for about twenty years, and then apparently the Government of India will be able to decide, as Lord Rawlinson stated in February, 1923, 'whether units officered by Indians will be efficient in every way'. A college has been opened at Dehra Dun where these officers obtain their early education. Some proposals for speeding up this process were made by the

[1] Sir George Arthur, *Life of Lord Kitchener*, Vol. II, p. 177.

Indian Sandhurst Committee, under General Skeen. Their report, issued in April, 1927, suggested doubling the number of vacancies at Sandhurst, instituting a similar establishment in India in 1933, and training a few Indians for commissions in the artillery, tank, and air force. No action has yet been taken on these proposals, the result of which would be that half the total cadre of officers in the Indian army would be Indians in 1952.

It seems clear that the Government of India is merely 'playing for time', and adopting the same policy towards the Indianisation of the army as it pursued towards the Indianisation of the Civil Service at the end of the nineteenth century. The reason is the same in each case. The British are not steering for some definite objective, but drifting vaguely along, and thankful when the weather is calm. The lack of an objective is even more demoralising in the army than in the civil administration, for in peace time an army must always be training and organising for some future work, and, as Lord Bacon wrote, 'to take a soldier without ambition is to pull off his spurs'. The Indian politicians, who are merely the opposition, cannot be expected to put forward definite proposals for a military programme, and usually confine their demands to the more rapid Indianisation of the Commissioned ranks, and to extending the facilities for training Indians in the territorial force. They also want to bring down the expenditure on the army, partly because it is absorbing too much public money, but also because they feel that its expensiveness is due to it being an army of occupation. It is absurd for English officials to adopt the patronising attitude of the latest annual Report, and magnanimously suggest that 'the lessons taught by the War, and their own ambitions for Dominion status for India, have compelled Indian politicians to give serious thought to the problems of national defence, the importance of which they now perceive, although adequate recognition of their complexity and difficulty is yet to come'. [1]

So long as the army is mainly a garrison, controlled by the British, the Indian educated classes cannot be expected to take any lively interest in its efficiency, and they certainly will not do so until the Government has definitely stated its intention of building up a national army, and shown clearly the steps by which it means to accomplish this object.

The Indian, before he can co-operate in this work with any enthusiasm, must have some idea of the organisation and functions of the army in, say, 1940. Returning to Lord Rawlinson's division of the army into three groups, he may legitimately ask what will be the future of each. Is the Field Army to remain one-third English, and organised for service abroad, and, if so, against whom is it intended to fight, the enemies of the Empire or of India? If the Covering Forces, which contain six Indians to one Englishman, are considered good enough to defend the Frontier, would not a completely Indian force, with Indian artillery, suffice for the purpose? Finally, if India is to be given any real measure of self-government, is she to be saddled permanently with the Internal Security Troops, a garrison army, containing five British to every four Indians, and clearly organised as an army of occupation?

Any attempt to answer these questions only emphasises

[1] *India in* 1926–27, p. 264.

the vague and uncertain basis of British policy in India. It might be argued, for example, that attack is often the best means of defence, and that a Field Army of mixed troops is therefore a necessity. It is not easy to see who these potential enemies will be, against whom an expeditionary force may be necessary. India's earliest conquerors poured in through her North-Western frontiers driven by three great motive forces, pressure on the land, love of plunder, and missionary zeal. Her later conquerors were European Powers, with naval armaments, who came to trade and remained to govern. The danger from both sources seems to be much smaller to-day. India's land frontiers, though 6,000 miles long, pass through difficult and often inaccessible country, and divide India from weak and undeveloped States. The thousand miles of Chinese frontier, the six hundred miles where India touches Siam, and the corner of distant Baluchistan which borders on Persia are too wild and too far from the centres of the other Governments to cause any anxiety to India, even if these three countries showed the least signs of aggressive tendencies, which at present they do not. There are no longer hordes of fanatical tribesmen ready to follow in the footsteps of Mahmud of Ghazni. The Covering Troops are considered strong enough to deal with the frontier tribes, and behind them there are only two States to be considered, Afghanistan and Russia. The first is an oriental, the second a semi-oriental country. Both have repeatedly proved themselves difficult to invade, but weak and impotent as aggressors. Afghanistan is a small barren country, with a population[1] about a quarter as large as that of the Punjab,

[1] The population is 6,380,500.

which would be quite capable of defending itself. The English have always used the Russians as a bogey to keep the Indian nationalists in order, an unfortunate policy which led to a complete misunderstanding in India about the Russo-Japanese war, and to considerable disillusionment during the last war, when Indian troops first met the scarecrow Cossacks who drifted into Mesopotamia, and stories reached the *bazars* about their defeats in Europe. Similarly the frequent and exaggerated references to the spread of Bolshevism which emanate from official sources merely encourage a certain section of Indian politicians, like Mr. Jawaharlal Nehru, to look North for a possible deliverer from their bondage. It will never be easy to make Indians believe that any serious danger of invasion threatens from the North, and in this they are probably justified.

India has no resources for defending her sea coast from any of the larger European Powers, and it is unthinkable that her peasants should have to bear the cost of a modern navy. It is almost equally unthinkable that the efforts of the League of Nations, of which India is a member, should not be sufficient to protect her from any deliberate act of aggression by a naval power. The attitude of the civilised world has changed entirely during the last fifty years, and the old policy of 'trade follows the flag' has been changed into one based on the idea that 'trade follows the funds'. At any rate, India would probably have the benefit of a kind of Monroe doctrine extended to the Peninsula by Great Britain. In the absence of any definite object most Indians look upon the Field Army as an Imperial convenience rather than as an Indian necessity. This idea has received some confirmation from the fact that the only use of the Field Army since 1921 has been to supply a brigade for Shanghai.

There is the same uncertainty and confusion of thought about the Internal Security Troops. Is this predominantly British force intended to check at the outset another Mutiny, or to protect as many European lives as possible in the case of a general rising, or to be used as a kind of armed police? In the first case it should be concentrated in the Punjab, in the second it should be divided between the great ports, in the third it should be scattered in small units throughout the peninsula. Is it to be a permanent feature of Indian military organisation, or is it merely a temporary arrangement to tide over a transition period? Indian politicians, who take an interest in these matters, search hopelessly amongst the reports of commissions and the *obiter dicta* of Commanders-in-Chief to find some statement of general principles. At one time they hoped that the new territorial force, now consisting of some 12,000 men in twenty battalions, would form the basis of a national army, but the committee, appointed under Sir John Shea in 1924, did little to define its future position, or to destroy the suspicion that it was not taken seriously by the authorities, who in time of internal stress would always turn to the analogous European body, the Auxiliary Force. The mentality of the Mutiny times still survives in such details as the apportionment of armoured cars to the Auxiliary Force, but not to the Territorials, and it would be fair to say that the Territorial Force is a second line to the Covering Troops, and the Auxiliary Force to the Internal Security Troops. This policy makes the former still more definitely Indian, and the latter even more preponderantly British.

Like most nationalists the Indian politicians are not much interested in theoretical pacificism. Many of them honestly believe that the general effect of British rule, and especially the policy of confining recruiting to a few races, has, to use their favourite word, 'emasculated' a great section of the population. There is certainly no evidence that further transfer of responsibility to the Indian legislatures would lead to any deliberate weakening of the army, but attempts would be made to place the existing army on to a more logical basis. The Field Army, organised for foreign service, would have no further justification, for it would clearly be useless except to a country with a powerful navy, and India can never hope to defend her long and exposed sea-board against a modern European power. Her army would be organised against oriental enemies, especially the tribes of the North-West, and India will look to the League of Nations or to England for support against acts of deliberate aggression by any of the civilised Western powers. The present Covering Troops would form the basis of a national army, with the small European personnel being gradually replaced by Indians. The Territorial Force, once it was definitely recognised as the second line of a national army, would be capable of great expansion. Very little objection would probably be raised to the continuance of the Internal Security Troops and the Auxiliary Force, so long as it was made clear that they were a temporary expedient to tide over a transition period, and that they were limited in their scope to certain large European centres.

## CHAPTER IV

# ADMINISTRATIVE EFFICIENCY

THE last three chapters have dealt with certain general questions which must arise if there is to be any real transfer of political power to the Indian Assemblies and to Ministers responsible to them. It is also necessary to consider the view, which is widely held in England, that the withdrawal of responsible British officers would lead to inefficiency and corruption in the administration, and possibly to a revival of the anarchy of eighteenth-century India. There is no reason to assume that there is anything insincere or hypocritical about these forebodings, though they are often based on very superficial reasoning. It is a natural and perhaps an amiable weakness of all officials to imagine that they are indispensable, and the Europeans in Government services are inevitably keen critics of those Indians who are now taking over so many of their functions. Certain facts give an edge to their criticism. The English do most of their work through Indian subordinates, often ill-paid and badly trained, whose habits they find exasperating, and whose anomalous position since the spread of nationalism has not encouraged loyal service. They are often unduly affected by the petty corruption prevalent in Indian public life, for they are drawn from a class which is usually ignorant of the not dissimilar conditions in English commerce and until recently in English local administration. They may have noted the rapidity with which some of the smaller Indian States have relapsed under a bad ruler into mediæval barbarism. Their pessimism is reflected amongst the small section of the English nation which takes any interest in Eastern affairs.

While the educated Indian looks back to a mythical Golden Age, the Englishman remembers the erection of a stable government in India on a foundation of savagery and disorder. Brought up on the romances of Mr. Kipling they picture the present administration as a piece of cultivated land carved out of the surrounding forest, and they fear that our withdrawal will mean the 'letting in of the jungle'.

There is no need to discuss the historical accuracy of either point of view, or to consider the problem as hypothetical. For some years Indians have taken a large and increasing part in the administration, and the process of 'Indianisation' has been very rapid in those departments which have been transferred since 1920 to the charge of Indian ministers. Recent developments in certain Indian States should also prove a useful guide to the capabilities and limitations of Indian administrators. It will be best to consider each of the chief departments in turn, taking first those 'nation-building' subjects which have already been transferred, like education, and then dealing in the next chapter with those subjects which are still reserved, such as Land Revenue, Justice, and those various activities which in England are controlled by the Home Office. With regard to the first group it has already been emphasised that the powers of the Indian Ministers are limited, and that there is no popular control over the apportionment of the Budget.[1] Within these limitations there is, however, some evidence on which to forecast future developments.

Local Self-Government is the cumbrous title of a department which is as important as any in India, but whatever may be the future of decentralisation it has made

[1] See p. 161.

little progress before the Reform scheme, and the subject was transferred in an embryonic condition. The network of municipalities, of District and other local Boards, with which India is covered, was a bureaucratic conception. The system was so obviously modelled on English lines, and was an importation so exotic that it was remarkable that it functioned at all. As Dr. Johnson said of a woman preaching: 'It is like a dog walking on its hinder legs. It is not done well; but you are surprised to find it done at all.' For many years the various boards were under the chairmanship of British officials, and were usually managed on the lines of the town council in that almost forgotten classic, *The Chronicles of Dustipore*. The Municipalities of Calcutta, Bombay, and a few other Westernised cities soon developed into powerful and fairly efficient bodies, but in the Mofussil towns they have often been a complete failure. Since 1919 elected chairmen have nearly everywhere taken the place of the District Magistrate or other official, and their work is now controlled by an Indian Minister in each Province. At present there is not sufficient evidence to show whether there has been any real change. It would seem that local bodies are now showing more enterprise, but are also more inclined to get into financial difficulties. The most recent reports are typically contradictory:

'In the Bombay Presidency both municipalities and local boards are working on the whole in a not unsatisfactory manner. Some of the municipalities have now taken to raising loans in the open market for sanitary and other improvement schemes, and the net income of municipalities generally seems to be on the increase.'

On the other hand,

'municipal administration in the Province (of Bihar and Orissa) is in a deplorable condition. Apathy, neglect, and faction have brought the majority of towns into discredit. Patna city is one of the worst . . . Darbhanga, the second largest town, is in a state of chaos owing to neglect and peculation. The ordinary measures of conservancy and sanitation have not been taken, with the result that plague and malaria are rife in the town.'[1]

If local boards are a doubtful success under Indian control, there would seem to be more hope in the attempts to revive an old form of self-government indigenous to India. Village *panchayats* or councils of the elders have a remarkable history. They were a feature of Indian life in the time of Alexander the Great, and for many centuries were an Aryan institution almost as characteristic of Hinduism as the caste system. The *panchayat* administered such public buildings as the temple, school, and rest-house, punished minor offences, regulated the common grazing, and arranged for the repair of the tank or pond which plays such an important part in village life. As Sir Charles Metcalfe wrote in 1830, the system made the larger villages into 'little republics, having nearly everything they want within themselves, and almost independent of outside relations'. Such a system of village autonomy was admirably suited for a pioneer community settled amongst aboriginal tribes, but it left the country very open to other invaders, and undoubtedly helped the successive Moslem conquerors.

It is an axiom amongst Indian nationalists that the

[1] *India in* 1926–27, pp. 298, 299.

*panchayat* system disappeared as a result of the British occupation. This is only partly true, and the Indian ministers and politicians who are working to revive them would have an easier task if these village councils had really flourished only a century ago. The *panchayats*, as might be expected, did not thrive too well under Moslem rule, and over most of Northern India and the Deccan the orderly routine of village life must have completely disappeared in the anarchy of the later Moghul Empire. It survived longest in the South, for the *panchayat* is essentially a Hindu institution. Those who blame the English soldiers and administrators of pre-Mutiny days for not reviving the *panchayat* system should remember that they were a handful of men attempting to wrest some sort of order out of chaos. They would have been glad enough to use any existing organisation which was strong enough to function, but they were forced to centralise justice and to get help from individuals like village *patels* and *zemindars* in order to cope with the dacoits, cattle-raiders, Thugs, and other wandering criminals, who were far outside the scope of the village councils and village watchmen. Probably the conversion of the village head-man into a Government servant helped to end the *panchayat* system in parts where it had survived, but the question is now of little more than academic interest. It is more important to consider how far the tradition has survived, and whether the system can be used and fitted into the administration. There is little doubt about the second question. It would be extremely valuable if local village councils could deal with petty offences, like thefts, allowing cattle to stray, and minor assaults, which are now brought before the magistrates. There is also some municipal work which could be undertaken in the larger villages, such as the disposal of rubbish, the cleaning out of the 'tanks', sinking of wells, clearing of prickly pear, and all the host of little jobs round a village which are everybody's business and nobody's business. Since 1919 Village Panchayat Acts have been passed in nearly all the Provinces, but they have not proved a great success except in the south and east. Both in Madras and Bengal the larger villages have shown that they could collect a local 'cess' or rate without difficulty so long as the money was spent in the village. In these parts the tradition of the *panchayats* is probably more recent than in the Punjab or the Deccan where considerable official encouragement was necessary to make the new bodies function.

Efforts to revive the *panchayat* system were, of course, made long before the 1919 scheme. It would seem, however, that this is one of those reforms which can best be introduced through the agency of Indians themselves. One of the main problems of rural India, to which it will be necessary to return later, is that the ordinary villager pays little towards local administration and gets practically nothing from it. This can only be cured by beginning with small areas, so that the ryot can actually see something tangible as the direct result of the cess which he pays so unwillingly. If the Indian Ministers and the politicians can start this process in the larger villages, then the comparative failure of the municipalities and local boards will be of less account.

State education is another transferred subject which never flourished under British control. Ever since 1835 when the 'Anglicists' – inspired by Ram Mohun Roy and Dwarkanath Tagore, and led by Macaulay – forced their views upon the Government, and Lord Bentinck agreed that India should learn of Western culture through the medium of English, education has been one of the Government's least satisfactory offspring, an ailing and complaining child. The Filtration Theory upon which Macaulay founded his system was based upon the assumption that Western education, taught intensively to a small class, would spread slowly down to the masses. Incidentally he expected to convert Bengal to Christianity.[1] His ignorance of the resisting power of Hinduism was as complete as his misunderstanding of the Indian social system. The Filtration Theory was doomed before any attempt was made to put it into practice, and thirty years after the memorable dispatch of 1835 Bengal was entering upon a great movement back to the Vedas and to orthodox Hinduism.

The nationalist movement was at first marked by a strong reaction against Western education. The enthusiasm for everything which was 'genuinely Indian' spread through the country, and attempts were made to provide by private means an education based on that religious teaching which had been so drastically excised from the Government schools. Some admirable institutions were ultimately founded, like the Arya Samaj *gurukul* at Hardwar, but the chief effect of the nationalist movement was to destroy the personal influence of the English teachers. There is little real demand for training in an institution, like Hardwar, which does so little to fit a student for ordinary life. Only a few appreciate the atmosphere 'saturated with the Vedas and Upanishads'. The first enthusiasm for a return to the *guru* and *chela* conception

[1] See p. 95.

of education was followed by a reaction for a more modern system, and political leaders began to realise that a knowledge of Western methods would be the best instrument for obtaining freedom from British rule. Time has its revenges. Less than a century has passed since Macaulay decided that 'a single shelf of a good European Library was worth the whole native literature of India and Arabia'. There has been time for India to discard his theories, and then come back to his practice by another route. Shortly after the last war 'national' schools were springing up in various parts of India. Though they were founded on hatred of English rule, their masters made a point of teaching English at an earlier stage than in the Government institutions.

From the official's point of view education has always occupied the same place as agriculture in England. It was 'the last subject on the agenda', presenting hopeless and insoluble problems which every one was anxious to shelve. There was a general feeling of relief when the Reform scheme made it possible to hand over education to Indian Ministers, and leave the administration as well as the teaching in Indian hands. There are still a few English masters and professors at the Universities, at the larger secondary schools, and at the so-called Chiefs' Colleges, but for better or worse the policy of filtration, the dissemination of Western culture from a few gifted Europeans, has been abandoned. Indian education Ministers have suffered from weaknesses inherent in the system of dyarchy, and from having no party to support them, and no voice in the Budget allotment for their subject, but they have brought new enthusiasm to their work, and they can undoubtedly get local bodies to help them in a way which English officials found impossible. Apart from the allocation of funds by Provincial Governments the chief obstacles to progress are the dislike which all local bodies feel towards raising the local 'cess', the prejudice against female education, the apathy of the ryot, and the dearth of teachers. In nearly every province the Indian Minister has made some new and definite contribution to solving these difficulties by their personal contacts with people of local importance, thus following the example set in Mysore and Baroda. In Madras, for example, schools are being opened in over a third of the four thousand largest villages which were shown to have none in the 1925 survey. In Bihar and Orissa the number of pupils in primary schools has increased by nearly a quarter of a million since the introduction of the Reform scheme. In Bombay, where Professor Paranjpye was the first Minister, they are experimenting with compulsory education, and three local boards and six municipalities have submitted schemes. In the Punjab compulsory education has actually been introduced into 42 towns and 450 rural areas, and seems to be working well. There is, in fact, no evidence of any deterioration in the administration under dyarchy, and the first years have been marked by a considerable speeding up of the vast bureaucratic machine which has been created during the last seventy years.

In some directions the results of 'Indianisation' have been disappointing. There has been no tendency to evolve a more indigenous type of education, and none to bring back religion into the schools from which it has been banished. Education thus remains curiously divorced from the national life of India, and the student, especially in the secondary schools, undergoes a training which never touches at any point his ordinary home life. 'Knowledge without conscience is the ruin of the soul', and our schools have left the most important part of education to the chance ministrations of the *guru* and to the superstitious talk of the *zenana*.

Over the strife of the schools
  Low the day burns,
Back with the kine from the pools
  Each one returns
  To the life that he knows where the altar flame glows
    and the *tulsi* is trimmed in the urns.

It may be necessary to destroy before rebuilding. An unfortunate legacy of the British connection are the many colleges which were founded on the lines of the English Public Schools. Most British officials in India are either the product of such schools, or belong to a class with an exaggerated and somewhat snobbish admiration for these institutions. They felt that something was lacking in the Indian upper classes which they themselves possessed, and repeating Macaulay's mistake of two generations before, they transplanted into India a parody of the system which they believed to be so beneficial. The Chiefs' Colleges, which cater for the children of the very wealthy and the sons of ruling Princes, give their students the feeling of social exclusiveness, the inordinate love of sport, the false standards and distaste for work which were the worst features of the more expensive English schools. Many Indian leaders now realise that the rising generation should have instilled into them a German love of efficiency and an American keenness for experiment, but they are far from evolving any system of education which could build up these qualities on an Indian foundation. Only at the Universities are there signs of a new spirit. Even those which are definitely sectarian, as Benares and Aligarh, are doing much to quicken a sense of responsibility for the future. The transference of education into Indian hands may in time ease the old racial bitterness and preoccupation with politics, and allow the next generation to develop along lines more consistent with their religious and social traditions.

The other 'transferred' subjects do not provide much evidence which is pertinent to the question under discussion. Sometimes the Reform scheme has merely added another cog to the existing machine. The Indianisation of the Public Works Department has increased the overhead expenses, but not added anything to the amount of money available for roads and buildings or produced any noticeable alteration in its methods. That fearful architectural product of the official mind, sometimes known as 'Dak Bungalow Gothic', still regulates the style of minor Government buildings, and Indian Ministers do not seem able to prevent the old scandal of money being wasted at Headquarters, on the Governor's houses, and on the multiplication of office buildings. On the other hand, there is no evidence that the corruption, always prevalent amongst the lower grades of the Department, has grown worse. During the last few years it has become painfully clear that the employment of European subordinates does nothing to prevent bribery either in the Public Works and similar departments or in the Police. Two recent cases [1]

[1] The acquittal of Mr. Nariman in Bombay, and Mr. Reddi in Rangoon, on charges of libel. Both accused European officers of corrupt practices, or of allowing such practices.

have drawn attention to this matter, but they may perhaps be taken as pointing to an increase of public interest in the administration, and to a growing number of people willing to call attention to peculation and bribery.

There are certain transferred departments which have been founded on European lines, and have up to recent years been controlled by Englishmen. Some of these, like Co-operation and Industrial Development, are quite modern. Others, such as Forests and Public Health, have at times run counter to popular or nationalist sentiments. There is some doubt about the way in which these will be managed when staffed entirely by Indians and under an Indian Government. European medical practice, for example, has been severely attacked by many nationalists, including Tilak and Mr. Gandhi. One may well ask what will be the future of sanitation if based on the Ayurvedic system. Possibly some compromise will be found, and it is worth noting that the Lahore Municipality has aroused a fierce controversy by giving a larger grant to 'popularise and encourage the Ayurvedic and Unani systems of medicine' than to the Mayo Hospital in Lahore, which is the most important in Northern India. Similarly the methods of the Forestry service have been castigated by every Indian politician for interfering with village grazing, and the ryot's only source of fuel. Now forests are the foster-mother of agriculture, and every Province can show the evil results of their neglect, but the Report of the Linlithgow Commission again points the way to a compromise.

It is possible that there will be some lowering of the technical standard in certain subjects, but there are two other factors which have to be considered. In many ways England has not been the best interpreter of the West. In agriculture, in rural co-operation, in the planning and sanitation of great cities we lag behind some countries of Western Europe. Apart from politics India shows no disinclination to seek European and American advice, and it is probable that after a little time the various departments would avail themselves of the services of experts from all over the world. It is also clear that most of the 'nation building' services are dependent on co-operation with various organisations and groups, composed for the most part of upper-class Indians. It is not easy for an English official to get into close touch with caste *sabhas* and voluntary movements for social reform. Even in his dealings with individuals, like religious leaders and landlords, he must frequently employ intermediaries. In practice few can avoid that attitude of aloofness, that ignorance of the best method of approach which alienates so many people to-day. The Indian Ministers and officials, though sometimes hampered by caste or religious conventions, have many ways of smoothing over difficulties, many channels through which they can work, which are unknown to the foreigner. Even if the withdrawal of English officials leads to an increase of nepotism and corruption in high places, these evils are only of relative importance, and it is sheer affectation to pretend that they are confined to the East. Up to quite recent times the direction of English affairs was controlled by a few families, and a country can be happy and prosperous, like the United States to-day, in spite of a low level of ministerial and official integrity. To an educated Indian, with a sense of humour, there is something delightfully ridiculous in the spectacle of the two opposing leaders in the House of Commons, both of whom avowedly owe their position to the sale of honours, agreeing about the need for retaining English standards of political honesty in India. It is true that the joint family system which prevails in India has such a deep religious significance that nepotism can easily appear almost as a sacred duty, but it is doubtful if the claims of a second cousin to promotion are stronger in India to-day than they were in England a century ago. There will always be plenty of people who believe that '*ceteris paribus*, one should give a job to a relation', and a few who agree with the cynic that '*ceteris paribus* be damned'.

It would be absurd to pretend that the usual forms of corruption in India, bribery and the taking of commissions, are characteristically oriental. Throughout the world these practices are the dirty oil which helps to make the commercial and administrative machinery run smoothly. Only of recent years have a few countries of Western Europe begun to pay their officials so well that it has been possible to eliminate corruption from the public administration. The process is far from complete, for the years which followed the War were marked by a considerable increase in peculation amongst minor officials in England and France, while the rapidity with which the formerly impeccable German civil service began to take bribes during the 'valuta' crisis proved that the general standard of honesty is partly dependent upon a decent rate of wages. The world has yet to see a country in which indirect bribery is unknown, or in which the urban police force is above taking money from the purveyors of illicit delights.

The future of the 'reserved' subjects is considered in the next chapter. In the other 'transferred' branches of the administration corruption is often little more than a wasteful and silly way by which underlings raise their salaries to a more reasonable figure. *Dasturi* is a recognised system of illegal commissions, very reprehensible, but, as the name implies, governed and limited by custom. The *zemindar's* clerk, who collects the rents, is often paid some ridiculous sum like five rupees a month. It is tacitly understood that he will acquire another thirty by underhand means. The municipal octroi clerk who gets twelve rupees a month for stopping and examining the bullock carts as they make their way into the towns, probably looks upon his pay as merely the 'rice for his curry'. It is like the English system of paying a waiter some inadequate salary and expecting him to make his livelihood from 'tips'. The difficulty experienced in England about getting rid of the 'tipping' system, and in enforcing the Act against illegal commissions suggests that *dasturi* will be a long time dying in India. Certainly it has flourished under British rule up to the very doors of the European official. Our further withdrawal can make little difference to the practice amongst the lower grades of clerks and 'peons', though it may mean the extension of corruption into certain higher spheres. On the other hand, we must remember that there will always be a very free-spoken and jealous opposition, and also that certain forms of corruption which we connect with the administration in America do not seem to be incompatible with a very high standard of efficiency and enterprise.

Too much criticism of Indian administration is based upon the idea that 'progress' must necessarily be along English lines, and that the development of, say, the Provincial Governments can be measured by the extent to which they imitate the virtues and limitations of the British

Parliament. Anglo-Indian society, using the phrase in its colloquial sense, has been little affected by the scepticism so rife in England concerning the efficiency of our Parliamentary institutions and of our local administration, the integrity of our police, and the disinterestedness and impartiality of our judges and magistrates. In twenty years' time Indian politicians may be looking to Turkey or Persia for models of efficient administration suitable for an Asiatic people living under Oriental conditions.

CHAPTER V

# LAW AND ORDER

IF, as seems probable, the Simon Commission makes proposals for granting a further measure of provincial autonomy, criticism in England will be chiefly directed against the weakening of the district officer's authority. Such knowledge as the English have of Indian affairs is seldom up to date. They still picture the British official riding round his district, dealing with land questions *en grand seigneur*, settling disputes between ryots, planning roads, relieving famines, thwarting the moneylender, and trying the criminal. As a matter of unromantic fact the districts have always been so large, containing from one to three million people, that there was never very much direct personal contact between the district officer and the people, and most of his dictatorial powers have long been shorn away. He does, however, still retain nominal responsibility for law and order, he controls the police as well as the administration of land revenue, and it is the transference of these reserved subjects of the 'Home Department' and Land Revenue which have now to be considered.

The magisterial and police functions of the District Officer will be discussed as part of the judicial system. The importance of the Land Revenue work is often exaggerated. Except in the newly-developed irrigation areas the work has become completely stereotyped. Many experienced administrators, realising this, have always held that it was a mistake to 'reserve' this subject, and not retain under British control some of those modern and technical departments in which further development is possible, and in which contact with Western ideas might have been more valuable. The building up of our land administration was a remarkable achievement, but the department is now a machine which could be allowed to run itself. Even the conduct of famines is bound by codes which prescribe with incredible parsimony the exact measures to be adopted, the size of the wattle shelters to be erected at relief works, and the amount of *atta* which will prevent a man from dying of starvation. Such work as the granting of loans, the revision of land revenue, and the routine inspection of villages have for many years been competently done by Indian officials. Some district officers, especially when dealing with backward areas or aboriginal tribes, have been able, from sheer missionary zeal, to use their official position to accomplish valuable social reforms. Even in such cases they have usually been able to do this work better when, like Mr. Starte at Bijapur, they have been relieved from the routine of revenue work.

The future of the judicial system and the maintenance of 'law and order' raise very difficult and contentious questions. It will perhaps be best to adopt frankly the position of *advocatus diaboli*. The establishment of the *pax Britannica* throughout an immense continent is a great achievement which only the superficial will underrate. The English are perfectly justified in watching with a jealous eye any change of policy which may endanger their work. It is necessary to inquire how far an autonomous India would maintain the integrity and proper conduct of the criminal and civil courts, whether the criminal code would be relaxed, and what will be the fate of the police force and the machinery for preserving the peace.

It will be best to deal with judicature first, though the old saying *tant valent les juges tant valent les lois* is only partly applicable to countries in which most of the inhabitants are poor and uneducated.

The extent to which the higher judicial services have for some years been staffed by Indians is not fully appreciated in England. The Royal Commission, appointed shortly before the War, emphasised this point. 'Practically the whole of the original suits up to Rs.2,500 in value, and six-sevenths of the original suits above that value, and considerably more than half of the civil appeals were disposed of by Indians.' [1] In Madras four of the ten High Court judges, six of the twenty-two Sessions judges, and all the twenty-four subordinate judges were Indian.[1] Since that date the proportion of Indian Sessions judges has increased throughout India, for the Indian members of the Civil Service are inclined to prefer the judicial side. The High Courts have still a majority of Europeans because of a curious and anomalous rule under which a third of their number are recruited from the English Bar, an unfortunate arrangement which leads to the elevation of many quite obscure and mediocre barristers. Meanwhile the number of English barristers practising in India is decreasing, and many important cases are argued and decided throughout by Indians. Although the criminal and much of the civil law is English in origin and practice, there is no doubt that in the higher courts the Indian judges have earned the praise bestowed upon them some forty years ago by a Lord Chancellor: 'In respect of integrity, of learning, of knowledge, of the soundness and satisfactory character of the judgments arrived at, the

[1] J. Ramsay Macdonald, *The Government of India*, p. 197.

judgments of the native judges were quite as good as those of the English.'[1] This opinion was given at the time of the controversy over the Ilbert Bill, which first proposed that Europeans should be triable by Indian judges, and it has been fully justified since that time. No deterioration of the formal practice of law is likely to follow the continued replacement of English judges. The system is, of course, entirely artificial, a foreign law administered in a foreign tongue, and on the criminal side the law has often little relation to justice. Within those limitations the appellate side of the Indian judicature is scrupulously fair and free from corruption.

Unfortunately the administration of justice is only partly dependent on the accurate and scientific interpretation of the law. A famous economist once argued that the 'higgling of the market' and the relatively stronger position of the landlord against the tenant had 'eaten up' the doctrine of economic rent. It is even truer that the elaborate and costly machinery of British courts and British legal processes and the immense advantages which they give the literate minority against the illiterate cultivators and craftsmen have completely elbowed out of Indian courts all real justice founded on equity and common sense. The undoubted corruption which has always existed amongst the lower civil courts is really a small matter compared with the advantages which the present system gives to the moneylender pressing his unlettered client, to the dissolute landlord bringing a false charge against a poorer neighbour or tenant, and to every wealthy evildoer who enters the Courts either to commit an injustice or to escape the consequences of a crime. Just as the manu-

[1] See also Strachey, *India*, p. 119.

facturers of explosives are continually improving their methods in order to defeat the makers of armour plate, so the lawyers have struggled against and finally rendered ineffective each successive measure to protect the cultivators from the effect of our legal system. No legislation, such as the Deccan Agriculturists Relief Act, or the Punjab Land Alienation Act, has given more than a temporary respite to the peasant, for whom 'our legal system presents a maze as complicated as the Hampton Court Maze'. There is therefore a real danger lest the money-lending classes and the professional politicians, with their strong lawyer element, may combine to increase this legal burden. Similarly the weak Trades Union movement, which at present enjoys certain advantages for which European workmen have had to fight, may have to face a series of legal attacks which it would have no power to reverse by legislation. On the other hand, the present party divisions, which are usually along nationalist or communal lines, are likely to be modified in most of the Provincial Governments if they became autonomous. Ultimately the peasants should be able to exercise considerable political power.

Portions of the English criminal law have little support from the people, and sometimes it is opposed to their religious views. A free India would never have agreed to the death penalty being imposed except on the lowest castes, and the whole system must seem to the masses essentially a foreign innovation for which they have no real responsibility. It is, in fact, not unlike the agricultural machinery which Provincial Governments have, from time to time, introduced from England and shown to a sceptical peasantry. It is powerful and in some ways efficient, but usually too heavy and not much suited for the work. One dreads lest the mighty engine of the law should suffer the same fate as a certain steam plough which was sent to the Deccan. After being a nine days' wonder, garlanded and almost worshipped by the local ryots, it broke down, and was long left derelict and forgotten with the strings of the garlands still hanging forlornly round the funnel. Every magistrate who has had to apply the Indian Criminal Code to a witchcraft case, or wasted days listening to false evidence about some trumpery village quarrel, must have envied Ulysses meting out 'unequal laws unto a savage race'. A return to the paternal justice which is still administered in many Indian States is unthinkable, but it is a matter for consideration whether the present system, already so very bad, can get any worse.

It may also be questioned whether an entirely Indian judicature would enforce certain laws and enactments which have been passed, as it were, over the heads of the people. The objection to capital punishment has already reduced the jury system to a farce in certain areas. In some districts practices which are highly repugnant to Europeans, like infanticide and 'suttee', are viewed in a totally different light by sections of the people. The abolition of the death penalty would make little practical difference, and apart from humanitarian reasons would probably be an improvement. Transportation is, to a Hindu, a deterrent almost as effective as capital punishment. A slightly higher proportion of convictions would do more to prevent murders, for they are very common and frequently unpunished. Infanticide, a common practice amongst all primitive people, is undoubtedly still prevalent amongst the Rajputs, Jats, and Gujars, though the method may not amount to the actual murder of the girl babies, but only to the feeling that the parent 'need not strive officiously to keep alive'. The matter is dealt with at length in the last two census reports,[1] and there is sufficient evidence to prove the 'existence of a practice of this sort in large sections of the people which must be generally known and must necessarily influence the sentiments of others towards the value and sacredness of infant life'. Infanticide is purely utilitarian, like the drowning of unnecessary puppies and kittens, and is almost entirely confined to the unlettered classes. Any increase in the practice would therefore be due to the connivance of the police rather than to a change in outlook on the parts of the Courts.

*Sahamarana*, whereby widows immolate themselves on their husband's pyre and become *sati*, is a religious rite of great antiquity. It has been the subject of a recent monograph by a very keen and sympathetic student of Indian affairs.[2] The abolition of 'suttee', as the rite is usually called, is a typical example of a law passed against popular opinion. At the end of the eighteenth century *sahamarana* was a practice fairly widespread throughout India, but commonest amongst the highest Brahman clans of Bengal, and the leading families of Rajputana. Most of these had several wives, and other reasons besides religion may have led their families to look favourably upon a rite which so drastically reduced the number of their dependents. The English at first made no attempt to stop the practice, though individual officers would sometimes come across a

[1] Report of 1911, pp. 215–17. Report of 1921, App. VI.
[2] Edward Thompson, *Suttee.*

case and prevent it. About 1811 orders were made to regulate the *sahamarana* ceremony, and officials had to attend to see that no compulsion was put upon the widows. There is some evidence to show that the effect of this indirect official sanction was to encourage the rite, and a growing feeling of indignation amongst Europeans and a small section of Indians culminated in an order by Lord Bentinck in 1829. Although this prohibition did not provoke the popular excitement which was expected, there was bitter opposition from the religious leaders of Calcutta and an appeal was taken to the Privy Council against the legality of the order. It is interesting to notice that even Ram Mohun Roy, a valiant fighter against the practice, thought that Bentinck's order was premature.[1] The extension of the prohibition throughout India and the Indian States was very slow. *Sahamarana* did not become illegal in the latter till after the Mutiny.

Throughout most of India the prohibition probably killed for ever a custom of which people were already growing ashamed. In some parts, however, the memory undoubtedly survives, and nearly every year an illegal 'suttee' comes before the courts. 'Bihar had cases in 1901, 1903, 1904, 1905; there was one in a small village in the Punjab in 1905; and in 1906 there were suttees in Cawnpore and Calcutta.'[2] There was a famous case at Jarauli in 1913, and one or two have been reported since the War in Bihar, the last being in the autumn of 1927. They would be of little importance if they did not obviously arouse great popular enthusiasm. The 1927 *Sati* was the heroine of the countryside, and vast crowds visited the

[1] Miss Collet, *Life and Letters of Raja Rammohun Roy*, p. 146.
[2] Edward Thompson, *Suttee*, p. 122.

place of her immolation.[1] Similarly the frequent cases in which widows commit suicide in their own homes, usually by burning themselves with paraffin, are often commented upon with great approbation by the Bengali Press. It is difficult for a European to appreciate the manner in which the idea of the *sati* appeals to the Hindu mind. The voluntary sacrifice of the widows upon the death of their hero husband is the natural and fitting end to many of those traditional stories of Rajasthan which take such an important place in Indian history and legend. It is easy to see a mystic beauty in these

> Indian widows, gone to bed
> In flaming curtains, to the dead.

It may seem offensive to suggest that there is still any sympathy with this practice amongst those classes who are bound to take a continually larger part in the ruling of India, but it is necessary to face the unpleasant fact that this ancient rite has never troubled the Hindu conscience in the least, and that it has considerable popular support in Bihar, and in some parts of Bengal and Central India. Whether we agree with Mr. Thompson that the withdrawal of the English control would lead to a revival of the practice in certain parts depends upon the view we hold about the inevitable struggle which must take place between the orthodox Hindu leaders and those with a more modern and Western outlook. Europeans interested in Indian affairs have a natural tendency to under-estimate

[1] Ten of her relatives were tried and acquitted by the Indian jury at the Sessions Court. On appeal they were tried and sentenced by the High Court at Patna. See *The Times*, June 15, 1928.

the numbers and strength of the former. There is, of course, an important section of the nationalist movement which is led by Mr. Gandhi, and is strongly reformist in character. If the next generation of politicians is under his influence then there is little fear of any reaction in the direction of the old Hindu rites. The future would be more assured, and certain difficulties in the way of political change would be removed if Hindu leaders would emphasise their abhorrence of certain mediæval barbarities connected with their religion. It would also help to clear thinking if they would realise how great an obstacle these practices have been in the past to the recognition of the proper status of India in the civilised world.

Although there are other laws of a social character which were originally passed in the face of considerable opposition, few of them are still the subject of controversy. The English have always shown a marked reluctance to interfering with anything connected with the religious life of Indians. In a country where religion is so intimately bound up with every domestic happening and every social activity this policy has prevented the carrying through of various reforms – reforms that is to say from the English standpoint – which most other European countries would have enforced. It is difficult to imagine that the Germans would have allowed, without a bitter struggle, the continuance of the caste system in its present form. The Dutch would probably have interfered with the laws of inheritance so as to prevent the fragmentation of land, and they would, if one may judge from their administration in Java, have taken drastic steps to remove those religious difficulties which prevent the improvement of Indian cattle. British innovations have been so cautious and so tentative that they have seldom been much in advance of the ordinary practice. A great social evil in India is the custom of early marriages, or rather the early consummation of child marriages, and the frequent marriages between middle-aged widowers or married men and young girls of twelve. An influential group of social reformers have fought for many years against these practices, but very little support has come from the Government, which seems to grow more and more diffident about encouraging legislation which is in any way opposed by orthodox Hindus. Since 1892, when the Age of Consent Act fixed twelve as the age before which marriages could not be consummated, there has been no further development of the law in British India. For some years Sir Hari Singh Gour has been the chief protagonist of raising the age of consent, but the Government, after repeatedly blocking his measures, has recently [1] appointed a committee under the chairmanship of Sir Moropant V. Joshi, to inquire into the subject. It is probably felt that the new constitution will be in existence before any further action need be taken. At least two Indian States are in advance of British India. The Baroda Act of 1904 prohibits marriage before twelve years for girls and sixteen for boys. In Mysore the marriage of a girl under eight is forbidden, and also that of a man of fifty with a girl of under fourteen. The census, however suggests that a considerable proportion of infant marriages still takes place in both States.

The same caution has marked the Government's legislation dealing with factory conditions. Though a series of Acts have been passed regulating factory conditions, child

[1] June, 1928.

labour, workmen's compensation, and mining conditions, yet these lag very considerably behind the standards imposed in Western Europe. The Government's efforts in this direction have been hampered because of their old policy of helping Lancashire by the cotton excise. Any measure which might increase the cost of production was traced to the same motive by nationalists anxious to repay the help which they had received from the mill-owners. They could always claim that 'the voice was the voice of Exeter Hall, but the hand was the hand of Manchester'. Progress by legislation has indeed been so slow that any reactionary measure imposed from above at the instance of the employers would probably be fought by means of those disorganised but comparatively effective strikes of which India has recently had so much experience. It may safely be said that the Government of India has never supported any legislation to help one group of persons against another, whether tenants against landlords, ryots against moneylenders, workmen against employers, or even little girls against middle-aged voluptuaries unless the need was very great and there was a strong measure of support from the educated classes. For these reasons it does not seem that there is much fear of reactionary legislation, but only that in certain areas magistrates and juries may be loath to enforce laws which they dislike or a criminal procedure which is foreign to them.

The future of the police and the maintenance of good order both present considerable difficulties. It is, of course, the habit, and may even be considered the privilege of all oppositions to attack the police, especially in their dealings with political crime. In India there is a permanent opposition, and criticism of the police accordingly plays an unduly large part in public affairs. The present system has grown up in a haphazard manner. At the time when Sir Robert Peel instituted his police force in England, men like Sleeman were putting down the Thugs and dacoits who, like jackals followings tigers, were harassing a countryside already laid bare by the Pindaris and other marauders. Military methods had to be used for there was no indigenous organisation except the village watchmen. This was in accordance with Indian custom, for the ordinary Hindustani word for criminal is *faujdari*, which suggests that in early days the *fauj* or army was expected to deal with serious offences. When the country became more settled, and it seemed advisable to have a separate establishment for ordinary crime, the new police force appears to have been modelled on the lines of the English constabulary in Ireland. The country was gradually parcelled out into areas, in each of which there would be a *thana* or police station, and several of these *thanas* would be under an English officer.

Some control of the police was necessary, and inevitably this work was handed over to the District Magistrate. He was the only representative of the Government, except the Judge, who was present in every station and was not doing some definitely technical job. It would have been unthinkable to entrust the supervision of the police to anything corresponding to a 'watch committee' or a 'standing joint committee'. The system, however, has not worked very well, and obviously could not be incorporated into any future scheme. There are strong theoretical objections to entrusting a single man with appellate powers as a magistrate and also assign to him the duty of instituting criminal proceedings and controlling the police.

Although Englishmen are rather good at 'keeping two separate sides of their heads', and the cases of actual injustice are neither very frequent nor important, there is something fatal to the proper working of local administration in a grievance which is generally recognised but which is allowed to continue. This feeling has been intensified by nationalist sentiment, and by the conduct of certain 'political' cases. The idea of having in each district a single individual, responsible to the Government for the maintenance of order, is quite in accordance with Indian traditions, and it is unfortunate that the political objections to the District Magistrate's powers have obscured the question whether every district does not need an official Prefect or Head, such as is found in most Latin countries. Apart from racial considerations there would be many advantages in having as the official head of each district a man who could control the police, collaborate with any system of self-government, but not exercise magisterial functions. Lord Ripon probably made a mistake when he chose the British system of self-government as his model for India, for it places too great a strain on a countryside which is not very well provided with men of weight, leisure, and public spirit. Once Indian politicians have forgotten the connection between bureaucracy and the British connection it is possible that they will look more favourably upon the Latin system of self-government, a system which is really more indigenous to India.

The position of the police force is also far from happy. As so often happens in India their troubles tend to form a vicious circle. They are unpopular and receive little help in the detection of crime. In many parts they are socially boycotted, and the difficulties which they experience in collecting evidence make them *zabrdasti* or high-handed in their methods. It is an old joke against the police that their first lesson is how to torture without leaving a mark on the victim. Because they are unpopular every effort is made to cut down their estimates. Actually they must be quite the cheapest constabulary in the world. The cost per policeman in the United Provinces is about £19 yearly. In England it is about £270. The wages of a constable are often under thirty shillings a month, and the service only attracts a poor and uneducated type of man. His poor wages tempt him to be corrupt, which does not help to make him popular, so that the trouble begins again.

Unfortunately many Indian politicians encourage this attitude. However much they may dislike the methods employed in dealing with political offences in Bengal and elsewhere, it is impossible to deny the existence of much violent crime which has no connection with nationalism, and which would continue under any Government. Police work has never been a kid-glove affair in India, and the War was followed by a serious increase in dacoities and murders. In the United Provinces alone five policemen were killed and ten officers and seventy-two men wounded during the year 1926. The courage and loyalty of the rank and file are remarkable considering the odium to which the force is exposed, but certain offences, for which special areas are notorious, like cattle-raiding in the Punjab and murder in Burma, are still increasing, although crime generally seems to have reached its highest point in 1922. At present the motive force behind all measures taken to stamp out these offences is European. The Indian educated classes are indifferent, the poorer classes look upon the activities of the police as they look upon those of the tax collectors. In view of this attitude there is some doubt how far the existing machine would function in Indian hands, or whether another could be evolved which was more suitable for Eastern conditions.

There are several factors which justify a certain optimism in this matter. It is the experience of all successful nationalist movements, whether in Italy, Ireland, or Persia, that the political poacher turns gamekeeper very rapidly and fairly efficiently. It is also true that the cultivators and craftsmen, however much they may dislike the police, hate the dacoit even worse, and a sudden increase in violent crime will soon make a peasant prefer King Log to King Stork. The experience of a very able investigator in Gujerat may illustrate this. He had gone to some villages near Broach at the height of the Non-Co-operation Movement, and was talking with cultivators in order to see how far the movement had spread. He found that they would talk about nothing except the increase in dacoities.

'We tried them about *khaddar*, about the spinning wheel, the Punjab, and the other favourite topics of the Non-Co-operators, but we could get no sign of interest from them. They were too angry about the thieves. They even spoke disrespectfully about Mr. Gandhi.' [1]

Indian Ministers and officials should be able to enlist some popular support for the police where the British have signally failed. A small measure of such support would go far to counterbalance any deterioration in police discipline or technical efficiency. In practice the ryot

[1] J. T. Gwynn, *Indian Politics*, p. 103.

wants little more than protection from wandering groups of *badmashes* or bad characters, and it is not easy for Europeans living in India to realise how little security the police provide at present for the ordinary villager. There is no possibility of policing the Indian countryside according to the standards of Western Europe, nor would it be advisable. If petty criminal justice is to improve it will only come from developing village tribunals. Against the dacoits an armed and mobile force is needed, and such a force is also needed to deal with possible communal disturbances and outbreaks of political anarchy. Some unarmed police would be required for ordinary routine work, for the detection of individual crimes, and for keeping order in the towns. These would be best left as a Provincial service under the charge of the Head of each district. The armed police might well be an all-India service, but placed at the disposal of the Provincial Governments, especially if the Provinces are reduced in size. There may be sporadic outbursts of political and religious violence, but in the absence of any nationalist question the bulk of the population will probably be affected but little by them, unless they are sufficiently common and widespread to become a nuisance. In this case the ryots can be trusted to vent their wrath on the politicians, and they will have the machinery to do this.

## CHAPTER VI

# THE MACHINERY OF DEMOCRACY

MANY authorities, including Mr. Rudyard Kipling, have prophesied that India would never vote. Actually the Indian electors, on their present very limited franchise, go to the poll in numbers which compare very favourably with many older democracies. Most of the provincial constituencies and nearly all the Imperial constituencies are of a size and nature which would break the heart of any English election agent. The system of communal voting has, of course, further increased the geographical area of the constituencies. One stout-hearted member, for example, has to represent the urban Sikhs throughout the Punjab. An English country constituency, forty miles by thirty, is considered very difficult to organise, but in India the distances may be five times as great, and the electors be scattered amongst hundreds of villages with few roads. Many of the villages will be eight or nine miles from the polling station. A candidate's troubles are made infinitely worse from the fact that three-quarters of his constituents are illiterate, and therefore cannot be reached by letter or pamphlet. In spite of all these obstacles to proper organisation 350,000 electors out of 800,000 polled their votes in 1924 for the Central Legislature, and in many of the provincial elections a poll of 50 per cent. or more was recorded. In the French general elections or in English local elections the proportion is often considerably less. It seems that the fairly prosperous Indian cultivators and the middle-class townsmen who make up the bulk of the present electorate are quite prepared to play their part in the mechanical side of democracy. Not only will they vote, but they are willing to walk much farther to the poll than most Europeans.

Most English critics of democracy in India have spent their lives in the East, and have had little or no experience of politics in other countries. They are inclined to compare the first tentative efforts to obtain direct representation in India with memories of an ideal democracy obtained from textbooks on political science. There is no reason to expect that India will do better than attain by slow degrees to the standards of democratic control reached in other scattered agricultural areas. The system of direct voting is at best a rough-and-ready way of choosing legislators and testing public opinion. At present it functions in India about as well as in many country parts of nineteenth-century England, indeed the lines on which the elections are fought are curiously reminiscent of certain phases of English politics. Many are based on communal and caste feeling, and are not unlike the Church and Chapel contests of a generation or so ago. The type of candidate is usually successful who can

> 'prove his doctrine orthodox
> By apostolic blows and knocks'.

On the other hand, the elections in the *zemindari* areas of Eastern India are more like those struggles which still take place in the hunting counties between a Conservative landlord and a Labour or Liberal opponent. One constituency in Oudh was contested by a friend of the writer as a Nationalist, and a description of the election campaign may explain some of the practical difficulties which make the democratic machine hard to work in the East.

The area was, of course, dominated by the Talukdars,

who are glorified country squires, each exercising almost feudal control over several villages. They are often absentees, leaving their estates to be managed by agents, but politically they are fairly active, usually combining in a general support of the Government, except on those occasions, now unhappily rare, when the latter interferes on behalf of their tenants. The Talukdar candidate starts therefore with two great advantages, he has the moral support of the other Talukdars and during the election can use their agents. The Nationalist candidate had the greatest difficulty in getting any foothold in the villages, and as soon as he became at all dangerous the law was invoked against him. He was accused of rousing the tenantry against their landlords, and thus setting class against class, an accusation with a not unfamiliar ring. Unfortunately the Indian Penal Code was designed to meet revolutionary movements, and to forestall communal disturbances. It was found possible to bring much ordinary political propaganda within the term 'sedition'. Cases were heard, and some decided against the Nationalists, but they carried on their work until the election, when fresh difficulties arose.

Most of the voters were tenants, cultivating land for which they paid fifty rupees or more a year. They lived in the 600 villages which made up the constituency. Three-quarters of them could not read or write, and many could not even recognise their candidate's name on a polling-card. The first difficulty was to get them to the thirty polling-booths, which would be often eight to ten miles from their homes. The Talukdar candidate used his own agent and also those of his friends, for this purpose. The Nationalist candidate when he reached his first polling-booth found a large camp pitched outside it. These were the tenantry of a group of villages. They had been collected by the agent on the previous evening, had been given some food, and were being led to the polling-booth in batches to vote.

Inside the polling-booth there would be more trouble. At the first elections, after the introduction of the Reform scheme, the English system was adopted. Two local and presumably neutral men were in each booth, and on them fell the task of advising the illiterate ryots where to put their cross. This led to abuses, for in country areas no one could be found who was both independent and neutral. Each candidate was therefore allowed a representative inside the polling-booth. The tenant as he entered would see some land agent, possibly the man who worked for his Talukdar. He would be told how to vote, and might receive a hint about the value of his tenancy if the cross went into the wrong square. The system sounds absurd, but it is not easy to think out an alternative method in a country where so many voters cannot read. In some areas they tried giving each candidate a sign, either a colour or an animal, so that the voter could put his cross against an elephant or a scorpion. The system did not work very well, for the ryot has a strange but lively sense of humour.

In spite of the long distances to be travelled on foot in these country constituencies the polling is quite high, and even in Oudh the Talukdars or *zemindars* are not consistently successful. It is probably easier for anyone who is neither a landlord nor has the landlords' support to get returned in the *zemindari* areas of India than in certain English constituencies. There is ample evidence that the illiterate elector can decide and vote upon a simple issue. The chief drawbacks to the present system come at a later stage. The organising and 'nursing' of these huge constituencies must be an expensive and arduous task, especially for a candidate who has no territorial hold. It requires at least twenty helpers to make any headway in an area containing several hundred villages. The candidate himself must spend some months travelling about the district addressing meetings in the larger villages and market towns. Even if the helpers give their services free they must be provided with ponies, and by the time the most economical candidate has made any impression upon his constituency he will have spent 5,000 rupees. His wealthier rival who indulges in such forms of indirect bribery as gifts to temples – the Oriental equivalent to cricket and football club subscriptions – will often spend six times as much.

Five thousand rupees is a large amount for an Indian of the professional classes to provide, and contests will be confined to men of considerable private means, and to those supported by some party or organisation. The methods by which these organisations obtain their funds are likely to be one of the less happy features of Indian democracy. Industrial organisation will only touch an insignificant fraction of the people, and up to the present there have been few serious attempts to collect the ryots and cultivators into political groups. Unless there is to be a repetition in Indian agricultural areas of the political conditions now prevailing in rural England, which is almost entirely represented in Parliament by wealthy men of one political persuasion, it is essential to make the candidate's task as easy and as cheap as possible. Indirect voting is often advocated, especially by those who know the South of India, where the corporate life of the village is strong. It has been proposed to group villages together and make them vote through delegates, while some enthusiasts would like to use the village *panchayat* in order to discover the views of the inhabitants. There are, however, many practical difficulties, and the writer has discussed this point with Indians of different political views. They nearly all agreed that as the direct voting system had been introduced it would be best to continue along these lines. It is possible that the smaller ryots may ultimately organise themselves politically in opposition to those with larger holdings, or tenants will combine against landlords. This would mean that each village or group of villages, which had to choose delegates, would be divided much more fiercely than they are by an ordinary election.

An extension of the franchise would help to mitigate the effects of bribery and intimidation, but it would not make the candidate's task any easier. Opinion on this subject is divided, some people contending that there are already too many voters who can be bought for four annas, others that a wider electorate will encourage the 'spell-binder', but most progressives favour the larger franchise because it is theoretically fairer, and because there is little use in delaying an inevitable extension. It would certainly give a much larger voice in public affairs to the rural districts. These are at present badly handicapped by the assistance which the means qualification gives the townsman, and also by the dearth of candidates who have any interest in agriculture except as an industry which exists to pay rent and the interest on mortgages. It is interesting to notice that the Commission on the Constitution of Ceylon has recommended what is virtually manhood suffrage, with votes for women at the age of thirty, thus going considerably further than the demands of the Ceylon National Congress.[1] One of the main grounds for this decision was their belief that a vote would raise the status of the depressed classes, who will be in a better position to obtain redress for their grievances, and also gain in self-respect.

Another method by which the practical difficulties can be minimised is one which has been discussed in another connection. The size of the larger Provinces not only complicates the question of the Indian States, but it also imposes a serious handicap upon the system of democracy. The men who divided up India into its existing provinces never dreamt of the introduction of autonomous governments based on a popular franchise. The provinces were the 'satrapies of a vast oriental dependency', and their boundaries were often decided by some historical accident, such as joined Sind and Aden to Bombay. The areas and population of the nine chief Provinces are too large to make them suitable units for social administration. The history of the last twenty years has gone far to prove that 8 or 10 millions is the limit of population which can be conveniently and efficiently managed by a single democratic Government. England is an exceptional case. The United States would have been a much better model for India. Her population of about a hundred million is divided amongst forty-eight States, and the largest has a population of rather more than 10 million. In a State of this size a legislature of, say, 250 members can be based on constituencies which are of a convenient size, and need not be inordinately expensive to contest. In Denmark,

[1] Report of Special Commission on the Constitution, pp. 87–9.

Norway, and Sweden it is possible for a local agriculturist to stand for Parliament with a fair chance of success. The smaller Provinces would also do away with the need for a candidate to be bilingual, which he must be at present, if he is to have any influence in the Bombay or Madras Assemblies.

If this principle is conceded the formation of the smaller provinces would present no insuperable difficulties. In many cases the existing provincial boundaries could be retained, in others a few districts, *talukas*, or *tehsils* could be included when advisable for linguistic or racial homogeneity. Thus Bihar would be separated from Orissa and from Chota Nagpur, and Orissa could be reinforced by Ooriyan districts from the Madras side. Bombay is at present hampered by having four vernaculars, Sindhi, Gujerati, Marathi, and Canarese. Sind and Gujerat would make suitable units, the Marathas could unite with some of their own race in the Central Provinces, and the Canarese join with others who speak their beautiful but difficult language in the north-west of the Madras Presidency. These divisions may seem drastic, but there is little provincial loyalty, and the provinces, except the Punjab and Bengal, have no historical basis.

Elections for the Central Legislature present an entirely different problem. It is difficult to conceive of any system by which a population of 300 millions scattered over an immense continent can intelligently select 200 or even 600 direct representatives. The system only works at present because of the extremely restricted franchise, and it must be remembered that each slight lowering of the qualifications will bring in millions of new voters. In this case some system of indirect voting seems most desirable, and the obvious method would be through the Provincial Legislatures.

The first committee of inquiry held into the working of the Reforms reported strongly on the lack of contact between members of the Legislatures and their constituents. This difficulty is common to all countries in which the inhabitants do not read newspapers regularly, and are scattered amongst isolated villages. The party system tends to mitigate this evil because his fellow-politicians will soon advertise the defection of one of their own party, but it still exists throughout Europe. In England there is no method by which a Member of Parliament who changes his opinions and his Party, can be compelled to resign, and in other countries there have been cases of men sent to a legislature to represent one interest who have consistently voted the other way. It is a weakness in democracy rather than in the Indian politician. Most of these problems will tend to straighten themselves out with the slow spread of education, and an increase in public spirit. In Victorian times few country Members of Parliament troubled to explain or justify their actions to their constituents except at elections, and a County Councillor who did so to-day would in most parts of England be considered very eccentric. It is absurd to criticise Indian democracy on the basis of some Utopian ideal. The Indian voter has already shown that he is far from apathetic, but at present his only function is to choose between candidates all of whom he may cordially distrust and dislike. Improvement will come when the ryots, who form the bulk of the population, begin to organise themselves into peasants' parties along the lines which have already been successful in parts of Europe.

# PART IV

# THE FUTURE

CHAPTER I

# THE NEW CONSTITUTION

MODERN India has suffered as much as any country from the use of those 'masked words' which, as Ruskin once wrote, 'nobody understands but which everybody uses and most people will fight for, live for, and even die for, fancying they mean this or that or the other of things dear to them'. Chief amongst these words, which are continually bandied about with various shades of meaning, are 'self-government', '*swaraj*', and 'self-determination'. Perhaps their vagueness is due to their all commencing with the word 'self', which raises obvious difficulties in a country with 300 million inhabitants. To some the word self-government merely suggests the emancipation of the Government of India from the control of Parliament or of the Secretary of State, to others it entails the progressive substitution of Indian for British officials. Some would hold that the Indian States enjoy self-government except for such control as is exercised by the Central Government, but others would insist that Government of Indians by Indians is not enough. They would consider that self-government must be based on elected legislatures, even if they are uncertain about the extent to which they are prepared to entrust themselves to democracy. Many Indians, even amongst those who most insistently demand self-government, would privately agree with Lord Milner,

'I, of course, take off my hat to everything that calls itself Franchise, Parliament, Representation of the People, The Voice of the Majority, and all the rest of it. But . . .

I cannot shut my eyes to the fact that popular Government, as we understand it, is, for a longer time than one can foresee at present, out of the question.'[1]

On the other hand, there are many Indians, and with them some experienced British officials, who are prepared to support the application of the full democratic principle, province by provincc, but would deny India's claim to speak as a unit, holding that such an amalgamation must follow and not precede the building up of the provincial governments.

Self-determination is an equally vague phrase, which is often used to support the claim of India, considered as a unit, to choose the terms upon which she will or will not remain in the Empire. It might equally be used to disrupt India into a number of small communities, or be the grounds upon which any little Indian State could claim complete independence. The continual employment by all parties of catch-words, like 'India demands this' or 'India is not fitted to do that', have helped to confuse the issue. There would seem to be some five methods by which the Simon Commission and ultimately the British Parliament can proceed with regard to the future of India. Because of the fog with which sentiment and political propaganda have enshrouded the whole subject, it will be best to consider them under separate headings.

### I. A RETURN TO BUREAUCRACY

When the late Mr. Montagu brought his Reforms scheme before the Parliament of 1919 there were many supporters of the Coalition Government who held that

[1] *England in Egypt.*

his proposals were too ambitious and were also premature. In order to appease these the path for a retreat had to be left open, and the Government of India Act makes it clear that the Simon Commission can recommend a return to the old system, if they consider dyarchy to have been a failure. The important Section 84A lays down that the Commission shall 'report as to whether and to what extent it is desirable to establish the principle of responsible Government, or to extend, modify or restrict the degree of responsible government then existing. . . .' It is, however, inconceivable that such proposals should be made, nor is there any serious body of opinion in England or in India which would advocate or support such a course. The rather truculent mood, which marked in England the years immediately following the War, has grown weaker, and the House of Commons which will be elected in 1929 is likely to be dominated, even more than its predecessors, by a desire to relieve England from as many outside troubles as possible in order to concentrate on difficulties at home. In India few of the educated classes would care to see an uncontrolled bureaucracy even if it was almost entirely staffed by Indians. Although the old attacks upon the bureaucracy were racial in origin, the jealousy of the politician towards the new Indian official is almost as marked as that which used to be felt about his British predecessor, and it is probable that a dislike of too much Government interference will now spread to classes which would formerly have looked upon it as something foreign to their ordinary life, and hence, like fate itself, not worth resisting. Uncontrolled bureaucracy has done India some good and much harm, it certainly cannot be restored.

## 2. A MODIFICATION OF DYARCHY

Although dyarchy has few friends there are certain arguments in favour of continuing the system. Like the Morley-Minto reforms of 1909 it will have been in existence for just ten years when the Commission reports, a period which is too short for its benefits to be appreciated or its possibilities exploited. The British policy in India since the beginning of the century has been compared with a man trying to plant an orchard but continually digging up the trees to see if the roots are healthy. The rapidity of the changes have thrown a great strain upon the public services, and the glamour of political reforms, followed by disputes about their sufficiency, have tended to obscure all other issues, and to give undue importance to abstract questions rather than to the dull and prosaic work of administration.

It is possible that if the Montagu reforms had been initiated under more favourable circumstances, and had not been branded as a temporary expedient by the promise of a Commission after ten years, they might have worked satisfactorily in most Provinces, and even been capable of great development. It would have been difficult to resist the pressure of those Responsivists who came into the Assemblies and took office if they had set themselves from the first to win responsible government through the constitution. They could, in many Provinces, have forced the Governor to recognise the principle of collective ministerial responsibility for the transferred subjects, and by that means extended their influence over the reserved subjects by establishing a rudimentary cabinet system. The transfer of certain other departments could have been arranged so as to prevent the overlapping between transferred and reserved subjects which causes many of the anomalies existing at present. Some other reforms, such as an extension of the franchise, could have been introduced.

The Liberals have made no attempt to gain their ends through the constitution. They lacked the cohesion to form parties in the Councils to support the Ministers, and help them to improve their status. They preferred to treat the newly appointed Minister as a lost leader, and join in the game of 'sniping' at him on all possible occasions. Dyarchy, apart from certain fundamental defects discussed previously,[1] failed because of its transitional character. It will never seem to the Indians as anything but a compromise scheme, and it is asking too much of human nature to expect the educated classes to take it seriously. The European Association and the keenest Nationalists would agree that the next step is to establish a system which is neither temporary nor experimental, and which must contain the machinery for future development within itself.

### 3. A TREATY WITH INDIA

Most books written from the Indian standpoint about responsible government are based on a conception of India as a single unit, and it is assumed that this unit can be considered as represented either by the Central Legislature, or by the various political bodies now in existence. This is essentially the outlook of those who have been described as the All-India politicians, and would apply equally to a Liberal like Sir Tej Bahadur Sapru or to the

[1] Part II, Chapter V.

Congress Party. It has some measure of support in England, especially from those members of the Labour and Liberal parties whose personal contact with India has been, for the most part, through these politicians. The claim to speak for India has long been put forward by the Congress Party, and since the appointment of the Simon Commission they, and many Liberals, have concentrated their efforts upon evolving paper constitutions by which the British Parliament will be relieved of all control over India. There are several of these constitutions in existence[1] describing, sometimes in great detail, the method by which the Speaker of the Central Legislature is to be elected, and exactly who is to be responsible for the lighthouses. Nearly all of them are modelled on the constitutions granted to the Dominions, or the 'Treaty' made with Ireland. A Committee of the All Parties Conference, under Pandit Motilal Nehru, has produced the ablest and best sponsored of these schemes. Unfortunately their proposals are a reply to Lord Birkenhead's challenge rather than a serious attempt to outline a new form of government. Their 'Constitution' envisages an Assembly of 500 members, directly elected by constituencies of over a quarter of a million voters, not one per cent of whom are at present enfranchised. To this fortuitously chosen body and to the first Prime Minister are to be transferred almost sovereign powers only limited by a paper constitution which would have no popular basis or support.

It is most unlikely that an advance towards responsible

[1] Mrs. Besant's 'Commonwealth of India Bill', S. Srinivasa Iyengar's 'Swaraj Constitution', 'Outline Scheme of Swaraj', the Independent Labour Party's draft Bill.

government will be made along these lines. The Dominion precedents are not really apposite. In every case the object of those constitutions was to transfer power to a small and comparatively homogeneous group of people. It should also be noted that even in the case of Lord Durham's famous Report, which recommended the introduction of responsible Government into the Canadian Provinces, he did not advise that any attempt should be made to establish a national government until the separate provinces were running satisfactorily. The South African parallel is an unfortunate one, for the effect of the constitution has been to hand over a large native population to a small white minority. In this country also the different provinces were strong and independent before the Union was formed. The analogy of Ireland is equally far fetched. The size and diversity of the population is of the very essence of the problem, and certainly India cannot afford to have a number of Ulsters amongst the provinces and Indian States. Nor, on the Irish analogy, would it be easy to find the politicians who are able, in Mr. Churchill's phrase, 'to deliver the goods'. No one could take seriously the claim of the Congress Party to represent India. The other parties, like the Hindu Mahasabha, the Moslem League, etc., are groups of politicians rather than sections of the electorate. The Central Legislature, based on its 800,000 franchise, has the best claim to speak for India, a fact which might have been more fully recognised in the appointment and procedure of the Simon Commission, but which hardly gives its members the right to negotiate a general constitution apart from the provinces. There are over seventy Mohammadans and sixty Hindu outcastes for every individual on the franchise for the Central Legislature, and probably a majority of both these groups would strenuously deny the claims of the Legislature to speak for them. Many of the All-India politicians have also lost much of their hold on their own provinces. Mr. Lajpat Rai is undoubtedly a more important person in Delhi than in Lahore. This does not mean that the provincial politicians are less nationalist or less impatient of British control, but only that a process is now taking place in India which could be paralleled in nearly all reformist movements. The old propagandists are being succeeded by a new generation who are brought up against the practical questions of administration. There is something pathetic about these veterans who are now being pushed into the wings of the political stage, and spend their energies on abstract schemes, and on chiding, quite fairly, some of their old friends in England. Their attitude towards the provincial politicians is not unlike that of the old-time Socialist to his convert who has been elected on to a local council, a wistfully reproachful 'Been three months on the Council and not slung out yet, Bill?'

### 4. PROVINCIAL AUTONOMY

Most of the provinces, including hesitant Bengal, have passed a vote in favour of co-operating with the Simon Commission. Although this measure of support has usually been due to the Government *bloc*, it will assist the natural tendency of the Commission to work out some measure of responsible government in the various provinces, and then to deal with the Imperial Government at Delhi. The Commission will have to consider whether the remaining 'reserved' subjects can now be transferred to

Indian Ministers, whether any adjustment of subjects is needed between the Imperial and the Provincial Governments, and finally what type of constitution is best suited to give real responsibility to the provincial electorate, and through them to the Assembly.

The provincial subjects, which are at present reserved, are finance, land revenue and irrigation, law, justice, and the police. Financial control is the key to provincial autonomy; the lack of it made it impossible for the Ministers to take dyarchy seriously. The chief objection to its transference disappears when there is no question of competition between the two sides of the Council, but it will mean a very clear and definite separation of provincial and central finances. Probably the Meston award with some modifications might be allowed to stand, but it is essential that the provinces should be given all residuary financial powers. The claims of the central government must be limited, and the development of taxation will be one of the most important functions of the provinces. All public services are starved, and one of the chief virtues of a government which is in any sense representative is that it can raise taxes which an autocratic government would not dare to impose or be able to collect. This has been seen both in Ireland and also in South Africa, where General Botha imposed taxes which neither Lord Milner nor Lord Selborne would have considered practicable.

Land Revenue in itself presents few difficulties, the actual administration is largely in Indian hands, and the assessment and collection have become almost routine. The work of the Department is, however, carried on in most districts by the Indian Civil Service, which is an

All-India and not a provincial service. The same difficulty has already arisen in other departments, like Agriculture and Education, but the number of All-India officials was smaller, and the problem has been solved, not altogether satisfactorily, by employing provincial officials in their place. As a permanent arrangement it is obviously wrong that Ministers should be served by men, often of another race, whose pay, promotion, and conduct are not under their control, but under that of the Secretary of State. There are, however, many practical reasons why District Officers should retain some of their position and status, and the same argument applies in the case of the police. Although nationalists are very anxious to obtain control of the police and of the initiation of prosecutions, an All-India force controlled in each district by men in an All-India service would undoubtedly add to the security and stability of the country during the transition years. Possibly a reasonable compromise would be a division of the police force into armed and unarmed sections. The first to be an Imperial force, a kind of militia taking over part of the work and functions of the Internal Security Troops, while the second should be under the Provincial Governments. It is impossible to avoid all chances of friction between Ministers and District Officers, but these will be reduced to a minimum if the Ministers are in a strong enough position, and not continually exposed to attacks from local wire-pullers. There may be a period of controversy over the assessments of land revenue in the *ryotwari* districts, for the nationalists are unchaining very dangerous forces in their support of the Bardoli refusal to pay the increased assessment. They may find, as the Russian Government is finding, that the passive resistance of the peasant is almost invincible, and that just when they should be persuading him to pay more for public services they are teaching him a way to avoid payment altogether. The sooner provincial taxation is in Indian hands the better it will be for the country, for racial animosity added to every one's natural objection to paying taxes is a combination too strong to be healthy.

The transference of 'law and justice' have been discussed in a previous chapter and do not arouse any special difficulties. Provincial autonomy would be based, then, on the administration of all the departments and subjects which are at present entrusted to the Provincial Governments, with the exception of the police or of one section of the police. There does not seem any need to transfer other subjects from the Central Government, which should properly be regarded as the agent of the provinces, doing work which is either very technical, or which is necessarily 'All-Indian', like controlling Customs, organising credit and currency, and maintaining an army.

Whatever may be the geographical basis of the Provinces, it is essential that the Ministers should be sure of some measure of support during their tenure of office, and that the electorate through its elected members should realise its responsibilities. The first point is one of great difficulty. No stable Government is possible if a Minister may find one morning that he has not got a friend left in the Assembly because he has taken some necessary and honourable action which may have offended Nationalist sentiment, or has upset his own religious community without of course getting the support of the others. Under the English cabinet and party system a Minister is spared this indignity so long as he can carry his cabinet with him, for his party are not likely to force a general election on some small issue. There is, however, little prospect of many Indian provinces evolving a two-party or even a three-party system. Where such divisions exist, e.g. in the Punjab and Madras, they are on a communal basis, which, it is to be hoped, will not be permanent. When the parties in India begin to divide along economic or social lines it is quite possible that they will break up into seven or eight groups as in Germany. It must also be remembered that the two-party system in England and the United States is far from evoking that universal admiration which it received in the nineteenth century, and a strong feeling is growing up in both countries that it has a deadening effect upon its members, and is not sufficiently responsive to public opinion. The English system is probably little suited to the Indian temperament, unless the back benches of its provincial assemblies are filled with landlords, who may perhaps share that placid temperament which made the old English landowners into 'the finest collection of brute votes in Europe'. The work of the Provincial Councils will be chiefly administrative, much of it will resemble that of an English County Council rather than a Parliament. It would seem, therefore, that the most practical procedure for the Provincial Governments would be that suggested by the Commission on the Constitution of Ceylon. Each department would be under the charge of a standing committee, and the chairmen of these committees will form a Board of Ministers which will act as cabinet, prepare the Budget, and consider the requirements of the standing committees. The rejection of the Budget, a defeat on supplementary estimates, or a vote of no confidence would involve a general election. The Commission on Ceylon recommend seven departments, and the addition of three officials who will act as advisers rather than as executive officers, but it is doubtful whether such a course would be advisable in India, where racial tension is more severe, and where the presence of European officials amongst the Ministers immediately rouses old memories, and incites the 'back-benchers' to form themselves into a permanent opposition. There is no reason why a provincial government along these lines should not work as well, say, as the London County Council, which deals with a population of many millions through such Committees, but it is undoubtedly best suited to a comparatively small area and population. If provincial autonomy is to be a permanent success it must be part of a larger scheme.

### 5. THE DEMOCRATIC REORGANISATION OF INDIA

Nineteenth-century statesmen of Liberal tendencies delighted to talk about the time when the 'colonies' being ripe for self-government would drop from the parent tree. It does not seem to have struck them that they were describing the most wasteful and foolish kind of husbandry. The wise man would surely pick his fruit before it was ripe enough to fall, but England has still to learn how to rid herself of Imperial responsibilities with the greatest advantage both to herself and the people whom she governs. At present the tendency is to think that 'democracy' can solve all difficulties, but a long period of foreign occupation invariably upsets the natural balance between the different classes, and this cannot be rectified merely by applying the ordinary machinery of democracy, and then leaving the people themselves to evolve some order out of confusion. If the new India is to be built up, as now seems inevitable, on a basis of autonomous provinces, it is the duty of England to see that her development is not handicapped from the start by the *débris* of our former rule.

The first necessity is a very wide franchise for each province. If the recommendations of the Ceylon Commission are accepted it will be difficult to avoid a similar almost universal suffrage in India. It would be a ridiculous anomaly if the Tamil coolie should have a vote in Ceylon, but not in his own home. This system should be introduced immediately, for the history of the native franchise in South Africa shows how difficult it is to correct injustices once the democratic machine has begun to function on a restricted electorate. The English owe something to the lower classes of India. Though we claim to be solicitous for the welfare of the outcastes and the small ryots, it is possible that the *pax Britannica* has indirectly contributed to their unhappy lot. It certainly cannot be said to have done them much good. The outcaste's vote will limit the power of the village 'headman', who is too often the 'jackal of the government', it will weaken the caste system, and bring a little *izzat* or self-respect to many who badly need some moral support. At worst the vote may be worth four annas, also badly needed. The same argument applies to female suffrage. It may reduce the proportion of votes polled, but it will do no harm, and will act as a mild solvent for certain social evils.

For many years the Indian electorate will have very little say in the preliminary choice of candidates, a most important part of a well-found democracy. It is of little advantage to have a vote if it means putting a mark against one of several unknown names, the lucky winner then disappearing to a distant capital where complete oblivion covers his deeds and actions. This is a weakness of all democracies, but it can be minimised by having small Provinces, so that constituencies are of a reasonable size and never too far removed from the seat of government. Take the case of Chandappa Basappa, a fairly intelligent Canarese villager in the Dharwar district. He may have learnt to read slowly and with difficulty the printed word, and in 1930 he receives a vote. If the Bombay Presidency is left as it is at present, and universal suffrage introduced, Chandappa will be a member of a large and scattered constituency with somewhere about fifty thousand voters. His candidates will all have to be at least bilingual if they are to talk to Chandappa and also to their fellow-members at Poona, some 300 miles away in the middle of the Maratha-speaking country. When his member is returned and Chandappa obtains a paper describing what happens in the Council he will probably find that the discussion turned upon conditions in the Ahmedabad cotton mills or the 'salting up' of land in the Sind irrigation areas, in which he is about as interested as an English farm labourer in the Ruhr coalfields or the Shannon power scheme. Suppose, on the other hand, that the Provinces are broken up, and Bombay is divided into, say, four parts, Chandappa becomes a person of slightly more importance, for his new constituency is decidedly smaller, perhaps a quarter of the old size, and his village will probably receive a visit from the candidate, who may not be able to talk three languages but may possibly know considerably more about local conditions, about agriculture in those parts, and other matters which interest

Chandappa intensely. The Council at Belgaum, though more modest than that which met at Poona, has all its doings recorded in the local papers, and Chandappa has no longer to puzzle his head over the strange grievances of Moslem tribes on the Baluchistan frontier. Can there be any real doubt in which of these two forms the democratic machine is most likely to work effectively?

It may be argued that the division of the present satrapies should follow and not precede the grant of provincial autonomy, but history and our knowledge of human nature suggest that these separate institutions would never come into being if the matter was left to the members of the larger assemblies, and their officials. Our bilingual lawyer who represents Chandappa at Poona, and enjoys the prestige and influence which comes from membership of a Council administering a population four times as large as that of Australia, is not willingly going to sacrifice his position to fight some rustic worthy for a seat upon the Belgaum council. The Governor and the officials will be equally keen to scotch any separatist movement, for these small provincial governments will have to do without the pomp and high salaries which tradition justifies in the case of the older provinces. Nor would there be very much strength in such a separatist movement, because the people of India have no memories of any form of democratic Government, but only of living in these large satrapies under foreign control. Chandappa Basappa would have no very clear ideas about the Bombay Presidency, and some of the outlying parts would seem completely strange and foreign to him, but some one would have to press the idea of a Canarese province upon him very hard and persistently before he took much interest in it. It is essentially a reform which must come from above.

The first two measures suggested are both constructive. The establishment of an electorate on a very wide basis, and the division of the existing provinces should not be difficult innovations owing to India's amorphous and malleable condition after a century of foreign control. The third step, which is even more necessary, presents much greater difficulties because it is destructive. The communal system of voting must go, and the only people who can get rid of it are the British. If the Legislative Councils in the autonomous provinces are elected on a communal basis the members will be a perpetual obstacle to any alteration, for they themselves will belong to the very class who thrive upon religious dissensions. Those who have followed the various attempts made during recent years to arrange some working compromise between the Hindus and Moslems must have realised the presence of sinister influences fighting desperately and successfully to prevent these 'pacts' becoming a reality. The need for action from outside is obvious, the patient cannot operate upon himself, and the malignant growth will become worse each year. There is only one possible alternative to an immediate abolition of the system and that would be the fixing of a time-limit in one or two provinces, like the Punjab, where the feeling is greatest. It would, however, be almost impossible to devise a satisfactory method for enforcing such a time-limit, for every year in which men look to their communal leaders as the proper dispensers of Government appointments, including jobs like that of sub-postmasters or platelayers' foremen on the railway, will help to rivet communalism on to public life, and the evil which is serious under dyarchy would be fatal in an autonomous government.

'The young disease, which must subdue at length,
Grows with his growth, and strengthens with his strength.'

It would undoubtedly be best if these three necessary reforms, the enlargement of the electorate, the subdivision of the provinces, and the abolition of the communal system of voting, could be inaugurated simultaneously, for the first two would help the introduction of the third. Thus in many of the new and smaller provinces the communal trouble would hardly exist, for the people would be more homogeneous. Returning to the example of the Bombay Presidency, the Canarese province would be predominantly non-Brahman Hindu. The few local Moslems have always behaved much like a Hindu caste, taking part in Hindu festivals, but also celebrating their own. At the other end of the Presidency Sind is almost entirely Moslem. In neither Canara nor Sind would there be any serious demand for communal protection which is only brought forward urgently when the opposing groups are in a proportion of about six to four or seven to three, or when some minority has important financial interests which it considers entitles them to a special consideration. The sudden extension of the franchise would also completely alter the numerical relations between the religious sects, and in many districts would bring in a mass of voters, like the depressed classes, who had not been previously considered by either of the communal factions. This would undoubtedly help to relieve the tension.

None of these three reforms would involve any great

expenditure. The land revenue system already necessitates keeping elaborate village records, and a staff of touring officers to inspect them. The preparation of electoral rolls on the basis of universal suffrage would not entail any great difficulties in British India. The smaller provinces should ultimately lead to economy. Though the number of ministers would be increased, the administration would be on a very modest scale, and salaries could be proportionately smaller. More could be done on a voluntary basis when attendance on a committee did not involve any great expenditure of time or money, and many establishments could be substantially reduced. There would be no possible excuse for the enormous sums spent upon the Governor and his semi-regal entourage, and for the gubernatorial pomp and extravagance which have done so much to set a false standard in Anglo-Indian society and also amongst the Indian wealthier classes. The Governor would remain the formal head of the Province, and in him would vest a considerable reserve of power as a safeguard if the principles of the constitution were violated, or there was a deadlock between the Provincial and Central Governments. His importance would tend to diminish, for, as in all constitutionally governed countries, his powers, lying perpetually in abeyance, would atrophy. Ultimately his position would be not altogether unlike that of a Lord-Lieutenant in England. There would be no reason to have European Governors, even in the transitional stages, though it might be advisable for an Englishman to be Governor of those Provinces which contain the great ports, where there is a large foreign trading population, and the possibility of international complications.

Another reform, which needs considering before the

establishment of provincial autonomy, would deal with the matter of Government appointments. We have allowed the 'spoils' system to enter far too largely into Indian public life, and it would be advisable to entrust all appointments above a certain value to a special commission of which the Governor himself would be a member. In this way Ministers would be relieved from the continual importunities of their family and of their caste fellows, and though Nationalists might object to the innovation on general grounds they would probably be secretly relieved.

The problem of the Central Government would become simpler once its main function is understood to be that of agent for a number of autonomous provinces, and also of the Indian States. Ultimately the question of India's relationship with England will solve itself, for as soon as the provinces are able to govern themselves they will be too strong for the Secretary of State. England's duty will be to provide the proper machinery for setting up a Central Legislature and administration on the basis of these Provinces and States, and also to arrange for the maintenance of good government during the transition stage when the local governments are settling down to their work. Almost certainly the personnel of the Central Legislature should consist of delegates from the provincial governments and the States. Any system of direct election raises insuperable difficulties. Assuming that the principle of universal suffrage is adopted a Chamber of three hundred members would have to be based on constituencies numbering several hundred thousand electors. Such an arrangement in a backward country would be farcical, and would also put a premium on great wealth.

It is difficult to avoid something approaching dyarchy

in the Central Administration, for it seems desirable to retain three subjects under British control during a transitional period, the Army, the duty of negotiating with the Indian States, and the power of interference if the government breaks down in any province. Apart from these subjects the Central Government, organised perhaps on the system of standing committees like the provincial governments, might well carry on the other administrative duties such as the State railways, Customs, irrigation, etc. For the three subjects which are reserved a very definite time-limit might be placed. Probably few Nationalists, once they were convinced that the English intended Provincial autonomy to be a real and genuine transfer of authority, would oppose the temporary reservation of certain powers, nor would they object to the assignment of some fixed amount, say fifty crores, to the yearly expense of the army so long as the general control of finances was left to the Assembly, and it had the right to criticise or refuse any further demand from the military authorities. The question of the ultimate control of the armed police would also need consideration, but the writer believes that the intransigent attitude adopted by many prominent Indian politicians is due to our failure to show them clearly the steps by which we propose to reach a definite goal, and that the relations between the Central Government and the Secretary of State would dwindle into comparative unimportance as soon as it was understood that where autonomy had been granted it was real and complete.

CHAPTER II

## INDUSTRIAL DEVELOPMENT

In the first chapter of this book Indian public life was compared with a stage upon which a few actors played before a vast and silent audience. In those subsequent chapters which dealt with the growth of Nationalism, its aspirations, its struggles, its failures, and its hopes of success one must never forget Sita Ram, the ryot, who has been sitting quietly, like Christopher Sly, watching the drama being performed for his benefit, and wondering perhaps 'Do I dream, or have I dreamed till now?' We must not do as Shakespeare did, and become so engrossed in the play that we forget its purpose, and allow the characters of the Induction to be bundled ignominiously off the stage. Let us assume that Katherina and Petruchio have settled their disputes, that political reforms have been put into operation, that the Indian educated classes have forgotten their quarrel with England, and that the machinery of government is working smoothly. Greatly daring, let us imagine that the wisest Indians are at the head of affairs, and that the deadening effects of racial animosity and religious communalism are but memories of the past. The political play is over, and we turn to the audience. Is Christopher Sly to become a lord or remain a drunken tinker? Is Sita Ram to become a prosperous and independent cultivator or remain a starved and ignorant drudge?

The real problems of modern India are social and economic. They spring to the eye of the most casual observer. The general standard of living is appallingly low, housing and sanitation are bad, the people generally engulfed in an ignorance of which illiteracy is but a small part, millions are perpetually degraded by the caste system, and others suffer as the result of certain evil social habits. There is an immense waste of energy and time owing to the lack of employment amongst the educated classes, and in every class there is a narrowness and stringency of life which kills ambition and destroys hope. In considering how far these evils can be mitigated by public and private endeavour, it must be remembered that less than a century ago none of them would have been considered as coming within the scope of State action. Public health only became a matter of political interest in England towards the middle of the Victorian era. Disraeli's joke about 'Sanitas Sanitatum, omnia Sanitas' dates the change. School boards were not established till 1870, and compulsory education followed some years later. State housing and government action to mitigate unemployment are even more recent innovations. The old doctrine of *laissez-faire* naturally died hard in India, and modern politicians are often guilty of an absurd anachronism when they blame the early English administrators for not introducing social reforms into India at a time when similar experiments in England were being tried tentatively, and in the face of much opposition. A single generation has seen a considerable revolution in our ideas about the duties of the State, but it was inevitable that in India, where there is a permanent opposition, the Nationalists should assume from the first that the Government can cope with every evil and satisfy every need. Much of this is mere propaganda, but it has had the unfortunate effect of deadening the incentive for industrial development and also for social reform amongst the Indian educated classes. Although most responsible Indian politicians and all administrators would agree that there are very definite limitations to State activities in the East, yet an atmosphere has been created which will force an autonomous Government to undertake many rash experiments, and which must lead ultimately to a period of disillusionment. On a smaller scale this has occurred recently in Ireland, and it is perhaps an inevitable and salutary stage in a country's development.

Most of India's social problems turn ultimately upon the status and condition of her peasants, for not only do they form the great bulk of the population, but the remainder are for the most part dependent upon them. Some of these difficulties can only be solved by a change of outlook, a kind of renaissance such as Turkey, and to a less extent Persia, have experienced since the War. Others are mainly economic, and these lead one back to the pressure on the land and the means whereby this can be relieved. The standard of wages in factories is governed by the amount necessary to tempt the poorer type of cultivator from his holding. The position of the village craftsmen depends upon their difficulty in getting land as an alternative occupation. Although the population of India is increasing slowly compared with most European countries or with Japan, there is a sufficient surplus each year from the rural areas to make it difficult to develop a higher standard of living either in the towns or the villages themselves.[1] India has to absorb about a

[1] Census of 1921, Vol. I, p. 7. The real increase is only about 20 per cent. in the last 50 years, but the influenza epidemic of 1918–19 has made the figures unduly small. Japan has increased 83 per cent. in 24 years, and England 39 per cent. in 40 years.

million and a half increase annually, and her great problem is to prevent her inhabitants being pressed down to the level of a family living entirely from a small plot of land, and a plot which tends each year to grow smaller.

Before discussing the various ways in which a solution to this difficulty may be found, it is necessary to say a few words about State finance. Every proposal is more or less dependent upon assistance from the Government, and it is often assumed that a change in the constitution will produce a large surplus which can be used for social improvements. As this question can only be treated in general terms it will be best to adopt the method of the yearly report on India, and combine the provincial and central budgets. The first question is how far the revenue can be expanded.

Apart from the railways, about half of which are managed by the State at a fair profit, the chief receipts are from Customs, land revenue, excise and income tax. There is a salt tax which has been much attacked because it falls on a necessity of the poor, but the 6 crores, which it brings in, form only 3 per cent. of the revenue. Most of the other smaller items, like the return from irrigation works, are not capable of much alteration. The alternatives would seem to be either increasing the four main heads of revenue, or finding new sources of income. Excise may be omitted because most keen Nationalists are vehemently opposed to the present policy which is really aimed at getting a maximum income from the drink trade. There is also a strong prohibitionist movement. If this was successful it would not only stop this source of revenue, but necessitate a large increase of expenditure on preventive measures.[1] Land revenue is a comparatively small proportion of the ryot's output, about 4 per cent in Madras and 8 per cent. in the Punjab, but Indian politicians have identified themselves with movements against small increases at the time of re-assessment, and it would be a bold Minister who would raise the amount taken directly from the cultivator in order to help his industry. India is, of course, a protectionist country, and the tendency will be to increase the tariffs still further, but the amount raised from customs cannot be increased indefinitely. Cotton manufactures and machinery are the most valuable imports, and any further tariffs on these will fall almost entirely on the consumer. Taxes on imported luxuries might well be increased, but it is doubtful whether the receipts would rise substantially. The demand for goods of this description varies very rapidly with the price. The most elastic item on the revenue side is the Income Tax, which at present brings in under 10 per cent. of the total. There is no doubt that the successful business and professional men are much too lightly taxed, but no one with any practical experience of assessing direct taxation in India is likely to under-estimate the practical difficulties of obtaining money from shopkeepers and *sowkars*. It would seem that no very startling increase in revenue is likely to follow a change of Government, and that some of the effects of raising the tariffs must be counterbalanced by a reduction of the receipts from Excise and the Salt Tax. The other possible sources of

[1] The Bombay Government held an inquiry in 1928 about the loss of revenue which would follow prohibition. This was reckoned at 6 crores (£4,500,000), including the cost of prevention, an amount equal to 40 per cent. of the Provincial revenue.

income which would be considered by an autonomous Government are duties on agricultural exports, and the abolition of the Permanent Settlement in the *zemindari* areas. The first is open to the objection that it would probably injure the more enterprising type of ryot, and might throw some land out of cultivation. The second raises the difficult question whether democracy in India is likely to deal more severely with its landlords than democracy in England or France.

Most Indian politicians look to a lower expenditure rather than a higher revenue for the surplus which they will need. It is unfortunate that such questions as the reduction of the army and the cost of the administration have been so distorted by propaganda that it is difficult to form an independent opinion about them. Compared with any European country India has a cheap and unenterprising Government. This makes the framework of administration, the bare necessities of any State, seem unduly large, like the bones of a half-starved horse. Thus 'Police, Jails, and Justice' total 10 per cent. of the total expenditure. In a Budget well padded with the costs of social services, pensions and local grants this would seem a high proportion, but considered as a charge of under four annas per head of the population these Home Office expenses are very moderate, even for the present meagre services. The same argument applies to the military expenditure of about 54 crores, which forms 28 per cent. of the total. If the present proportion of British troops is to be maintained no further reduction is possible, for there is little doubt that if the army had to take the field again it would be nearly as badly equipped and as unprepared as in 1914. The only way in which substantial reductions could be made would be by altering the basis of the army, and retaining a force strong enough to keep order on the Frontier and within India, a possibility which was discussed in a previous chapter.

The other items which are open to criticism are the salaries paid to high officials, especially Europeans, and the amount spent on public buildings. It is most unfortunate that the British should have adopted the evil traditions of the Moghuls, and that the idea is now firmly embedded in the minds of many Indians that pomp and display are a necessary part of administration, and that officials should remain aloof from the people. There is a serious danger of bringing into existence a new Brahmanism, based on European standards of life, and separating its members as definitely from their fellow-countrymen as the old. An autonomous Government would have to resist a demand for larger salaries and larger staffs as well as having to cut down those which are already disproportionately high. The total reductions possible would only be in the nature of five or six crores a year, an amount which could perhaps be arranged by paying High Court Judges about Rs3,000 a month, and scaling down the other salaries. If the Provinces are broken up, it will be essential to reduce the number and importance of the officials. Such economies would, however, only be in the nature of 2 or 3 per cent., and it must be confessed that the first effects of 'Indianisation' have been to increase rather than reduce the number of offices, clerks, and the 'overhead expenses' of the administration. A liberal estimate of the economies possible by the conversion both of the army and the administration on to an Indian scale would be about 20 per cent. of the total expenditure.

Unless some revolutionary action is taken, equivalent to dispossessing the landlords without compensation, imposing a levy on capital, or repudiating the State debt, there can be no very large surplus available for expenditure upon social services. £30 million a year, or two shillings a head of the population, would be an extremely optimistic figure, only obtainable under very favourable circumstances, and by drastic economies which would cause much hardship amongst certain classes. A reduction in the army, for example, would increase the pressure on the land in the Punjab.

The activities of autonomous Provincial Governments and of the Central Government are likely to be severely limited financially, and the question will arise as to the best means of assisting the ryot. The first and strongest demand will be for assistance in developing commerce. The rural exodus in Western Europe and America is usually ascribed to the establishment of large-scale factories. This has led many Indian leaders to look upon Western industrial methods as the best way of relieving pressure on the land and improving the general standard of living. The obvious corollary was a demand for the assistance of existing industries by tariffs, subsidies, loans at low interest, and freedom from factory legislation.

At present Indian industrial development is not absorbing her surplus population. If every workshop employing over twenty men is reckoned as a factory, and many seasonal milling and ginning concerns are thus included, there are still under one and a half million men, women, and children who can be described as factory operatives. The number is sufficient to entitle India to be considered as one of the eight large industrial countries of the world, but the proportion of factory workers and their dependents to the rest of the population is infinitesimal, certainly little more than 1 per cent. There are still twice as many beggars as there are factory hands, and the progress of industry is slow and irregular. The textile and allied industries employ the largest number, but though they are developing, they only increase their staffs by about 5 per cent. yearly. The progress of the other industries, paper-making, brick-works, etc., is on the same scale. Unless there is a complete industrial revolution in India it will be many years before 2 per cent. of the population are engaged in large-scale production. At present the progress is so slow that only about 40,000 more workers are employed each year, and this can have no appreciable effect in absorbing the annual surplus from the rural areas.[1] Clearly Indian industry is doing nothing to relieve the increasing pressure on the land.

Although Government action in the past may have hindered large-scale production in India, it is not easy to see how any help from the State can bring about a rapid development. There are to-day only three industries employing more than 200,000 workers, – cotton, jute, and coal-mining – and the last two are financed and managed for the most part by foreigners. The cotton industry can be protected against imports, but at present only a quarter of these imports are in competition with the Indian producer. The remainder are the finer kinds of yarn and cloth, the demand for which drops rapidly with any in-

[1] Numbers employed in factories:

| | |
|---|---|
| 1923 . . . . | 1,409,173 |
| 1924 . . . . | 1,455,592 |
| 1925 . . . . | 1,494,958 |

crease of price. One may expect a gradual development into this latter field when a longer stapled cotton is produced in India, but no advance on the present tariff of 11 per cent. is likely to help the industry substantially. The mills of Bombay and Ahmedabad already depend far too much upon the advantage gained by the low rate of wages paid, and the sixty strikes which have occurred in that area during the last year suggest that this item in the cost of production is likely to rise rather than fall. Short of a system of bounties which the Government could never afford, or the granting of loans at an easy rate to an industry which is already over-capitalised, it is difficult to see how the most sympathetic Government is going to accelerate the development of the cotton industry.

Perhaps the best example of the limitations which economic facts set to Government assistance can be seen in the history of the steel industry since the War. The founding of Tata's works at Jamshedpur is one of the romances of Indian commerce, for it is less than twenty years since the late J. N. Tata decided upon an unknown Santali village as the site for his factory. Most other Indian industries have sprung up in a haphazard fashion near the great cities. These new iron and steel works started with a clear field in a district close to iron, coal, and good water. The directors sought all over the world for efficient managers, and have always used the most modern plant and methods. Here were the leadership and power of organisation so often lacking in India. The Company could obtain skilled labour at about Rs3 a day, and unskilled at twelve annas. We have the evidence of their General Manager, Mr. Tutwiler, that the hands trained in his works were fully competent to replace British workers.[1] The War brought them some very large contracts for railway material at lucrative rates. They received a Government order after the War on very favourable terms for all the steel rails which they could produce. In 1922 their position was further strengthened by a Customs duty of 10 per cent. on imported steel and iron, railway plant and rolling stock. In spite of low wages and protection the firm found itself unable to stand on its own feet. A series of bounties were given to the steel industry from 1924 onwards, and the tariff was again raised. In September, 1925, Sir Charles Innes stated in the Legislative Assembly that this one company had received bounties amounting to 20,300,000 rupees, and the benefit of a protective tariff which had cost the country about 1½ crores of rupees. The details of the Protective policy adopted by the Government has been the subject of much criticism, but the outstanding fact remains that an industry, starting with every apparent advantage, employing labour at rates about a fifth of those paid by its foreign competitors, and receiving considerable protection from tariffs, still needs to be financially supported by the Government. It is true that the firm has suffered from labour troubles, but that fact rather strengthens the general conclusion that nothing except a measure of protection which would hold up all railway construction for some years, and would place an intolerable burden on other industries, is likely to bring any real measure of prosperity to this key industry.

Most of the smaller industries in India are subsidiary

[1] Evidence before Industrial Commission, Vol. II, Cmd. 235 of 1919.

to agriculture. Over half of the 7,000 factories are engaged in some seasonal operation, like jute pressing, cotton ginning, oil and rice milling, etc. There would not seem to be much room for further development of these except in the newly-developed areas. In the older tracts, especially in Burma, the rice mills are already too numerous,[1] though in other districts the Linlithgow Report considers that the mills could be increased. There are, of course, many new openings for minor industries, but the Indian capitalist class shows little inclination to embark upon such enterprises, or even to invade such established industries as jute which are mostly in European hands. The landowners prefer to invest their money in the traditional manner. The Marwaris and other wealthy business communities are too fond of purely speculative ventures, and there is a tendency to leave, either to the Government or to foreigners, the work of building up the industries which are not immediately profitable. Possibly agricultural co-operation will ultimately force the large money-lending class to invest their money in productive industry, but the process will be very slow, and it would seem that no Government action, short of starting and financing speculative commercial ventures, is likely to cause any rapid development of India's minor industries.

It is possible that the Government's recent currency policy may have injured the large producers, but they have had plenty of time to adapt themselves to the higher value of the rupee. If this was lowered to, say, 1*s*. 4*d*., it might give a temporary stimulus to industry, but only at the expense of the wage-earners. In a short time costs would again adapt themselves to the altered value. The

[1] Census Report of 1921.

factors which prevent the economic progress of India cannot be altered by juggling with the exchange. The same limitations govern the future of State participation in industry, a policy which the British administrators in India, though usually reputed Conservative in politics, have sometimes encouraged to an extent which would be considered very advanced in England. From the days of the East India Company the Government suffered from the difficulty of getting local supplies for the army and for the administration. It was forced to open its own factories, and it now has workshops for the State railways, makes saddlery in Cawnpore and ammunition in several arsenals. It does its own printing, and the Public Works Departments makes bricks and tiles, and does much work by direct labour which in England is normally given out to contractors. The Forestry Department sells lac and other products worth three or four millions annually, and shows a considerable profit on its working. The Government has also experimented with various commercial processes, and in 1905, when Sir John Hewitt was Director of the new Department of Commerce and Industry, factories were started for making aluminium goods, for chrome tanning, and other technical work. In 1908 the Madras Government proposed a great extension of such commercial ventures, but further enterprise was checked by Lord Morley. Following the true Liberal tradition, he would only allow State expenditure upon

'familiarising the people with such improvements in the methods of production as modern science and the practice of European countries can suggest; further than this the State should not go, and it must be left to private enterprise to demonstrate that these improvements can be adopted with commercial advantage'.[1]

Old-fashioned Liberalism thus placed a heavy foot upon an interesting experiment, and though the War caused some revival of such State enterprises, the Government's activities are normally confined to giving expert advice and to demonstrations. It is doubtful if any large body of Indian opinion would be in favour of extending such State incursions into the field of competitive commerce. There is, however, a very general demand for the investment of public money in private enterprises, and, as this policy has been advocated by most Indian leaders, an autonomous Provincial Government would be forced to experiment in this direction. There are two obvious objections to such a policy. It is difficult for the Government to exercise any real control over the firm in which it has invested money, and if the system was extended it would mean that the Government was using its ability to borrow money in the foreign market at a reasonable rate in order to finance ventures which were not sufficiently safe or remunerative to attract private capital. The inevitable result would be the lowering of its credit, and either a higher rate of interest would have to be charged upon the industry, or the difference be met by the taxpayer. The tentative experiments of certain Provincial Governments in making such investments have not been very fortunate, and acceptance of the principle would undoubtedly expose a popular Government to very strong pressure from interested business men, and lay them

[1] Despatch No. 50, Revenue, 29th July, 1910. See Pillai, *Economic Conditions in India*, p. 311.

open to political blackmail from men with wild-cat schemes.

Apart from this doubtful policy of direct investment, an Indian Government might assist industry by the mobilisation of savings, and by encouraging a different banking system. Though the extent of hoarding in India has often been exaggerated, and at the highest estimate does not exceed Rs.25 per head· there is a great field for extending banking facilities, and for encouraging the small investor. Some good work has been done by the Post Office Savings Bank, which has two million depositors with some twenty millions in their accounts. The resources of the Co-operative Banks are stated to total 50 crores.[1] There is, however, a great need for developing the type of business now handled by Shroffs, Mahajans, and Chetties, most of whom operate in the towns. Barely 10 per cent. of the 2,253 Indian towns with over 5,000 inhabitants are served by the banking systems of the country. One of the arguments advanced in favour of the much debated Reserve Bank was that it would leave the Imperial Bank of India freer to extend banking facilities throughout India. Unfortunately the history of Indian joint-stock banks has not been very encouraging, and a middle course seems necessary between the conservative methods of the English banks and the speculative course of action adopted by the People's Bank, the Indian Specie Bank, and other ventures which ended in liquidation. It would probably be best to model Indian banking on German or Japanese lines, with power to underwrite issues and to place loans, and even to float new companies instead of leaving India to the mercy of the company

[1] Report on Moral and Material Progress, 1925–26, p. 292.

promoter. Unfortunately any proposals for reorganising Indian banking are complicated by a number of political considerations, and by the extreme 'touchiness' of Indian opinion on the subject of indigenous banking.

An extension of industry and the absorption of men from the rural areas are not the only advantages which might follow from more large-scale production. In England and other industrial countries a rise in the general standard of living has resulted from the higher wages which were paid in the industrial centres, and from the discipline and self-reliance which follow from trade-union organisation. The parallel is only partly true of India. An improvement in factory conditions, though urgently needed, cannot have much general effect in a country where so few work for wages, and there are special reasons which make it difficult to get any sympathetic response from the employers. In India, that land of paradoxes, the immediate effect of a rise in wages is to reduce the supply of labour. Most operatives look upon their factory work as a temporary occupation by which they can earn certain sums of money which they need for their families and for life in their villages. If they can earn the money quicker than they expected, then fate is kind and they can escape the sooner. Thus, instead of an increase in wages acting as a stimulus, and leading to a rise in the standard of living, the first result is often that the workers drift away from the mills quicker and stay away longer. Taking a long view, which is difficult for the individual mill-owner to do, high wages will ultimately bring a settled population round each factory, and it might be possible to get a more stable type of workman. Shorter hours and better conditions will also increase output, but such improvements will only come from State action or from the growth and improvement of the trade-union movement. The weakness of the trade-union movement has been discussed in a previous chapter. It is probable that the exploitation of workers for political purposes is only a passing phase of nationalism, but it must be remembered that the number of men available for union organisation is proportionately very small, and unions will have little political power unless they can enlist the sympathy of the ryot. Otherwise their only weapons will be their ability to hold up certain vital services, like the railways, and the pressure which they can bring upon the individual employer.

In case this chapter may seem unduly pessimistic about the future of large-scale production and the possible relief which it may bring to the cultivators, it may be worth quoting a few figures dealing with the drift from the country into the towns. During the thirty years from 1891 to 1921 the number of factories increased fivefold. The number of operatives rose from 316,000 to nearly a million and a half. The rural population, however, remained almost exactly the same proportion of the total population. It was 90·5 per cent. in 1891 and 89·8 per cent. in 1921, and the actual number of people living in villages (defined as having less than 5,000 inhabitants) had risen by nearly 24 millions. From these figures it seems clear that large-scale production would have to increase at a rate out of all proportion to its present progress if it is to have any appreciable effect in reducing the pressure on land. At present it does little more than absorb the increase in the urban population. For reasons suggested above, this rapid change is unlikely to occur whatever political transformations may take place. It must also be remembered that any relief which the agricultural community might receive, being in the nature of 1 or 2 per cent. of its surplus population, would easily be swallowed up by a very slight decrease in the rate of infant mortality or be nullified by the injury which the cultivator would suffer from a high industrial tariff. It does not seem that Sita Ram the ryot is going to be saved either by being transported to an industrial centre, or by a higher standard of living amongst the urban workers. One must turn to remedies which deal with him, and also with the craftsmen, by helping them in their own villages.

## CHAPTER III

# THE FUTURE OF THE RYOT

THE general policy of drawing the surplus population from the countryside into industrial centres would appear to be an inadequate, slow, and expensive method of relieving either the pressure on the land or the poverty of the cultivators and village craftsmen. The alternative is to deal with the rural population without uprooting the countryman, without, in the words of Mr. A. C. Chatterjee, making him 'travel long distances, in many cases hundreds of miles, to tracts where a different language, a different climate, and an entirely different environment confront him, in addition to the strangeness of unfamiliar, continuous, and sometimes dangerous work in closed buildings and areas'. The most practical methods which suggest themselves are helping village industries, supporting the ryot financially, increasing the area available for cultivation, encouraging intensive farming, assisting migration and emigration to other agricultural land, and improving local administration. British policy has tended to concentrate on these agricultural developments, partly for selfish reasons, because the English have always looked upon India to supply raw materials, but also because most administrators find the countryside problem more interesting and more hopeful than that of the towns. The Indian politician, who has a distinct urban bias, naturally ascribes the worst possible motives to the Government, and it is one of the unfortunate results of foreign occupation that a period of disillusionment will be necessary in India, as well as in Ireland, before the politicians discover that the hardest problem of all is to make a country of small farmers prosperous.

A very important report upon Indian agriculture was issued in July, 1928, by a Commission under the chairmanship of the Marquess of Linlithgow. It is a valuable document containing a useful analysis of the position, but the Commission find no royal road to prosperity, and have few suggestions for Government action except on the lines of research and propaganda. Anyone acquainted with agricultural conditions in England and India must have foreseen that the report would be along these lines, for the problem of the Indian ryot is not unlike that of the Russian peasant and the Irish small farmer. The urge for improvement must come from the villagers themselves, and the administrator's problem is to help them to help themselves. The Commission could not discuss the interesting question whether this new spirit on the part of the governed as well as the governors was more likely to develop under a more definitely Indian administration. The main lines of advance may be best considered under separate headings.

### 1. VILLAGE INDUSTRIES

The resuscitation of village industries in India is not the sentimental and uneconomic business which we are apt to connect in England with the making of unwanted raffia work and the keeping of Angora rabbits. The present position of the full-time craftsmen was discussed in a previous chapter, and it was suggested that though their position had deteriorated to the level of the poorer cultivators they seemed to have reached their nadir and were now holding their own. They live on in the villages, bring up their sons to their trade, and show no marked tendency either to die out, take up other occupations, or drift into the towns. There is not the least reason to suppose that the next generation will see any appreciable alteration in their numbers – 8 to 10 million men and their dependents. There is an immense field here for the work of a really sympathetic Government. The craftsmen have two great needs, which are intimately connected with each other. They require financial assistance to relieve them from the toils of the *mahajans* or middlemen. They also want better and more modern implements and some training in their use. Much could be done by co-operation to relieve them from debt, or at any rate to regularise their debt, but the field for co-operative selling is more restricted. The Indian craftsman, unlike the Indian ryot, has to sell his produce in a market where there is considerable foreign competition, especially if he is a weaver. Co-operative selling agencies will therefore meet the same difficulties as are experienced by English farmers when they combine to market their goods. The craftsmen's work is on the borderline of being uneconomic, but the same is true of the Indian steel industry. It should be recognised that the small workshop is bound to be a permanent part of Indian industrial life, and that a certain measure of help is owing to the craftsman after a century of neglect. There is nothing reactionary in this idea, and it is worth remarking that in a typically agricultural but highly civilised country like Denmark 80 per cent. of the industrial establishments employ less than five workers apiece.

The immediate need is for small technical schools where young craftsmen can learn the use of the flying shuttle for hand weaving and of other modern tools for carpentry and the smithy. Advances for purchasing such implements would probably have to be made through societies, and support is needed from the Government to see that the small workshop is not hampered by the new tariff policy. India has adopted fiscal protection at the behest of large-scale producers, and their tariffs may frequently injure the handicraftsmen, who are at present politically impotent. Already this difficulty has occurred owing to the imposition, in 1922, of a 5 per cent. duty on cotton yarn. The extra cost fell, almost entirely, upon the handloom workers who are the chief users of foreign yarn. They were, of course, too weak economically to hand on the increased charge. Similarly the present arrangement is that some, but not all, agricultural implements are imported free of duty. Thus power-driven machinery for crushing sugar-cane and making sugar is admitted free, but not such as is worked by hand.[1] The ryot therefore gets certain implements cheap, but for others he must usually pay the full amount of the tariff, and when he wants repairs done by his village *lohar* he or the craftsman will have to pay the extra 15 per cent. on the iron or steel. The present policy, therefore, hurts the ryot a little and the smiths a great deal, and it will hold up the development of that most hopeful of village industries, the making and repairing of agricultural machinery and implements.

An improvement in the position of the village craftsman would only help the cultivator indirectly by providing for him a better local market for his produce. There seems little prospect of developing that other important type of

[1] Linlithgow Report, p. 115.

village industry, the spare-time occupation, the *Nebenbeschaeftigung* which plays such an important part in German rural life. There is not the least doubt that such work is badly needed, especially in the dry-crop areas where the ryot has much less than six months' work to do in his fields. Mr. Mukerjee,[1] who is perhaps an enthusiast in this matter, suggests basket-making, rural woodwork, bamboo and straw weaving, but to an English country dweller most of these have a painfully familiar sound. Only in a few parts of India does the villager seem to have the energy to tackle more than one job, and the extremely small number of cultivators who undertake weaving or spinning has already been noted.[2] The land worker prefers a secondary occupation not too unlike his ordinary work. Just as it is best to help the craftsman in his own shop, so it is difficult to raise the status of the cultivator except through his holding.

### 2. FINANCIAL HELP FOR THE RYOT

It is most improbable that any future Government will reduce substantially the amount which the cultivator pays directly to the State. With all the 'nation-building' departments crying out for money, and local bodies developing their activities and demanding larger grants, few Provincial Governments are likely to abandon a source of revenue for which such elaborate machinery already exists. A popular Government will, of course, be subjected to considerable pressure, for most of the prominent politicians have identified themselves, more or less, with the refusal to pay the higher assessment in Bardoli. Probably some alterations will have to be made, for the

[1] *Rural Economy of India*, p. 236. [2] See p. 38.

land revenue offends against modern ideas. It is based on acreage, and so takes the same proportionate amount irrespective of the ryot's capacity to pay, but grading would be difficult, for it would be very easy to multiply the number of small holdings by dividing up those at present held under the joint family system.

A more hopeful line of attack is to help the ryot in his struggle against those great sources of financial trouble, debt and dependence on middlemen. The machinery for this purpose, the co-operative movement and the system of *takkavi* or loans, is already in existence. It only needs development. The experience of the last fifty years has shown that legislation directed against the moneylender and the middleman seldom achieve its object, nor is it likely to be more effective under a popular Government, with a full proportion of lawyers in the Assemblies. The solution lies in building up separate and alternative institutions by which the ryot can market his produce and finance his little business. So far only the latter side of co-operation has been developed, yet India is a country admirably suited for co-operative selling. It has a considerable export trade, and there is no import trade in agricultural produce to give the middleman that immensely powerful lever which he possesses in England. In many parts of India there is considerable buying of cotton, jute, and wheat by foreign firms, usually through the agency of innumerable *beparis*, *mahajans*, and other petty dealers. All of this could be done cheaper and more efficiently through 'pools' and societies, but on this point, where the Linlithgow Report was expected to take an original line, the Commission does little more than commend the Berar system of regulated markets for the cotton trade, and the Bombay legislation for controlling the establishment of unauthorised markets. The whole trend of modern agricultural organisation suggests that, for the export trade, markets should be eliminated and not encouraged, and, for the home market, towns should own and manage their own markets by committees upon which growers are represented.

The other side of co-operation, the granting of loans to members, has made definite headway. Initiated by an Act of 1904 co-operation on the Raffeisen plan has advanced rapidly in the *ryotwari* areas, but the progress is much slower in the *zemindari* districts, owing to the tenants having no land to pledge. So far the movement has set up an efficient rival to the *sowkar* rather than driven him from the field, and there have been areas where it might be said that the new societies, with their enhanced power of distraint, were only the old *bunniah* 'writ large'. Ultimately, however, the new societies will tend to drive the moneylenders, with their large reserves of capital, into more productive fields, a change which will be of great service to industry and the State.

India has undoubtedly suffered from being under the control of a foreign power which has always been backward in the organisation of its agricultural marketing. Just as co-operative banking is an import from Germany, so India will have to look to Denmark or to the Dominions for a model in co-operative marketing. Probably the 'pool' system would suit India best, all produce for export being collected and graded by a single authority, and the total receipts divided according to quantity and grade. An attempt has been made to work a co-operative jute-selling agency, but its history suggests that such bodies should have a semi-official status. They need capital, for deferred payments are the weak feature of many co-operative ventures. They also should be given a virtual monopoly, for if the matter is left to voluntary efforts, the present middlemen will fight the 'pool' in every direct and indirect way, and would probably win. Public bodies like Port Authorities or City Improvement Trusts would be the best model to follow, for they should be open to criticism and have a certain standing, so as to prevent disputes about the management. The State, as supreme landlord, has every right to bring pressure to bear on cultivators to dispose cotton, wheat, jute and other produce through specified channels. Home produce could be sold in municipal markets. Along such lines the ryots might be relieved of many of their business difficulties, but the necessary changes could only be made by a very autocratic Government, or by one which is controlled by the cultivators themselves. It might have been done fifty years ago, now it may be necessary to wait for another fifty.

### 3. INCREASING THE AREA OF CULTIVATION

The simplest and most direct method of relieving pressure on cultivated land is to extend the area, for this, unlike industrial development, involves no change of occupation. Statistics for the Indian States are incomplete, but taking British India alone there are just under 280 million acres cultivated, but of these about 45 millions are current fallow each year. There are another 152 millions of 'culturable waste', and about the same area of land classed as not available for cultivation. There has been considerable divergence of opinion about the extent to which these latter areas could be brought into use.

The Linlithgow Report states that much of the 'culturable waste' could 'in no conceivable circumstances be brought under tillage'.[1] There is probably little land in the west which is fit for dry farming, and not brought under the plough. Those who know the Deccan have seen how the plough-land creeps up the hill-side till it includes land so stony and thin that it will barely return the seed which has been sown. In other districts the pressure on land is not so intense, but over most of India dry farming has usually reached and sometimes overstepped the 'starvation acres' which mark the limit of soil bringing in a reasonable return. This was apparent after the War when the Government had to redeem its pledge, and find land for returned soldiers. Outside the new irrigation areas, and the Brahmaputra valley in Assam it was difficult to find any worth having. The missionaries and others who are trying to settle the landless outcastes and criminal tribes experience the same difficulty. The Forest Department still holds some land in the plains, but they have already released 3,000 square miles out of 5,500. The Linlithgow Report suggests a fresh inquiry into the deforestation of land which is under 'scrub' jungle, but the total area affected is probably under 1 per cent. of the existing cultivated area, and much of the land very poor.

Any considerable extension of cultivation in India would seem to be dependent on irrigation. There are two main types, according to whether the land is watered by 'flow' from canals, or 'lift' from wells. The first is naturally the most satisfactory, and there are some 28 million acres thus irrigated either from the perennial rivers of the North, or else from the huge storage 'tanks'

[1] Linlithgow Report, p. 605.

in Madras and the Deccan. Progress along these lines has been considerably accelerated lately, and there are five large schemes on which work has been begun. The Sukkur Barrage should irrigate 3 million acres of uncultivated land, and improve a further 2 million. The Sutlej Valley project should reach another $3\frac{3}{4}$ million acres. The Cauvery Reservoir and the new dams to supply the Pravara and Nira canals will turn about a million acres of poor 'dry' land into irrigated land. There are several minor schemes in every Province, and it would probably be right to accept the official estimate that when all projects under construction are in working order the total area of 'flow' irrigation will be 40 million acres, and this may 'ultimately' be extended to 50 million.[1] Against this must be set the undoubted danger that further irrigation may raise the water level in irrigated areas, and 'salt them up', a process which probably ruined Mesopotamia and which is already causing serious alarm in the Punjab.

Although these large irrigation schemes bring malaria in their train, they afford at present the most effective relief to the pressure on the land. Apart from the large demands for labour in their construction, another 12 million acres of irrigated land would allow the settlement of at least a million cultivators and their families. In most cases the new areas will be land which was previously bare desert, and if we may judge from the history of Lyallpur the cultivators will bring with them, not only their 2 or 3 million dependents, but also a number of craftsmen and shopkeepers. If these areas can be opened up within a decade the new colonies should absorb most of India's surplus population.

[1] Report of Moral and Material Progress, 1925–26, p. 271.

It is frequently asserted that this irrigation work would have been undertaken more rapidly under a popular Government. It is undoubtedly true that many schemes, which are classed as 'unproductive' because the returns would not cover the interest charges, might have been undertaken on national grounds. Part of the expenses would fall on the taxpayer, but as a means of relieving pressure on the land these irrigation works are clearly more effective than industrial development. The amount spent since the War in bolstering up the steel industry by bounties and tariffs is reckoned at six to eight crores, but it only supports about 30,000 men. The Sukkur Barrage scheme costs about twice as much, but will provide considerably over ten times as many men with fifteen-acre holdings, and be permanently remunerative.

The extension of 'lift' irrigation will not relieve pressure on the land in this way. Watering from a seepage well is a gardener's occupation, and a cultivator who grows ordinary field crops in this way is at a hopeless disadvantage. In most cases he is working a small area of old land, and the best use to which he can put his limited supply of water is to grow vegetables and special crops. For such seasonal work little improvement is possible on the leather *mot*, pulled by the plough bullock, which so upsets the economic soul of every Scotsman when he first visits India. Where, however, there is an inexhaustible supply, as from bore wells or wells connected with rivers, power pumps are more practical, but there are certain difficulties experienced equally on the banks of the Tigris and the Tungabudra. Oil pumping plants are not easy to keep running in hot dusty weather, and one day's breakdown will ruin the crop. The *takkavi* system of loans is already in existence for those who wish to invest in mechanical plant.

There are some 13 million acres under wells. The extension of this system should be encouraged, but the effect will be to convert part of the present dry-crop land into market-gardening plots, rather than to bring new land under cultivation. It means more intensive farming of the old land by the old ryots. The same is true of the small 'tanks', mostly dating from pre-British days, which are found in many parts of Madras and the Deccan. These tend to silt up, and with the decay of village life they have been allowed to fall out of repair. Improvements under this head come really into the next section, which deals with intensive farming.

### 4. INTENSIVE CULTIVATION

Most townsmen assume that it is the countryman's duty to produce as much as possible from each acre. As the former write nearly all the books this rather one-sided idea is generally accepted, but there is really no moral reason why the ryot should spend a rupee to get back twelve annas, any more than a manufacturer need produce goods which he cannot sell except at a loss. The only intensive farming that need be considered is such as will pay its way. This cuts out many proposals which find their way into books by economists and speeches by politicians. The activities of agricultural departments are of great value to the man with a large holding, but they leave the typical small ryot unmoved. The wealthier peasants, corresponding to the *kulaks* of Russia, work with an eye upon the export trade and the large cities. Ploughs which are too heavy for half-starved bullocks, cottons with longer staples, wheats suitable for machine milling, all these interest him more than they do the typical ryot with two acres of land upon which he has to grow food for his family, and have something over to sell. He cannot stimulate his hard-worked soil with nitrates at £12 a ton. Within a generation or two there seems no prospect of giving him more land. The only person likely to teach the ryot how to support a family and pay his taxes off a little plot of land is the man who can do the job himself. There seems only one hope for the poorer ryots, they must learn from the Chinese, who for centuries have been faced with the same problem and solved it.

The Chinaman's secret is fairly simple. It does not go far beyond the Southern Indian saying about 'lots of water and old muck'. The ryot with a small plot must use market-garden methods, at any rate on part of his land. He must save and use intelligently every scrap of available manure. He must allow no waste. This formula may seem simple, but it means reorganising village life, jettisoning a host of religious scruples, and revolutionising most people's domestic habits. At present the village cattle pick up their living from the jungle, or from the fallows which for this purpose are left unploughed, and thus lose nearly all the advantage of being cleaned and 'rested'. Most of the cattle are useless, their only valuable product being their manure, which is either wasted or made into cakes and burnt. Human excreta and the village sweepings are ceremonially unclean. Now the Chinaman attends to these unpleasant details. He sees that there are no idle mouths in the village, and that every scrap of waste product is carefully stored and applied to the field in proper condition. By these methods they have retained, century after century, the fertility of their little plots. They have, as farmers say, kept 'heart' in the land. Only in the new and virgin areas of India is this true, the rest is reduced to that low level which will produce small crops without much further deterioration. The Chinaman's land remains easy to work, so that he can grow a variety of crops, and use part of his holding for the more expensive and difficult vegetables and other crops which can be sold for cash in small quantities.

A ryot who wished to imitate such methods would find that his religion, if Hindu, prevents him managing his cattle on European lines. The village would object to his storing certain kinds of waste product. A shortage of wood tempts him to burn manure – a difficulty which the Linlithgow Report would partly meet by cheapening the freights on firewood from the Forest Department,[1] and by establishing village forests in suitable areas. Marketing difficulties discourage the ryot from growing small quantities of tobacco and other 'cash crops'. If these difficulties could be overcome, not only would each holding become more productive, but there should be no need to leave a fifth of the land fallow. A few good cattle would be worth feeding on specially grown fodder crops which could be supplemented, as in Europe, by dried grass or silage from crops or grass. Unfortunately silage, for which the Linlithgow Report foretells a great future,[2] is not very well suited for working bullocks, and a revolution in cattle-keeping will have to precede its widespread use for milking cows. It is also a method for the larger holdings, unless villages can combine to use the same silo. It is not practical to make silage in small quantities, but there are also

[1] See Report, p 264. [2] *Ibid.*, p. 206.

considerable reserves of dried grass which could be made available with proper organisation, and the small ryot, if he could be persuaded to adopt a new outlook on his cattle and his manure, should have no need to leave a fifth of his land fallow. The hot sun makes weeding easy, and the land can be kept clean without bare fallowing.

The advantage of introducing, what may be described as Chinese methods, is that they require no expenditure, public or private, except that the Forest Department should consider the supply of firewood and dried grass as one of its chief functions, and the railways should reduce their freights. The other changes necessary are in the mentality of the ryots themselves. The history of most countries shows that such popular revivals usually owe much to the driving force of a few trusted and disinterested individuals. Denmark in the middle of the nineteenth century had sunk into a miserable condition, her peasantry, we are told by Mary Woolstonecraft, seemed 'averse to innovation', they kept few cattle, fewer pigs, and according to a reliable writer 'had no idea of keeping poultry'. A handful of enthusiasts found the necessary formula for success, and had the energy to force their countrymen to accept it. In India the problem is infinitely harder, and there is an unfortunate lack of enlightened landlords who will do the work of Coke of Norfolk. British officials have sometimes had great influence over rather backward peoples, Outram and the Bhils being the classic example, and an extremely interesting experiment is being carried on in the Gurgaon district by Mr. Brayne amongst the very feckless Meos. It would seem, however, that the racial question will now prevent any widespread movement based on the missionary zeal of the English, and a popular government, with the courage to tackle both priest and peasant, might accomplish more than any number of voluntary associations and agricultural experts. Such a Government might be able to apply that element of compulsion which is so often necessary, and it is a significant fact that the only instance of such compulsion is not in British India, but in the State of Rajpipla, where certain regulations are laid down about the growing of cotton. Some one has to instil into the Indian peasantry the will to work, to rebuild their houses, clean their streets, clear out their 'tanks', forget a hundred foolish inhibitions, learn a few new ideas. It is not surprising that many intelligent Indians, while they play at politics as the best means to get rid of the English, think more and more about Lenin, Mussolini, Kemal Pasha, and King Amanullah.

### 5. MIGRATION AND EMIGRATION

The very dense population in certain agricultural districts suggests that some relief from the pressure on the land might be obtained by a better distribution of the population. The difficulty experienced by certain industries in obtaining labour would also point to a disinclination to try 'fresh woods and pastures new'. An examination of the census reports hardly bears out this idea of the static population. Movements between provinces usually entail a different climate, and a change of language, but they are on a very considerable scale. Bengal, with its increasing industrial and mining development, received nearly 2 million emigrants from other provinces between 1911 and 1921, but a third of that number left her. Most of the latter went to Assam, where the Brahmaputra valley provides one of the few large areas of waste land which is really worth cultivating. This attraction, combined with the prosperity of the tea gardens, brought Assam a million immigrants. This was a healthy movement, for most of the new colonists came from overcrowded districts like Mymensingh, and settled in sparsely inhabited areas. The other movements, however, are usually from bad land to good land, or from the Mofussil to the larger cities, and the tendency is towards concentration rather than distribution. The shortage of labour in industrial areas is due to the Indian's natural disinclination to 'stay put' in poor surroundings, rather than to any unwillingness to migrate. Disease, ignorance, and the moneylender combine to keep the villager at home, but the Punjabi is a born pioneer and the Tamils of the South have emigrated in large numbers to Ceylon and Malay.

The future of Indian emigration is very uncertain. At present it is on too small a scale to have much effect. Of the 2,282,000 Indians resident outside India, a million and a half are in Ceylon and British Malaya, both of which have for many years received Tamil-speaking immigrants from South India. The other Indians abroad have generally gone as 'assisted' labourers or as traders, but since 1917 the former type of emigration, which gave rise to great abuses, has been very strictly controlled, and very few are now going to Mauritius, South Africa, Trinidad, or British Guiana. Of these countries British Guiana is the only one which is capable of absorbing further emigrants from India. Sir Cecil Rodwell, the Governor, considers that the population could be increased from about 300,000 to 3 millions by extending the area of sugar-growing and plantations and that the only available source is India.

All development, however, is in the hands of European planters, and the formation of another Indian Labour Colony is a doubtful blessing. The old indentured labour was a failure, and was practically abolished in 1917, since which date over 2 million Indians have returned. Future movements depend upon the policy adopted by countries like Australia, Brazil, and others with large undeveloped areas. Whether these would be more disposed to admit emigrants from an autonomous India is a question too conjectural to be worth discussing, though this view is widely held by Indian politicians. The main objection to Indian emigrants is their tendency to lower the standard of living, but this is only true of certain classes. The Sikhs and other northern Indians in Canada and elsewhere make excellent pioneer settlers.

### 6. IMPROVING LOCAL ADMINISTRATION

One of the indirect disadvantages of the British occupation has been that so many social questions are considered with a political bias, and in India a political question is never free from racial bitterness. Taxation and expenditure on social services become inextricably confused with the cost of the army, high European salaries, and the poverty of the ryot. The Government has followed the line of least resistance, and collected taxes for the general administration, but troubled little about the money which in most countries is raised and spent locally on amenities such as roads, lighting, water supplies and sanitation, the type of expenditure which in England is met by the rates. The Indian ryot pays a negligible amount to his local authority, and receives very little in return. In this matter comparisons between India and industrial

European countries are useless, but they can fairly be made between India and the agricultural parts of Italy and Japan. Statistics were collected shortly before the War for two villages of the same population and size in Madras and Italy. The Government land revenue was much the same in each case, but Kanatalapalli in Madras paid Rs.250 in local cess, and Torre San Patrizia about Rs.9,000.[1] Major Jack [2] arrived at the same conclusion from villages in Bengal and Japan. He showed that while the incidence of taxation per head was very much heavier in Japan (£1 2*s*., as against 3*s*. 4*d*.), the amounts levied by the local authorities were out of all proportion, being under four annas in Faridpur and more than thirty-eight times as heavy in Japan.

The effect of this policy is visible to the most superficial observer. In Italian villages and those of other parts of Europe which have not been industrialised the peasant receives little more from the Central Government than he does in India. Civil justice is slow and expensive, the police and the criminal administration do not bear a very high reputation. Railways are neither very efficient, nor developed more extensively than in India. Main roads are better in Europe than in most parts of India, except perhaps the Punjab, but it is in the local conveniences supplied to the villages that the difference is so marked. The Italian village has probably a good water supply, electric light, proper sanitation, and a well-made street. Usually a doctor and a midwife are provided free for the villagers. Only very slowly and fitfully is the same work being done in India. In Assam an Act has recently been

[1] *More Truths about India*, p. 65.

[2] *Economic Life of a Bengal District*, p. 121

passed to create 'Village Authorities' for 'the execution of certain easy and simple duties including those connected with water-supply, roads, drains, jungle clearing, medical relief and sanitation'. In Madras the local boards maintain 109 hospitals and 513 dispensaries. The machinery exists, but it hardly functions because of a certain inertia amongst the people themselves and because of the lack of adequate funds. Thus in Bengal the average incidence of local cesses is under three annas a head, and has scarcely altered since before the War.

There seems little doubt that most Indian villagers would pay more in local cess if they could actually see the result in work being done before their eyes, schools being built, roads being improved, village sites cleared of prickly pear, tanks cleaned, and wells sunk. Mr. Gokhale, many years ago, held that taxation under a responsible government could be much increased, and he believed that local and municipal rates could be trebled. The weakness of the British administration has been that it was obsessed by the idea that a 'government's duty is to govern', whereas its chief work is to make the inhabitants govern themselves. The peasant, who saw his hard-earned rupees disappear into *tehsil* or *taluka* treasuries, naturally imagined that the government had vast sums available. In thousands of villages it would be difficult to find any trace of government expenditure, and the people are loath to pay any more to district boards until they see some concrete sign that these further sums are to be spent locally. Ultimately the ryot will probably have to pay considerably heavier taxes, but this change can only follow a grant of responsible government based on a very wide franchise. As Lord Cromer often pointed out, a dependency will only submit to a foreign government so long as the rate of taxation is kept very low. Much of the work which is usually called 'village uplift' can be done without any expenditure, merely by organising some of the wasted energies and time of the ryots and their dependents, but other reforms need money, especially if the services of outsiders like doctors and schoolmasters have to be secured. A complete change of attitude is needed towards voluntary work within the village, and also towards local cesses, and such a mental revolution is not likely to take place while the whole field of politics is occupied by racial and communal questions.

There would seem to be two sides to the problem of the Indian peasant, the pressure on the soil and the low standard of life. The first admits of no real cure except the limitation of births. It has been shown that industrial development, irrigation, village industries, and emigration are not likely to do much more than absorb the fresh yearly surplus, a surplus which may increase rather than decrease in the future. Accepting, however, the fact that Indian life will have to be based on peasantry living on areas too small to be real economic holdings, a condition which can be paralleled in many parts of southern Europe, in Japan, in China, and other more or less civilised countries, much can be done to improve the productivity of these small plots of land, and also to raise the standard of village life. The English model is an unfortunate one, for Indian agricultural life will never be dependent on the large towns and industrial centres. Villages or groups of small hamlets will have to be the units on which the India of the future must be raised.

## CHAPTER IV

# EPILOGUE

THE attitude of the English in India towards constitutional changes is perhaps typified by the pseudonym 'Khub Dekta Age' under which a government official has recently produced a useful book on the problems facing the Simon Commission.[1] Far better, however, than the implied advice of looking well ahead would have been the old monastic warning '*finem respice*'. England's shortcomings in India have seldom been due to any precipitancy in introducing changes, in fact the history of the last fifty years has been a succession of opportunities lost by delay. Her failures can usually be traced to the lack of any definite objective, the policy of drift which has led a famous writer to compare the British in India with a man perched upon an elephant, which he cannot control, and from which he cannot get down. It is not fair to blame the European official for this. It is not his duty to institute constitutional changes. Parliament is responsible for the general direction of policy, which is thus left to a body constantly changing its members and distracted by many other problems which seem more urgent and important. The English two- or three-party system has not worked happily for India. There has been little of that continuity which has marked the colonial policy of France and Holland, or of Germany before the last war. Probably most people who can claim any knowledge of Indian Nationalism would agree that the exasperation of the educated classes is due more to the lack of any settled policy than to the dilatory manner in which reforms are introduced.

[1] *India To-morrow.*

The Indian politicians ask for a definite programme but receive only vague and meaningless phrases. Some of them have been tempted to play one English party off against another, but they soon discover that Indian affairs are not an important issue and influence no votes. The opposition party might talk about 'self-government', but the Government would always add the qualifying 'by successive stages', and omit to say what those stages would be.

It seems essential, therefore, that any reforms which are introduced should be of such a nature that an Indian can visualise the type of government which will be in existence five, ten, or fifteen years ahead. It should not, for example, be impossible to picture the India which would result in, say, ten years' time, from the granting of provincial autonomy on the lines which have already been discussed. Certain areas would have disappeared from the map altogether. Burma, which has little affinity with the Peninsula, would have a separate Government, modelled perhaps on the lines of that proposed for Ceylon. Aden, and possibly Baluchistan, would be under the control of the Colonial Office. The remainder of the present Indian Empire would be divided into a number of Provinces and States. The Provinces, between thirty and forty in number, would have single chamber parliaments based on universal suffrage, and the administration would be in the hands of Ministers who would be the chairmen of standing committees in charge of the various subjects. Each Province would have a Governor, usually an Indian, but like his Ministers he would only require a comparatively small staff. The influence of the peasants' vote would be always tending to keep the Government cheap and unpretentious. The States would still be autocratically governed, but their Chiefs would be experimenting with various compromises on the road to democratic control, their willingness to do so depending on the prosperity of the neighbouring provinces. They would number just over a hundred, and most of them would be represented, either directly or jointly, in the Central Government. A few of the larger states might prefer to remain outside the federation, but their inability to control the tariff policy would be a very strong inducement to them to enter in on the same basis as the Provinces. Simla would remain, for the Indian politician does not love Delhi in the hot weather any more than the British official, but much of its glory will have departed. There will still be a Viceroy, but most of the Europeans would be experts brought out under contract, and with little temptation to form a society of their own. The Indian Members of the Assembly would be much more 'provincial' than at present. The method of indirect election through the smaller provincial assemblies and of delegation from the states must exclude many of the cosmopolitan lawyers from the larger cities. Proceedings would be more business-like, for there would be little excuse for impassioned rhetoric about the few and severely practical subjects which the Provinces would leave the Central Government to administer, and there would be no benches of European officials inviting criticism on racial and general lines.

The small provincial governments are likely to develop into bodies not very dissimilar from the largest of our County Councils, and the more prosperous type of working agriculturist should find his place upon them. Their influence will undoubtedly be in favour of the most rigid economy, and this should prove a valuable safeguard both locally and through their representatives at Delhi. The State railways, for example, may become more 'oriental' in some of their methods, and the Eurasian population have a hard fight to retain their position on them, but if the expresses become slower the agricultural freights will also probably come down, and travellers will find in India as in Denmark, a railway system run to suit the farmer. The Army Department will have altered least, but the position of the British officers in the Indian Army would be gradually approximating to that of the officers lent by European powers to weaker countries, like the British naval officers in Greece and the Swedish officers in the Persian police. The number of British troops would be considerably reduced, and they would probably be stationed near the large centres of European population at Calcutta, Bombay, Madras, and Karachi. In the Mofussil life will not have altered very much superficially. The districts have already been 'Indianised' to an extent which is hardly appreciated in England. A few European officials more or less will not make any great difference. Perhaps the office files will accumulate a little more rapidly, for the old bureaucratic machine will survive for much longer than a decade, but the official will tend to take his ordinary place in society as an Indian professional man amongst other professional men.

The country is likely to be as markedly agricultural as ever. Nine-tenths of the population will still live in the villages. In some areas the stirring of a new life will be visible, partly, as in English villages, for reasons not connected with politics. The cheap motor-car – usually a semi-derelict American lorry with the carburettor tied on with string – is already having considerable influence in opening up the Punjab and other areas where the roads are good. Wireless will follow, and India is fortunate because these amenities of country life are becoming popularised before there has been any marked rural exodus. Other improvements will depend upon whether a change of government will bring with it a new will to be prosperous as has happened in Turkey and elsewhere.

The future turns to a great extent upon the development of the Hindu social system. At present it is looked upon as a bulwark against foreign influence, and in this way an atmosphere is created which is very favourable for religious corruption and obscurantism. There are, however, many signs of a growing impatience with certain beliefs, religious or superstitious, which are undoubtedly harmful to the country, and the reformist element is likely to receive an immense impetus when it is seen that politics are not enough to save the country. It will not require ten years for the Nationalist politicians to discover that the absorption of India's surplus rural population cannot be managed by docking European salaries or by imposing heavy tariffs. The present yearly increase is in the nature of 2 millions, and a very moderate reduction in infant mortality – from the present rate, say, of well over two hundred per thousand to that of Ceylon which is 189 – would add another half million. It is clear that along with the struggle against bad obstetric methods, a legacy due to the ceremonial uncleanliness of child-birth, there will have to go a campaign against too early and too frequent motherhood.[1] This is as much a matter of religion

[1] According to statistics collected in Scotland and elsewhere, a delay of three years in marriage means on an average one fewer in the family.

as of economics, for though a high birth-rate accompanies extreme poverty, the vast majority of Indians will have to continue living upon their small plots of land, and the limited kind of improvement which can be expected is not likely to act as an efficient check to large families. The present religious connection between marriage and puberty will have to be erased from people's minds, and so also will the various religious prohibitions which have been discussed in previous chapters as preventing the improvement of agriculture. A decade should be enough to show whether a change of government will introduce that anxiety for improvement which is so needed in the villages, the joy and pride in a well-kept village site, in the good and sound products of the craftsmen, and in the rich and well-tilled field, so that even the bullocks may, if we are to believe Martial, find a greater pleasure in the harder work.

> 'In steriles nolunt campos juga ferre juvenci
> Pingue solum lassat, sed juvat ipse labor.'

The effects of a foreign occupation upon the subject people are subtle but devastating. The chief grounds for optimism about the future of India is a belief that there are certain forces, innate in the people, which would be released if the country were relieved from its present political and racial troubles. These forces are only indirectly connected with politics, and it is difficult for an Englishman to understand why the presence of a small British army and a few European officials should have such a disheartening effect upon any religious reformist movement, and such a deadening effect upon the initiative of the ordinary villager. He is inclined to be sceptical of any improvement, but the history of nearly every country which has thrown off the shackles of foreign control shows that some kind of rejuvenation invariably follows. It is not that these countries have always gained political freedom, or been well served by their politicians, but they seem, like Italy, Ireland, and Turkey, to have regained their youth and their ambition.

The educated classes should, of course, gain most directly by the diversion of nationalist sentiment towards the improvement of their country. At present, generation after generation of young men are being brought up to look upon the release of their country from foreign control as the natural and highest end of their ambition. This encourages a tendency, itself an inheritance from the Brahman tradition, to prefer literary and forensic triumphs to the more solid but also more obscure work of the doctor, engineer, scientist, and agriculturist. Just as our Governors and higher officials have set a false standard to the landowners and wealthier classes, so the Nationalist leaders have fired countless young men with feelings and resentments which would be of little value in a free country. There are immense forces waiting to be released, forces which will make or wreck the future of India. The most optimistic must, however, be prepared for some years of disillusionment while Indian politicians experiment along the lines of their old propaganda, and before the peasantry bring their steadying influence to bear upon the Provincial Governments.

# APPENDIX

## THE SIMON REPORT

THE intensity of Indian antagonism to the British connection is as periodic as trade prosperity and depression. If shown upon a graph the high points would be such years as 1897–1900, 1906–8, 1919–21 and 1929–30. Between these points there is usually a 'trough' marking a period of comparative quiet when moderate politicians are often in the ascendant, and the more advanced groups are divided. The years in which constitutional reforms have been introduced have been invariably those when nationalist feeling is most intense. This is not a mere accident, though the results have been lamentable, for the proper time to introduce constitutional changes is when moderate politicians are comparatively popular, and racial feeling is low. Unfortunately the English political machine works slowly and only under compulsion. A period of excitement in India produces the feeling that something more ought to be done, but the quiet years are spent in enquiries and bargaining, and by the time any measure of reform is introduced we are well at the top of another wave of popular feeling. We are, in fact, always a few years late.

The Simon Commission started its work during a period of comparative quiet. The 'seven English gentlemen', chosen for their complete detachment from Eastern questions, spent some three years in acquiring the kind of knowledge which any British Government can obtain from public bodies, and from individuals, official and unofficial, in India, for there was no subject which the Commission investigated which had not already been discussed almost *ad nauseam*. The only possible excuse for such a lengthy period of incubation would have been that the Commission were making contacts which could not be achieved by the Government of India, or that they were marking time until conditions improved. Actually there was a moderately effective boycott of the Commission, and the three years were marked by a rapid deterioration in every department of Indian life. The personnel of the Commission, and certain speeches and incidents which followed their appointment, were in themselves powerful factors in starting an agitation which had about reached its highest points when the Report was issued. Communal strife between Moslems and Hindus grew worse, as it always will when men's minds are unsettled. Innumerable incidents, including one of such small intrinsic importance as the publication of Miss Katherine Mayo's *Mother India*, all widened the gulf between British officials and the politically-minded Indians. Both in the Provincial and the Central Governments the tension became more acute, while the Congress fell under the influence of younger and more determined men like Subashchandra Bose, Srinivasa Iyengar, J. M. Sen Gupta, and Jawaharlal Nehru. This group, though far from united, think of the relations between India and England in terms of the Irish settlement. Their chief ambition is to acquire a new status for Indians, and they believe that the best way to do this is to insist that any settlement should be agreed upon by English and Indians acting as parties to a treaty. In this demand they have the support of many Indians who dislike their methods, and the financial backing of a large group of industrialists, who are fighting for India's commercial and fiscal independence. The Lahore Congress of 1929 marked the supremacy of the advanced section. Mr.

Gandhi placed himself, not too willingly, at its head, and the months preceding the publication of the Simon Report saw a rapid increase in lawlessness, the most noticeable features being the violation of Salt and Excise laws, and the arrest of several thousand Congress supporters. On the other hand, Lord Irwin could see, far better than any politician at home, that the demand for a different status was real and widespread, and that there was no possibility of any stable government until this had been settled. In this he clearly has the support of many officials, and also of a considerable section of the more intelligent business men. In October, 1929, he announced that the definite aim of the Government was 'Dominion Status', and also that a Round Table Conference would be held, at which the Government would meet representatives of British India and also of the Princes. There was, of course, nothing new about the acceptance of 'Dominion Status' as our goal. The phrase has been used by politicians of all parties during the last decade, and a Round Table Conference had been suggested as soon as it was clear that the Simon Commission was not going to establish those contacts with Indian politicians for which the optimistic had hoped. The effect, however, of this declaration and the publication of the Simon Report has been to leave the situation in complete confusion. The Report appeared in June, 1930. Most of the first volume was descriptive, but there are sections in which the Commission explained their attitude towards certain controversial matters, and the chapters dealing with recent events showed that they possessed a very superficial understanding of the Nationalist movement. It was a sound unimaginative document with a distinctly Conservative bias, and to everybody's surprise it was unanimous. All seven Commissioners agreed 'that want of consideration in social intercourse for Indian feelings cannot justly be laid to the charge of the average Englishman in India to-day', the communal riots in Bombay were ascribed to 'inflammatory speeches made by extremist leaders during a textile strike', and the Jallianwallabagh affair was the natural culmination of mob violence. The volume was immediately hailed by the English press as a safe document with great propagandist value abroad, and this was quite enough to damn it in Indian eyes. Indian annoyance was also roused by a certain superiority of tone. The analysis of difficulties was clear, and would be accepted by many Indian politicians, but the Commission's attitude was of a veterinary surgeon examining a horse rather than a doctor giving advice to an important patient.

The second volume of the Report was a far more valuable document. The Commissioners were all practical politicians, and they had been shown a piece of governmental machinery, partly democratic and partly autocratic, which was not functioning properly, either in the Provinces or in the Central Government. They set about their job in a professional manner. They appreciated the need of simplifying the problem, and advise the total separation of Burma. They discuss the subdivision of some of the Provinces which are unsatisfactory units, especially Bihar and Orissa. Dyarchy has not worked well in the Provincial Governments, and they propose to make all Ministers responsible to the Legislature, including the Minister in charge of 'Law and Order'. The system of the official 'bloc' has failed, and is to be abolished. Direct election to the Central Government has proved itself a travesty of democracy, and the Commission suggest indirect election through the Provincial legislatures. All these proposals are sound, and almost inevitable. It would, however, be a mistake to suppose that the Commission has recommended complete Provincial autonomy, for the communal system of voting is to remain, and the Governor of each Province is quite definitely to be his own Prime Minister. He chooses his own Ministers, including if he wishes one or two officials, and he is advised to take some Ministers from groups which owing to the communal voting system are likely to be permanent minorities. The Governor is also given very large emergency powers, and is, subject only to the Viceroy, the sole judge as to existence of an emergency. It is clear that there would be no real collective responsibility amongst a Cabinet chosen from opposing groups, and containing officials, even though they are nominally responsible to the Legislature. The suggestion is for a temporary form of government which might develop into something more logical and sound if there was no racial antagonism tending always to throw the Governor and his officials into opposition against the Legislature.

Unfortunately most Indians when they picked up the second volume of the Report would turn at once to the proposals for the new Central Government, and for the future status of India. They would search in vain for any mention of Dominion Status, or reference to the controversy which had engrossed so much of India's political activities. The Central Government is to remain almost exactly as it is at present, except that the Legislative Assembly is to be elected from the Provincial Councils. The only recognition of the Indian demand for a new status is that the Central Assembly is to be considered as the nucleus of a Federation for All India, and there are empty chairs to be left, at any rate in imagination, for representatives from the States, 'if and when' the Princes agree to send them. The Commission assumes that the separate existence of the Indian States and the present composition of the Army make it impossible to modify the autocratic powers of the Viceroy and the Executive. This was exceedingly cold comfort for the Nationalists. The Report suggests a solution of the Army problem by making Defence an Imperial Responsibility, but Nationalists saw their demands postponed until a group of Princes, for whom they have no great affection, should of their own free will accept certain conditions which are probably distasteful. Not unnaturally they argued that this Report was out of date, that 'Dominion Status' has been accepted as the aim of the Government, and they could quote the Prime Minister to the effect that a change of status was a matter of months, and not to be deferred until the fulfilment of some almost impossible conditions.

The enormous number of arrests which resulted from the Civil Disobedience movement have further complicated a position which was already sufficiently confused. Most of the recognised leaders of the nationalist movement were in gaol when the Report was issued. The industrialists would take little interest in a Report which would exclude them indefinitely from any chance of controlling the Departments of Commerce and Finance. The tendency therefore is to shelve the Report until the Round Table Conference has given an opportunity for the discussion of the question of status. There is no reason why most of the conclusions of the Simon Commission should not be reached by way of 'Dominion Status with safeguards'. Most Indian nationalists would allow, at any rate in private, the difficulties which the writer has attempted to outline in the third part of this book, and which are discussed in the Simon Report. It may seem absurd to the modern Englishman, whose liberty is never seriously imperilled, that the Indians should be so insistent about the terms on which they deal with the British Government, but history is full of such absurdities. If Englishmen have been willing to die for a flag or a scrap of paper, there is no reason why we should grudge the Indians their wish to negotiate their future constitution on equal terms, or be surprised that they are willing to struggle for a legal abstraction like 'Dominion Status'.

# INDEX

# INDEX

## INDEX

# INDEX